A STORY OF THE RUSSIA-UKRAINE WAR LONGING FOR PEACE

BLOOD
SOWING HUMANS

MAYANK TOMAR

BLUEROSE PUBLISHERS
India | U.K.

Copyright © Mayank Tomar 2024

All rights reserved by author. No part of this publication may be reproduced, stored in a retrieval system or transmitted in any form or by any means, electronic, mechanical, photocopying, recording or otherwise, without the prior permission of the author. Although every precaution has been taken to verify the accuracy of the information contained herein, the publisher assume no responsibility for any errors or omissions. No liability is assumed for damages that may result from the use of information contained within.

BlueRose Publishers takes no responsibility for any damages, losses, or liabilities that may arise from the use or misuse of the information, products, or services provided in this publication.

For permissions requests or inquiries regarding this publication, please contact:

BLUEROSE PUBLISHERS
www.BlueRoseONE.com
info@bluerosepublishers.com
+91 8882 898 898
+4407342408967

ISBN: 978-93-6783-032-1

Cover design: Daksh
Typesetting: Tanya Raj Upadhyay

First Edition: December 2024

Dedication

This novel is lovingly dedicated to the global family enduring the pain of unrest, violence, and wars that plague our world today. It draws strength from the early teachings of compassion, truth, and integrity imparted by the late Shri Major Ranvir Singh Tomar (Babaji) and the late Smt. Heera Devi Tomar (Dadiji). Their values remain a guiding light, and through this work, I carry the hope that humanity will rise above the shadows of outdated beliefs that fuel discrimination and strife, embracing a future of peace and unity with open hearts.

Acknowledgement

Writing 'Blood Sowing Humans' has been an odyssey steeped in the surreal, where every step forward felt like a negotiation with an unknown force, an inquiry into the nature of existence itself. Yet, even in this maze of uncertainties and shifting realities, there were luminous figures who stood steadfast, guiding me through the labyrinth.

To my parents, Harish Tomar and Neelam Tomar: you are the unyielding constants in a world that often feels fragile and ever-changing. Your support has been an immovable pillar in a landscape prone to dissolution. Your voices, echoes of an ancestral strength, have carried me through the strangest of nights, grounding me in moments when everything felt blurred and abstract.

To my beloved wife, Mamta Arya, who, like a steady flame in the dark, offered warmth and clarity amid the most perplexing turns. Your love is a tether, an unwavering presence that kept me from being swallowed by the void. To my daughter, Triambika, whose laughter is an enigmatic melody that somehow makes sense of the chaos, you are a beacon of innocent hope that defies the absurdities of this world.

With the utmost respect and deepest gratitude, I extend my heartfelt appreciation to Dr. Ashok K. Chauhan, the visionary Founder of Amity University, whose boundless foresight has created a monumental institution, providing me with the space to explore the profound intricacies of human existence. I also express my sincere regards to our esteemed Chancellor, Shri Atul Chauhan, whose quiet yet profound influence resembles that of a watchful architect, nurturing the foundation of countless dreams. To our honourable Vice-Chancellor, Prof. (Dr.) Balvinder Shukla, your exemplary leadership serves as a beacon of guidance and strength in a world often lacking direction. I remain indebted to each of you for inspiring and shaping the lives of countless individuals, including mine, with your unparalleled vision and dedication.

I owe a debt to my Director at the Amity Institute of Social Sciences, Prof (Dr.) Nirupama Prakash Whose mentorship is a map covering vast area of the subject without fixed points and holding a compass to cover the social world which seemed direction less.

This work stands as a record of disjointed yet intertwined realities, of dreams that hover somewhere between the known and the ineffable. It is a book that owes its existence to the confluence of the tangible and the spectral support of these remarkable individuals. My gratitude is complex, impossible to articulate in its entirety, but its weight anchors this acknowledgement. Thank you for believing in the dream when even reality seemed to defy understanding.

A Voice of Peace

Why War? I offer this novel to my intelligent readers, who can go into the intense inhuman background of this novel and feel the human tragedy and can give birth to those voices in their hearts filled with the deep desire for peace for a new world full of peace and cooperation, which is needed today for the existence of the entire human race.

The fearful human indifferent sensitivity around us needs an ideological support and a thought filled with strong intentions of peace. For a better society, better education and an environment of peace should be seen as essential freedom. The inclusive world of tomorrow will be born only on the strength of thoughts and actions filled with the idea of peace. This novel is just a glimpse of the destructive history accelerating across the world. Stories of destruction are scattered all over the world today, seeing them and remaining silent, standing away from the causes of destruction, is only a silent support and hindrance in the way of preserving human civilization. Let us all rise together and talk about a world peace based in the interest of humanity because turning away from the reality will be like an ostrich hiding its face in the sand.

Though finding a scriptural basis for truth and justice seems a bit inconsistent in today's world which is busy in structuring thousands of logics in favour of war, yet raising fingers for the protection of the entire human society would not be an act of injustice?

My job is to alert the masses who are suffering all kinds of inconveniences, pains and humiliations in various systems for whom every corner of this world is important from the point of view of peace and livelihood, on which the future of its future generations depends. Today, the security of man and his environment can be achieved only by targeting peace and the involvement of whole of humanity.

The foundation of war is laid by self-serving, privileged groups on the basis of differences that have been cultivated and spread in social contexts for years. Our agreement or disagreement with these differences depends on our education and understanding of human history, including its merits, demerits, and shortcomings. At its core lies narrow-mindedness, not human compassion. Changing behaviour requires a change in mindset, which necessitates correct education that is honest and dedicated to guiding humanity towards a better path.

The poor, farmers, labourers, women and common people on a global level have to bear the brunt of the weakening efforts for peace and humanity. The welfare structure of the states involved in war gradually collapses on its own.

I know that my strength and resources are negligible, so what else do I have except to give a call to the people of the entire world!

With respect to the great souls of Mahatma Gandhi, Martin Luther King and Nelson Mandela.

The fears are the manure and water of life.

Kharkiv, Ukraine

February 23, 2022

One cannot fully comprehend the terrifying scale and brutality of war until they experience it firsthand. The capacity to ignore these horrors gives people the strength to carry on, especially when war is imminent. Amid death, destruction, and pervasive fear, life must have adapted to tune out these signs of war, possibly reducing their impact for a while.

A woman stands in front of a large square black gate covered in black leather. Four bouncers in black shirts are positioned directly in front of the gate. Nearby, there's a booking counter with another woman standing behind it. Above the booking counter, the name "Euphoria Night Club" shines in white lights on the black gate. The woman approaches and stands in front of the booking counter.

She is wearing earphones, yet the sound is so loud that it spills outside. She hums along to a song, "To the lips of another, lending your song... Leave a mark, then move on from the world... One day, you will be sold for the price of soil..."

The girl at the booking counter says, "Welcome to Euphoria Night Club. May I know your name?"

She could only see the girl at the counter's lips moving. Removing one earphone, she asked, "What did you want to know?"

"Your name."

This time, she heard it. She took off the other earphone, held them in her hands, and said, "My name is Sandhi." As she tucked both hands into her overcoat's pockets.

"You have another booking with you."

"Yes, his name is Petrovich... He should be arriving any moment. I'm waiting for him."

When she finished speaking, a young man's voice was heard calling out as he ran, "Sandhi... Sandhi."

Her face broke into a smile as if the Lopan River in Kharkiv had been replenished by rain, and its ripples reached her lips.

Sandhi said with a slight anger, which was more for the show, "Between the two of us, who is the girlfriend? I'm always the one waiting for you. Why are you late?"

Petrovich replied, "Such is the life of a journalist. There was an important meeting, and it got a bit delayed. Even before the news happens, we need to be alert."

Sandhi didn't wait for him to finish and interjected, "You're always late. Was that meeting so important?"

"I'll tell you later at the hotel; leave something for then."

Watching him speak, Sandhi noticed his expression was flat, with no trace of a smile, worry, or irritation. Perhaps that's how one's face looks when they're regretful. She didn't press further, eager to get inside the club.

Petrovich bent all the fingers of his right hand and placed his other hand over it, bringing it close to his mouth and breathing out warm air. "Doctor! You seem more like a boyfriend to me."

Sandhi laughed, and Petrovich joined in her laughter.

Sandhi stopped laughing and said, "Now hold my hand, my girlfriend, and drop this cold act. Give me your hand."

Petrovich placed his hand on Sandhi's shoulders, and she tucked her hands into her overcoat pockets again.

Seeing this, Petrovich remarked, "Oh, so you can feel cold, not me!"

Looking at the white light on the nightclub sign bearing the club's name, Sandhi responded, "You're Ukrainian; you should be used to this cold. I'm from India. It doesn't get this cold there. Back home, we've already celebrated Makar Sankranti, and here it's -2 degrees in February."

"This is the magic of Ukraine; this weather makes us strong. Let's go inside the club, or are you planning to spend all night here?"

This time, she looked at him and said, "Yes, let's go, my girlfriend." Both approached the girl at the booking counter, who, after checking them, opened the gate for them and sent them behind that black leather-covered gate.

As soon as she pushed the heavy gate open, loud and numerous sounds emerged.

As Sandhi heard these loud sounds, she first covered her ears and said to Petrovich, "Look, outside this gate, you wouldn't even know that there's such loud music inside here."

Petrovich didn't hear her and brought his hand, which had been on Sandhi's shoulder, to his ears and asked, "What did you say?"

"Outside this gate, you wouldn't even know that loud music is inside. You couldn't even call it music."

Petrovich laughed hearing this and said, "I've never understood why you come to places like this when you don't enjoy them."

After removing her hands from her ears, Sandhi replied, "You're a man born in Ukraine, and I'm a girl born in India."

"I'm a journalist, but your talk is all indirect."

Listening to him while unbuttoning her overcoat, Sandhi responded just before she opened the last button, "Journalist, I'm not a doctor yet, but I will be within a year, and I know that it's necessary to keep going before life shuts down."

Saying this, she began to dance to Russian music... Yellow and blue lights illuminated her face. Petrovich also started dancing and watching Sandhi, and they slowly began to jump together, celebrating life. Perhaps both thought youth was a story about losing oneself for a few days.

While dancing, Sandhi and Petrovich reached the bar counter. When Sandhi realized they had reached the bar, she first noticed the circular bar table with the bartender in the middle, juggling bottles of alcohol.

Watching this, Sandhi remarked, "I don't understand; if you pour the alcohol into the glass in the end, why does the bartender need to perform all these tricks and take so long?"

Petrovich laughed out loud and gently lifted her onto a chair next to the bar table. He then also sat on the tall chair and said, "You were the one who said it's necessary to start before closing... He was spinning the alcohol a bit before its final destination."

Sandhi liked Petrovich's response and watched him intently without blinking. Various lights from inside the club were reflected in their eyes, but neither blinked.

Suddenly, Petrovich said, "Tell me, what will you drink?" as he leaned towards Sandhi, and she also leaned towards him.

Petrovich caught the perfume scent on Sandhi's neck, and all the tensions in his mind were erased momentarily. A thought flashed in Petrovich's mind that the war would steal all these tender moments of joy.

Sandhi, without blinking, said, "Since I'm in Ukraine, only vodka." Saying this, she looked again at the bartender.

Petrovich loudly told the bartender, "Two 60 ml-shots." The bartender said, "Just a minute, sir."

As the bartender prepared their vodka shots, they turned their chairs to watch others dancing. Sandhi, watching them, said, "Life is something no less than a celebration."

"Even death would be a celebration with you," he laughed. Sandhi also began to laugh, watching him.

From behind, the bartender called, "Sir, your order."

Petrovich and Sandhi turned their faces back to the bar counter and picked up their glasses.

Sandhi- "To life, cheers."

Petrovich- "To life."

They both finished their drinks in one go, and just before Sandhi finished the last drops, she said without removing the glass from her mouth, "One more round."

Petrovich signaled the bartender for another shot with just a gesture.

When Petrovich looked at Sandhi, she said, "Now, tell me what you were saying."

Sandhi still remembered Petrovich's flat expression, prompting her to ask many questions and express her concerns.

Petrovich again evaded the topic and started looking towards the bartender as if concerned about the vodka.

Sandhi said, "No, I need to know now."

Petrovich looked at her and realized he couldn't delay this question any longer; it had reached the point of being asked and told.

Petrovich said, "Our agency has received information that Russian forces are heavily stationed at the eastern and northeastern borders, and they might even attack."

"This means the army is just 25-30 kilometers away from us."

Petrovich nodded without saying anything. For nearly a minute, they both looked at their empty glasses, and suddenly, the sounds of the club were no longer audible. They must have contemplated all the 'ifs and buts' and denied that a war could happen. Amidst these thoughts, the bartender had placed another 60 ml-shots in front of them unbeknownst to them.

Sandhi picked up the filled glass a minute later and sipped slowly this time. While drinking, she turned her chair again to watch the dancing, jubilant people, thinking whether they were unaware of the war or didn't care. Petrovich was staring intently at Sandhi and then suddenly said, "If people couldn't end or lessen their consciousness with external means, then more than half of the population in every country would hang themselves from the fans in their homes because consciousness, governance, administration, and mismanagement all lead to the commoner being trapped in the intricate web of systems and causing distress. Bars and pubs are places that reduce the continuity of consciousness. They don't know what's going to happen, or why it's going to happen."

She listened to him without interrupting and finished her remaining drink with a jerk. Sandhi drank away the intoxication of his words.

Then, after a while, they both said, "No, no, war isn't possible. It just can't happen."

To further convince himself and Sandhi, Petrovich said, "If war happens this time, the world will end. Powerful countries won't let it happen... Even if there's a war, we will win."

Sandhi stared at him, and only disgust emanated from her gaze, saying, "So what if we win? War will still happen. If there's a war, people will die anyway. What will winning do? Will it stop the deaths?"

"Don't worry. There won't be a war."

"If there won't be a war, then why did you tell me about it in the first place?"

"I didn't tell you. You insisted on asking, and it's just news: the war hasn't happened yet."

Sandhi felt both relief and pain from this conversation and abruptly said, "Do you have a cigarette?"

Petrovich nodded 'yes.' He handed her both the cigarette packet and lighter.

Sandhi went silently to the club's smoking zone, thinking about when you start to believe that your life might end in the coming moment, but when will that moment come? That moment depends on countless other moments and facts, and your life becomes tedious because you're under the pressure of waiting for many things. Our consciousness can't handle the pressure of two desires, let alone a myriad of 'ifs and buts,' causing inevitable boredom. Whatever is there is now. Everything else is futile.

Thinking this, Sandhi lit a cigarette, and when she took the first drag, she saw Petrovich waiting for his turn.

Sandhi handed him the cigarette, saying, "Live it up, you too."

Petrovich smiled and said, "Yes, you're right."

Both mocked life's uncertainties by turning them into smoke or considered life entirely sure; it was hard to understand.

Petrovich took a drag and handed the cigarette back to Sandhi.

Sandhi took the cigarette, saying, "This democracy is a strange thing; if it's not in a country, it's a problem, and if it is, it's a different kind of problem. It exists in India but has many problems like poverty, unemployment, inflation, and corruption. It doesn't exist in Russia, so along with these problems, there's the problem of war. Anyway, war is a big problem in itself. I don't know if Russia is being pushed into war because of these problems so they won't be visible or because they've spent so much money on weapons due to the long-standing pressure of war."

Petrovich extinguishes the cigarette and says, "It's not easy to talk about these things. They're very complicated."

"I don't know if it's complicated; I just know that those who are instigating the war, leaving them aside, war is not beneficial for anyone. Whether it is democracy or autocracy, I only see big leaders making major decisions related to the people. The public only appears during or after a war, dying, being cut up, flying about, turning to ash, or crying over the loss of their loved ones, their homes, and their spirits breaking down. I want to see ordinary people's faces over these big leaders' faces. Are these leaders trying to become immortal in history with these acts, or why does history discuss these big leaders, why not those who were senselessly killed in wars? These leaders only want to grip history and the present because history helps make the public loyal and the present is presented as a revitalizing power, but at whose expense? At the expense of ordinary people, at our expense."

Petrovich, laughing, says, "Don't be so serious, Sandhi. And this is about wanting to see the faces of ordinary people—it's the ordinary people who want to see their big leaders on newspapers and TV. The day they want to see people like themselves, newspapers will print it, and we will show it."

Just then, the DJ announces from the mic that it's midnight and we're still dancing with total energy, and then the entire dancing crowd begins to shout in a frenzy.

Sandhi also checks her watch. She can't believe it is midnight already. She says, "Let's go to the hotel."

Petrovich says, "We'll book a cab outside." They both exit through the leather-covered door. Outside, Sandhi is walking with her eyes down. She can see her shadow on the immaculate marble under her shoes and stops herself from letting her face hit the marble. Then, her attention shifts to Petrovich's face, who is looking ahead, and she can only see half of his face reflected on the marble.

Petrovich asks, "What are you doing?"

"Nothing."

"Let's go inside the elevator."

Sandhi straightened her neck and entered the elevator.

More people were inside the elevator, all talking about the Russian army, believing war couldn't happen. Sandhi listened to their conversations and looked at their faces. They also looked at Sandhi, and both sides saw the fear of uncertainty on each other's faces. Suddenly, everyone started looking at the elevator numbers, which read that the elevator could carry a maximum weight of 2267 kilograms.

The elevator doors opened, and everyone stepped out. Just outside was a grand glass door, and right outside was a cab. Sandhi opened the cab door and sat down, and from the other side, Petrovich also got in. The radio was on inside the cab, talking about the Russian forces at the eastern border.

The cab driver hears this, runs his hand over his head, and says, "I've been hearing this since the evening. I don't understand why they don't talk about something else."

Petrovich says, "If something happens, they will tell us." The cab driver says, "There won't be a war; it's tough. If it were going to happen, it would have happened by now, and besides, we have NATO, America, and European countries with us. Putin won't fight us."

Sandhi was listening to Petrovich and the cab driver and thinking about how existence seems to depend on power everywhere, which doesn't seem to go against the natural principles of justice and the right to life. A weak person needs someone else to exist, much more dependent on others than a powerful person. A weak nation also needs more influential and powerful nations to maintain its sovereignty. Are both the state and the individual enduring the assaults of unjust relations?

The cab driver changed the radio channel, and various experts were discussing the situation on that channel. One expert said, "Putin is a self-made man; he didn't reach here easily." Another said, "In a democracy, leaders reach the top by making false promises. So, this war is between a self-made man and a system that has reached the top by deceiving the public."

Petrovich, hearing this, slaps the seat and says, "This is what you call propaganda."

The cab stops, and the driver says, "Your hotel, Oriental Palace, has arrived."

In those 7 minutes, Sandhi felt part of a discussion but was only given the task to think, not speak. Thinking this, Sandhi believed that the more explicit and honest the discourse between all men and women, the better the governance will favor human interests. However, this discourse must be protected from the pseudo-intellectuals often seen in newspapers and TV. Our arguments and debates should be driven and inspired by our robust thirst for knowledge, definitely not induced. Otherwise, they would have no more significance than a pile of garbage. Today, the art of distracting thoughts is the most fundamental method of attacking social harmony. Once the chain of thoughts breaks, she quickly leaves the cab.

By the time Petrovich gets out, she's already at the hotel gate. Petrovich, getting out, says, "Wait for me." Sandhi doesn't say anything; she stands there. Petrovich comes, and they take the room card key from the hotel reception and reach their room together.

As soon as they enter the room, Petrovich asks, "Do you like the room?"

Sandhi only nods and looks at the picture in front of the bed.

Petrovich asks, "Do you like modern paintings?"

"Yes, I like them because of what you see in them; no one else needs to see the same."

"What do you see in this one?"

After a long breath, Sandhi says, "I see that it's due to the failure of relationships and the resulting distrust that someone can become destructive and cause wars. The inability to immerse oneself in relationships or the absence of any capable relationships leads a person towards violence."

"You're right," and he comes closer and hugs her.

As soon as he hugs her, tears fall from Sandhi's eyes, absorbed by the overcoat covering Petrovich's shoulders. She remains hugged until the tear streaks dry up, and as soon as they dry, Sandhi removes her neck from Petrovich's shoulder.

Petrovich holds her face and kisses her forehead, asking, "Hey, where's your bindi gone?"

"I didn't even notice what's happening."

Petrovich, half-smiling, says, "Let's go to sleep; it's quite late."

"Let's sleep; we both have a flight tomorrow."

After a while, Petrovich agrees and asks, "How's your medical study going?"

Sandhi says, "Just one more year - then I'll be a full doctor." Then they both start laughing.

Petrovich, lying on the bed, says, "I brought you nightwear... you can change it if you want. But tell me, why don't you like carrying luggage?"

Sandhi, laughing, says, "It's a one-hour flight, so why carry luggage? I thought I'd wear what I came in. We'd party all night, and I'd catch the return flight in the same outfit. One shouldn't take too much stress in life. Life should be free, and now that you've brought nightwear, I'll change."

"Wow, doctor, you're still a student."

She nods and says, "I'm still free today, and tomorrow I'll try to be freer."

Saying this, she takes the nightwear from Petrovich's hand and goes into the bathroom.

After she leaves, Petrovich delicately takes off his clothes and neatly hangs them on a hanger. After that, he lies down on the bed and looks at the modern painting before it. Sandhi comes out of the bathroom, and Petrovich pulls himself out of his absorption in the painting, but Sandhi sees that Petrovich is also looking at that painting. Sandhi slips under the silky blanket and places her head on Petrovich's shoulder.

Petrovich kisses her hair and says good night. Sandhi also says good night. Long after saying good night, with their eyes closed, they start thinking about the war again. Sandhi, thinking about the war repeatedly, starts getting angry at herself, thinking whether she has ever thought so much about love. Why do we always think more about the things that threaten life?

Is life paramount, or is life arrogant enough to ignore everything else? The compost and water of life are the very fears of life, and both, in their ways, fall asleep slowly on the bed in front of the same painting, understanding freedom.

February 24, 2022

Suddenly, Petrovich's mobile rings. Startled, he gets up and notices the clock in front of the bed showing 4 AM. He picks up the phone and sleepily asks, "Who is it?" From the other end, a voice comes through, "It's Frank" (with shouting sounds in the background).

"Frank, what's happened so early, and why are there shouting sounds in the background?"

"The Russian forces have attacked... I was reporting in the eastern region; the attack had already begun. Russian troops have crossed our border, and they're using missiles. You must update our news agency's website; I'm stuck here..." Suddenly, a loud explosion is heard.

The noise was so loud that Petrovich's mobile dropped from his hand. The next moment, he picked up the phone again, put it to his ear, and started calling out, "Frank... Frank." No response came from the other side. Petrovich realized that the attack had begun, meaning everything would change, and he recalled how loud the explosion had been on the phone. Sandhi, sitting up, had drawn her legs close to her chest and clenched her fists tight around the bedsheet.

For a moment, their eyes met, and Petrovich felt nauseous. He bent over the bed and started vomiting. Sandhi watched silently; the explosion had traveled from the phone into her ears. Petrovich was vomiting, and Sandhi just watched him. Suddenly, Sandhi composed herself upon hearing her mother's voice in her ears, saying she was her brave child, heading so far from home for the first time. The echoing voice and Sandhi's clenched fist began to relax. She stood in her white nightgown and stroked Petrovich's back, whispering, "Nothing will happen to us... nothing will happen to us."

Then, suddenly, their entire room shook, and everything was thrown into disarray. Everything in order seemed to float in the air for a moment and then crashed down. Sandhi and Petrovich fell to the ground. The room was filled with dust and smoke. Both were coughing; Sandhi only began to grasp the situation when she realized that a shard of glass from the window had embedded itself in her forehead. She forcefully opened her eyes, dust entering them, and pulled out the shard, after which a drop of blood rolled down her eyelid, which she wiped off with her nightgown (no longer white but covered with dust, smoke, and blood). Petrovich lay in his vomit, now obscured by the dust.

Sandhi yelled loudly at Petrovich, though he was very close, as the shouting resumed between them. Without a word, both rushed towards the room's door. Sandhi reached first and opened it. Upon opening the door, she saw people choking, coughing, and running through the smoke. Some, who had recovered from the smoke's suffocation, were screaming. Smoke and dust now began to enter the room. Sandhi and Petrovich started calling each other loudly. Petrovich stood right behind her, but the smoke covered everything. Only people's torsos were swaying visibly.

They, too, joined the crowd and started running. Due to the number of people and their urgency, it became difficult to run, and soon, people began to trample each other. Seeing this, Sandhi stuck close to the wall, but perhaps Petrovich had moved ahead or stayed back. She called out again, but the screams drowned out her voice. Now, her voice, too, began to turn into a scream.

She started to cry, but she must have cried for barely a moment before she realized that it would not help; where terror was already rampant, what would her two tears accomplish? She continued running close to the wall, feeling people trample beneath her feet, knowing she could not stop, lest she be felt under someone else's.

Running, she reached the stairs leading to the hall below. There, she saw people falling down the stairs as others pushed from behind, and the hall below was also filled with smoke. She was descending the stairs, watching the people laid out on them, searching for Petrovich. At the last step, she saw a pregnant woman. Her gown completely covered her face, and her belly was fully exposed, making it visible, but her face was entirely obscured.

Sandhi couldn't bear it. Once, she left that step but returned to the last step and pulled down the woman's gown.

The woman's face was scratched, and blood was coming from her lips. Sandhi sat down next to her, wiping her blood with her soiled nightgown, and thought of Petrovich again. People's feet were hitting her head. Many were using her head for support, but Sandhi gently patted the woman's face, trying to revive her.

When she didn't regain consciousness, Sandhi spontaneously started tapping her more forcefully. The pregnant woman opened her eyes and stared into Sandhi's eyes without saying a word. Sandhi felt she was trying to recognize her, so she said, "I'm Sandhi."

Instead of frantically stating her name, she said, "My stomach hurts so much, my baby..." and while saying this, she passed out again.

Sandhi tried to revive the woman again, but all her efforts were in vain this time. She exerted all her strength to lift the woman, but she wasn't conscious, making it difficult for Sandhi to manage. Sandhi put the woman's arm around her neck and supported her on her back, dragging her along. She couldn't go far; Sandhi moved her to the side and began pulling chairs around her.

Now, she ran to a large aquarium nearby, pulled a chair up to it, and stood on it. Then, she removed the aquarium lid and scooped up a handful of water. Before the water could drip from her palms, she reached where she had laid the woman down. Sandhi threw the water forcefully on the woman's face. After doing all this, she observed. A few moments after pouring the water, the woman regained consciousness, and Sandhi felt alive for the first time in the past hour. Sandhi hugged her, and the woman probably wanted to hug Sandhi too. Sandhi placed the woman's arms behind her neck and picked her up again, trying to move out quickly.

The smoke had cleared, and Sandhi could see outside—firefighters, police, and the army. As she watched, another bomb fell, hitting a fire truck, which flew into the air like a toy and then crashed. The impact of the bomb and the falling fire truck was so intense that most of the glass at the main entrance shattered. Glass spread everywhere, embedding itself in people's skins. Blood began to flow, and screams came from all directions. Sandhi and the woman fell, too, but by now, they were not as frightened as they had been during the first explosion. When they lost, Sandhi had her hand on the woman's belly. It was unclear whether she did this because she was a woman or a doctor.

Sandhi and the woman got up and started to move out. Outside, they saw some people burning in the fire, struggling for life, and others who were not entirely dead but struggling to escape from the fire. A shoe lay outside the hotel gate, with half a foot inside and the other half across the street. The other pair of shoes was filled with blood instead of sock, and the blood was red on the black leather shoes. Fingers were moving, but the hand was separated from the torso. It seemed as if the hand was calling out to the torso. The sun was rising at the time of the explosion, but it was so filled with light and smoke that it darkened everything for a while. The sun's light was faint compared to the cloud of the explosion. Due to the unbearable burning, intense screams were heard. Holding the woman, Sandhi moved outside, but there was another difficulty now: where to go. Now, Sandhi was not alone; she was with another pregnant woman who was distressed and restless from labor pain.

Everyone was running. Sandhi also started following them without understanding anything. Although she couldn't move as fast as the others, she was trying to run. The faster she moved, the more pain the pregnant woman felt. Sandhi couldn't decide whether to run fast or saunter; both situations had a loss. Ultimately, she chose to walk fast and started talking to the other woman to distract her. But the woman, whatever had happened outside between those two explosions, was lost in terror. The trees on both sides of the road were burning, the leaves were burning and falling here and there, and with the winds, black dust-laden ash was flying, settling like the dust of time on the faces of every person there, alive or dead. Bodies were lying in piles everywhere. It seemed as if the bodies were being used like sacks for barricading. Some buildings' windows had burnt, half-naked bodies hanging, encapsulating human brutality, naturally falling due to their weight. As soon as they fell, fountains of blood were shooting out. Some people were standing crying, but they were so frightened and shocked that the desolation of their eyes could not be hidden.

The air was tainted with the distinct smell of burning flesh. With each horrific scene, her hand instinctively went to her womb.

Sandhi asked her, "What is your name?" The woman gave no response as if she hadn't heard at all. Sandhi asked again, this time turning the woman's face towards her. As long as she had seen the bodies and burned people on the streets, she had not even moaned in pain, but as soon as Sandhi turned her face towards herself, the spell of the catastrophe broke, and she said in shock, "Julia... Julia."

"Don't worry, Julia, everything will be alright."

Julia looked at Sandhi as if to say, "Don't lie; nothing can be all right now." Then she looked down at her belly and sighed, "Just let nothing happen to it."

Sandhi reassured her, "I'm a doctor, don't worry, everything will be okay."

Hope appeared on Julia's face, but the pain quickly snatched that happiness away. The pain was becoming intense, and in front of Sandhi was a sign - 'Ploscha Svoboda Square' and next to it - 'University Metro Station below.'

Sandhi realized people were running this way because the metro station was underground, a good place to avoid the bombs. Sandhi was very tired. Her pace had also slowed significantly, and she began to stroll down the stairs towards the metro. However, the crowd was so dense that her pace slowed even further. Bracing herself, she continued to descend, and Julia's pain deepened. The moaning sounds had turned into screams.

Sandhi once again drew Julia's attention to herself and asked, "Where is this child's father?" Upon hearing this, she began to cry even harder.

Sandhi felt that during the war, questions related to loved ones only brought pain. Perhaps sadness and the estrangement from loved ones are symbols of cursed times. After that, Sandhi said nothing more to the woman and slowly helped her down the stairs. Once down, the woman couldn't walk a single step and started to lie down. There was no space; people were standing, but Julia had nearly fainted. She fell among people's feet. Sandhi was holding her tightly but still couldn't prevent her from falling. The crowd made a little room for Julia; that was all they had then—space in the heart and space for Julia to lie down. Perhaps together, they were eager to write a human story amidst this catastrophe.

As soon as Julia lay down, her pain increased, and some fluid started leaking from her torn gown. Sandhi first thought that

Julia had urinated due to the excessive pain. People around her felt the same and moved back a bit, mistaking the fluid for urine. But when the leaking didn't stop, Sandhi lifted her gown and immediately understood it wasn't urine. It was amniotic fluid leaking from Julia's uterus. Sandhi was standing but sat down upon seeing this and suddenly started crying, saying, "I am not fully a doctor yet; I still have a year left. I can't perform this delivery. I don't have medical equipment or anyone to help. I can't do this."

People had initially kept their distance as she shouted, but when she broke down crying and started hitting her hands on the ground, some people stopped her. In a faint state, Julia murmured, "You can do it."

A young girl, about 15 years old, emerged from the crowd and said, "My name is Helga. I will help you."

Helga's innocence was less evident than her firm voice. Everyone started looking at her, but she was sure of her statement. The way she introduced herself made it seem like she had come for a job interview. Her clothes were like a school uniform.

Inspired by this young girl's enthusiasm, another helper followed Helga's example, saying, "My name is Ivan; I also want to help."

Sandhi slowly stood again and said, "Make a circle quickly." Hearing this, Helga started shouting, "Make a circle... make a circle."

"Move back... move back," Ivan began to say.

Suddenly, these three became the heroes of that subway station, and people began to listen to them. Sandhi slowly got up and suddenly climbed to the top step of the station. Julia was lying below the lowest step, and Sandhi stood at the top.

Sandhi looked at everyone and said, "This woman is in danger; we all are in danger, but that doesn't mean we should leave each other alone. This morning, the person I was with is not here now... I don't know where he might be. I am sad for him - but Julia is my priority now. We will all grieve for those we have lost and fear what will happen next - but truly, what we have now, like Julia and Helga, is our reality. We must save them."

There was something in her words. People carried Julia to the middle of the subway station before she descended. Suddenly, a loud explosion occurred outside the underground. The impact was felt even below. After this explosion, her screams became even more intense, and the pain accelerated unbearably for Julia. Julia's condition was worsening. Seeing this, Sandhi couldn't understand anything... she just kept looking at Julia. When Sandhi descended the stairs, she said, "I need some clean clothes." Instantly, people took off their shirts.

Then, a faltering voice came from the crowd, "I have some spotless clothes; I ran with these," and he started laughing.

"I will give my clothes on one condition."

Ivan asked, "What's the condition?"

"The condition is that you give them back to me clean," he said, laughing again.

Helga approached him, and before he could hand them over, she snatched the clean clothes from him and said, "What are you saying?"

A circle had formed with Sandhi in the center, Helga standing to her right, and Ivan to her left. The boy who had given his bag of clean shirts sat just outside the circle. Everyone was only looking towards Julia's belly, and Sandhi was looking towards where the light was coming from.

An old Ukrainian man approached Sandhi and said, "I will also help you."

Sandhi said, "The more people, the better; only by standing together can we survive this war."

Helga pulled a white shirt from the man's bag; the shirt was so clean that either it was that the clothes around were so dirty that the shirt seemed even cleaner. It looked like an Olympic torch. There, the spirit of the game, and here, the torch of humanity, were both burning.

Sandhi pressed gently on Julia's belly. Julia was already moaning in pain, and now the pain intensified. Tears were streaming from her eyes, her lips were dry, and her face had turned pale.

Sandhi told her, "Julia, put as much strength as possible into pushing the baby out."

Helga touched Sandhi's hand from behind. It was almost as if Helga was touching her to say, "Do what you can; I'm with you."

Julia was also looking at Sandhi. She told Sandhi, "I'll put all my strength into one effort, be ready. You also have to try; I'm dying of pain. If you don't do something, I'll die anyway."

Sandhi saw all the pages of the books she had read before her. Although she still lacked self-confidence, she told Julia, "I'm ready."

Blood started to spread very fast. Sandhi's nightgown was now completely red, mixed with light black spots of dust and smoke, and blood was coming under the soles of people standing in a circle outside.

Julia was unconscious and in pain. Ivan was trying to bring her back to consciousness, and the rest of the people, those who could bear to watch, were watching, and those who couldn't were standing with their eyes closed. They were waiting for the newborn's cry, slightly less sharp than a scream, utterly free from fear.

Sandhi called Ivan and Helga over, then she looked back and saw the older man, too. Sandhi asked, "What is your name?" The old man said, "Marco."

Sandhi said, "Marco, come over here." Marco moved two steps forward and stood beside Sandhi. Sandhi also saw the boy who had given the bag of clean shirts. Sandhi motioned to him, too.

He said, "I'm coming," and stood up. Sandhi asked him, "What's your name?" He said, "Vladimir." He took the white shirt from Sandhi and said, "You take the baby out... I'll keep him in this shirt."

Sandhi looked at everyone and said, "I'll need everyone's help; help me." Vladimir, looking at his shirt, said, "All right."

Sandhi pulled the baby out, and when the baby came out, it tore through all the fear with its crying sound and began to cry carelessly without any fear.

Sandhi had the baby in her hands, and a loud voice came from behind: "Sandhi... Sandhi." Sandhi turned around but couldn't see anyone because there was a lot of crowd. However, someone was making their way through the crowd towards Sandhi. When that person pushed the last person aside, Sandhi said, "Petrovich."

Tears were in Sandhi's eyes, blood on her forehead, and a newborn in her hands, crying. By then, the medical services people had also reached the underground place. Sandhi handed the baby to Helga and said, "You are fearless; you didn't even blink once."

"How could I blink? A little Ukrainian was coming."

By then, Petrovich had also passed through the crowd to Sandhi. During the entire delivery, Sandhi had not panicked, been afraid, or cried, but seeing Petrovich, she fell into his arms with her blood-stained hands. Petrovich and she both sat down and sobbed; Sandhi showed him her red hands and said, "Look at the blood of life... look at the blood of life. In the horrific moments of distrust in human history, unexpected courage has changed circumstances, and we have just started doing something similar."

2

Who will recount the aftermath of the battles in my life, revealing how many dreams were martyred and how many wishes were wounded?

Kharkiv February 24

The medical team descends the stairs of the subway station, their clothes a testament to the injuries sustained by many in the city of Kharkiv. Four to five medics hurriedly carry a stretcher down. They quickly place Julia on the stretcher and return to their van to fetch more medical supplies.

Sandhi watches all this from a distance. Petrovich, grasping Sandhi's blood-stained hands, says, "I can't believe you did this."

Showing her hands, Sandhi replies, "Look at these hands, even during war, I've brought life into this world. Anyone can do this; you have to believe. I didn't believe in myself initially either, but I trusted myself because these people looked at me with belief in their eyes. I didn't perform magic… I just did what one human can do for another. Life isn't that complicated, Petro; you must find the path that gives you peace." As she speaks, she gazes intently at Julia.

Julia's baby is with her, clung to her side. Julia's eyes are barely open, but she has not let go of her child.

Petrovich also watches Julia and then looks at everyone else's faces, feeling calm. He thinks about how important it is to cherish life, and perhaps Sandhi is one reason for everyone's happiness.

Petrovich remarks, "The medical team is treating Julia here; it seems the attack has intensified."

"Why don't you ask the medical team?"

Petrovich approaches a medical officer and inquires, "What's the matter? Why aren't you taking the patient to the van?"

The officer responds, "It is not safe outside. An attack could happen at any time. The Russian army has penetrated inside. They are clashing with our forces. Kharkiv is no longer safe." After saying this, he returns to attending to Julia.

Petrovich doesn't share this with anyone else. When others ask what the medical officer said, he reassures them, "Nothing much, just that Julia will recover soon."

He confides only in Sandhi, thinking she might panic upon hearing the news. However, after listening, Sandhi says, "This means nothing is safe, and since this place is in the heart of the city, we should stay here till tomorrow morning or even tonight."

"'We' means?"

Looking into his eyes, Sandhi asserts, "'We' means you, me, and all of us here."

Standing up, but only with support from her knees, she says, "Nothing is safe outside; everywhere there are either Russian missiles, soldiers, or tanks. If we go out, it won't be without risks. We should stay here until tomorrow, as this location in the middle of the city is the safest." After finishing, she looks into everyone's eyes and asks, "What do you all think we should do?"

After some quiet discussion, everyone slowly but firmly agrees that staying is the best option.

Sandhi then approaches the doctor. As soon as she reaches him, the doctor, alert and ready, says, "You did right. There was no other way to save lives."

"I'm not even a doctor yet; I still have a year left in my medical studies."

"You'll finish your studies. Your dedication to this profession reflects your nature to respect others."

"I never wanted to be a doctor, but what can I do? It's fate..." With these words, she walks away.

As she walks, Sandhi ponders why even a senior doctor gives her so much respect when she hasn't completed her degree. Talking to herself, she muses, 'This is war; normal rules of life don't apply here. Only the victor is considered the hero, but I don't want to be such a hero if it means people die because of me. What, then, am I supposed to become? What should I be?' Musing this, she sits down, and everyone else gathers around her.

The doctor approaches Sandhi and informs her, "We've stitched Julia up, but she has lost a lot of blood. Someone needs to give her blood."

"What's her blood type?"

"O positive."

Immediately standing up and gesturing towards Julia, Sandhi asks, "She needs blood. Does anyone here have O-positive blood? If so, please tell us so the doctor can proceed with a transfusion."

Everyone starts asking each other - Ivan, Helga, and Marco inquire, amongst others.

Helga asks Sandhi, "Vladimir is sleeping; should I wake him up and ask?"

Sandhi thinks for a moment, as no other options are visible. Nobody is revealing if their blood type matches. She says, "Ask him." Helga stands beside Vladimir; she calls out, but he doesn't hear.

Helga pulls a water bottle from her school bag and pours water over Vladimir's face. Cursing as he wakes up, Marco chides him, reminding him that Helga is just a kid and shouldn't be sworn at. Vladimir responds, "This is my reaction… if you wake up someone drunk like this, this is what they will do," and then he starts laughing.

Anger is apparent on Helga's face as she says, "You have no manners."

"I don't have manners, but I didn't do it intentionally. Were you scared when the war started, tell me?"

"What does that have to do with anything?"

"Just answer. Were you scared?"

"No."

"Tell the truth!" Vladimir takes his eyes off his scotch bottle to look at Helga for the first time. She meets his gaze and confesses, "Yes, I was scared the first time I heard the bomb, but not after that."

"Why weren't you scared after that?"

"Because it felt like a video game... except in this, once someone dies, they don't come back. I liked that concept, and now I'm enjoying it."

Scratching his head after hearing her response, Vladimir says, "You're crazier than I am."

"To you, this may be like a video game, but that doesn't mean I don't respect human life or dignity."

"So what do you think? I don't?"

Seeing the situation heating up, Sandhi interrupts and asks Vladimir, "Forget all this; just tell me, is your blood type O positive?"

"No, mine isn't, but would you use my blood if it were?" Vladimir's question made Sandhi realize what he was implying, yet she still asked, "Why, what's wrong with your blood?"

"I've been drinking since last night."

"Why?"

Standing up, Vladimir explained, "What do you expect? A man who came here on vacation was having fun. How was I to know all this would happen?"

Surprised, Sandhi remarked, "You're not from here, but you seem local."

"No, I am, and I am not. My mother lived here, but she was Russian. " Everyone's gaze shifted to Vladimir upon hearing 'Russia.' He continued, "Hear me out; my father was an American citizen."

As he spoke, Vladimir searched his pocket and pulled out a cigarette. After sharing this, he laughed and said, "Not every Russian is your enemy; your enemy is those standing on your land and killing your people."

Sandhi hummed gravely in response while Vladimir lit his cigarette. The crowd began to disperse. Ivan approached with a woman and a dog. The dog, seeing Vladimir, started barking. The woman called the dog "Hero... Hero."

Hero calmed down. The woman, who had called the dog 'Hero,' explained, "Hero saw a bomb explode. There was a burst of fire, and since then, he barks at anything that burns." Vladimir walked over to the dog, hid his burning cigarette behind his back, and gently patted Hero, saying, "Don't be scared, Hero. It's just a cigarette, not a bomb, and I'm not like them."

Sandhi looked at the woman, about to speak, but the woman with the dog spoke first, "My blood type is O positive. Ivan told me someone needed blood. I was behind and didn't realize what was happening here."

Sandhi responded, "It's great that you want to help Julia."

Realizing that Julia needed the blood because she was the only one on a stretcher, the woman approached Julia, her dog following. She declared, "I'm ready."

Sandhi asked, "What's your name?"

She replied, "Natasha."

Sandhi called for the doctor. The medical team was already attending to other injured people. A doctor approached Sandhi to treat her wound. Seeing him coming, Sandhi said, "Please treat Julia first. I only have a scratch."

Hearing this, the doctor returned to Julia. While doctors were with Julia, the rest of the medical team tended to other wounded individuals. After testing Natasha's blood, the doctor quickly inserted a needle into her veins. Natasha gasped, and Hero barked at the doctors. Natasha petted him, saying, "Hero, I'm okay." Hero listened intently with his ears perked.

Cautiously, the doctor inserted the other end of the needle into Julia's veins. The blood transfusion began. The doctor asked Ivan, "Can we move the dog a bit away?"

Ivan looked at Sandhi, who stated, "Ukraine is as much his as yours, doctor. He's scared just like we are." Perhaps regretting his words, the doctor silently continued treating Julia.

Outside, the sound of gunfire reached the underground, alarming Julia, Natasha, and Hero. Seeing that the transfusion had started and sensing their fear, Sandhi moved closer and stood by them. Hero licked her hand, which made her smile. She stroked Hero's head. Sandhi was exhausted and sat down, leaning back on her hands. Petrovich also sat down beside her. Vladimir's cigarette had gone out, and he, too, sat down, turning up the collar of his jacket to keep his neck warm. Marco was already standing by Julia. Helga had been sitting with Ivan but moved to sit before Sandhi when she saw her sit down. The others, already seated, were disturbed by Helga's action but were too tired to object and made space for her.

Gradually, only 8-9 people remained near the stairs; the rest had moved further inside the underground station. According to the activity hierarchy, those more active stayed near the stairs, while those less active moved deeper inside the station.

As soon as Helga sat next to Sandhi, Sandhi grabbed her shoulders and said in a playful tone, "You seem to be enjoying this concept."

Helga blushed a little and replied, "No... I didn't mean that... Initially, it felt that way, but after seeing Julia, I realized there is no fun in this... just troubles. There's fear, the fear of death."

Sandhi hummed softly and said, "Dear, only politicians find this amusing; you are just a little girl."

Helga changed the subject, "Forget all that... tell us something about yourself."

"What should I say?" Sandhi paused as she looked at Petrovich, who also said with a smile, "Tell us something I don't know."

Sandhi laughed and looked around at everyone sitting nearby. She heard the gunfire in the background and asked, "What do you want to know?" (She realized from everyone's faces that they all wanted to know about her, understanding that connecting deeply could help them through these tough times, so she took on that responsibility.)

Helga said, "Whatever you want to share."

Touching Helga's blonde hair, Sandhi replied, "I was like you once. Not just me; almost every girl and every woman is the same. Whether in India or Ukraine. We all go through unique struggles, like believing whatever we choose or do in life will be wrong without a man's advice. My father was just such a person who often dismissed most of my ideas... partly because he cared a lot about me and partly because he thought I would fail in them. He, my mother, and I were worrying through it all. Of course, there were other family members like uncles, aunts, and my grandmother, but they were not concerned about my future or their futures. My grandparents passed away when I was very young. I hardly remember them, except for one thing—my grandmother's handkerchief where she kept her money. But let's not trouble their memory by recalling them. Then, one day, I suddenly grew up, and my future became a concern for my father and mother. I liked to skip rope and run, and Dad had decided to put a stethoscope in my hands." (Sandhi drifted back to her old days as she spoke.)

Banaras

June 23, 2017

In Banaras, near the ghats, was the house of Vrindavan Rai. On the third floor of that house, a girl was sleeping diagonally across the bed with the door locked from the inside while the whole house echoed with the calls of "Sandhi... Sandhi." These were calls from Sandhi's father. There was continuous knocking at the door as her father tried to wake her.

From inside, Sandhi asked, "What happened?"

Her father responded, "Open the door. Are you still sleeping? It's already 11 a.m."

Sandhi got up, thought for a moment, and then went back to sleep. Her father knocked again and said, "Hey, open the door; why aren't you opening it?"

This time, Sandhi got up, picked up a T-shirt from the table piled with sports books, and looked at a poster above the table that read 'I DON'T CARE.' After putting on the T-shirt, she started looking for her sports trousers but her father's knocking didn't stop. She found the trousers under the bed, quickly put them on, stood in front of the mirror for a minute to fix her hair, looked at herself, and said, "Looks like your results are out."

With that, she yawned and opened the door. As soon as the door opened, her father exclaimed, "Does it take so long to open a door, and why do you sleep so late?"

"It's not that late, dad, it's only 11."

Sandhi's mom had also come upstairs due to the loud knocking. From outside the door, her mom glared at her.

"You were saying it's only 11. Do you sleep even later than this every day?"

Sandhi realized from her mom's look that she had said something wrong. She should have just mentioned the time. Sandhi slept late, and that was a matter between her and her mom.

Changing the subject, Sandhi asked, "Why were you knocking so hard... tell me that."

"Your NEET exam results are out."

From downstairs, Sandhi's uncle shouted, "Sandhi, give us your roll number, and we'll check it on the mobile."

Sandhi shouted, "I'll check it; it's my result."

Her father said, "Just give the roll number... he'll check it."

"I'll check it myself; wait." Sandhi went back into her room. Outside, her mom stood, and her father entered and sat on the bed.

Sandhi saw her father sitting, then looked at her mom standing at the door, and heard someone's voice on the stairs; it must have been her aunt. She quickly took out her mobile and said, "Before the whole neighborhood shows up, I might as well check the result myself."

She turned on the internet on her mobile and closed the open tabs from the night before while researching how to run 100 meters. She went to the NEET site and entered her roll number. Her mom was praying in the background, but Sandhi didn't pray to anyone. She just looked at the 'I DON'T CARE' poster. She saw the result and told her father, "Dad, I've passed."

As soon as her father heard this, he exclaimed, "Praise Lord Vishwanath!"

Sandhi looked at her father and asked, "Happy now? Can I go?"

Her father replied, "Yes... yes, go, but don't wake up late from tomorrow, and now find out which college you will get."

"Okay."

"Now my daughter will become a doctor; the world will see my stature."

Sandhi came out of her room to find her aunt congratulating her. Sandhi said, "Thanks, aunt. Now please get me a tea with ginger," she walked downstairs.

Reaching downstairs, she picked up a towel and stretched out, then lay down on a jute cot. Despite the heat, she lay in the sun, then suddenly got up and went into the bathroom.

After a quick shower, she came out, and her mom remarked, "How do you bathe so quickly?"

Hanging the towel in the courtyard, Sandhi replied, "I bathe like ordinary girls, but Mom, you bathe like a movie star for hours."

Her mom looked at her and said, "It's so difficult to talk with you."

Sandhi went upstairs, got ready quickly, came down, and told her mom, "Mom! I'm going to Roshni's house, and from there, I'll find out about the NEET colleges."

Sandhi passed through the courtyard to the outside, where her bike was parked. While wiping the bike, her eyes fell on her father's nameplate. She first wiped the nameplate, which read 'Dr. Vrindavan Rai, BDS,' then suddenly stopped wiping halfway and left on her bike.

Riding her bike, Sandhi thought about what she would do if she didn't get into a good college. Would she run for her dreams again or retake the NEET exam? But retaking NEET meant another year of studying at home. While riding, she shook her head, thinking, "Dad has trapped me in this medical study; first, I need to take coaching for medical, which costs so much money, and then the pressure is on me. I'm even more trapped in this cycle that might never end. I wonder, do those who don't have money not become doctors? Is becoming a doctor so essential? It's not essential; my track and 100 meters matter to me. Dad couldn't become one, so he implanted his dream in me. My heart is set on the sound of the pistol before a race starts and on my 100 meters. What a time it is to fulfill someone else's dream. She passed several temples on the way but didn't bow her head to any, just glared and drove past them."

Sandhi slowed down the bike and stopped as her friend Roshni waved at her. She asked, "What's your score?"

Sitting behind her, Roshni replied, "I'm getting a government college."

Hearing this, Sandhi said, "Let's have a pan to celebrate," then started the bike and drove off.

While riding, Sandhi asked, "So, where will you study?"

"I'll study here... Dad won't let me go anywhere else."

"Be free for once," then Roshni pinched her from behind, and Sandhi started laughing.

Sandhi stopped at a pan shop to get a pan and told the pan vendor, "Uncle, in the white kurta, please make two pans."

The pan vendor looked at Sandhi and laughed, "No one calls me that."

"You're all fools... you sit at a pan shop, make at least a thousand pans daily, and your kurta stays clean all day; isn't that amazing?"

The vendor laughed again. Then Sandhi told him, "Uncle, you're just like the government of India. No matter how many bad things happen, whether education is expensive, people are hungry, or there's a lack of jobs. Whatever they do, they're still the government. We have to listen to them. What can we do, uncle? Go ahead and make the pan."

The uncle quickly made the pans and gave them to Sandhi. Sandhi ate one right there and gave another to Roshni. After eating the pan, Roshni covered her mouth with a cloth.

Seeing this, Sandhi said, "You keep swallowing everything; won't you spit anything out?"

Sandhi started the bike again and asked, "Now tell me, where shall we go?"

"Let's go wherever you want to go."

"Then I'll take you to my most special place."

"No, not there."

"Why not there?"

"That's where they cremate bodies, not there."

"Whenever something inside me dies, I go there."

"What's dead inside you today?"

"You wouldn't understand, crazy... Being free is very hard, and when you know you won't be free, a lot ends. Let's go there and decide what to do with life."

Soon, they reached there and sat down in a corner on the ghat, and Sandhi just watched the Ganga and the burning bodies without saying a word. Then she said, "Smoke, smoke, smoke, that's all there is in life... Roshni, do you know when smoke rises?"

Roshni looked at her silently, then quickly said, "Yes, from a scientific point of view, smoke rises when something isn't burning properly."

Sandhi stood up suddenly and said, "Exactly. There's a lot of smoke inside me; I'm burning but not properly. Nothing is going right."

"What's wrong? Tell me."

"Man, I scored 440 out of 720. Now tell me, can I get into a good government college?"

Roshni was silent for a minute, then said, "That's very difficult."

"Okay, now tell me, how much would the fees be for a private college?"

"Forget it; it will be costly. At least seventy to eighty lakhs?"

Sandhi started laughing, then told Roshni, "Look ahead."

"What's there?"

Pointing towards a burning body, Sandhi said, "This is how dreams burn fiercely."

"Did you want to study medicine?"

"No, man, I didn't want to, but Dad borrowed money to pay for coaching. Then I did the coaching, and now I think, since Dad is doing so much, I might make it my dream."

"So our Sandhi has made peace between desires and reality," they said, and they both laughed for a long time.

"Let's go home. Otherwise, Dad will start calling."

"Okay, let's go."

"Have you ever come here at night?"

"No, I'll never come here at night."

"It feels good to come here."

"What feels good?"

"Watching the fire burn, even humans, you see the beginnings or the ends of cries here."

"I will never come at night; it must feel so scary here."

Sandhi laughed, saying, "Nothing is more beautiful and deceptive than death. It just has to come at your favorite moments." They laughed again and made their way to the bike.

Sandhi bowed before the Ganga as they left the ghat, then started the bike again and told Roshni, "Come on, get on, let's go home."

They both got on the bike, and Sandhi drove even faster this time. Roshni exclaimed, "Are you going to kill us today?"

"Don't die, I won't let you die... you're sitting with a doctor." This time, Sandhi didn't laugh; only Roshni did.

After dropping Roshni off at her house, Sandhi said, "Wash your face... you've eaten pan; otherwise, your dad will curse me," and sped off.

While driving home, Sandhi thought about what would happen when she told her dad that she wouldn't get into any government college. With this dilemma in mind, she reached home.

After parking her bike, she carefully cleaned her father's nameplate. Then, taking a deep breath, she went inside, drank water to lessen the pan's redness, and sat in the lower courtyard.

Sandhi thought to herself, "Is it okay to sit here? What will happen?" Then she answered, "Whatever happens, will happen... the sooner, the better."

She then played with her hair in various styles for a while. Suddenly, she heard, "Sandhi... Sandhi."

This time, she responded immediately. Her dad came and sat next to her, then turned on the TV and asked, "Did you find out? What happened? Which colleges will you get?"

Sandhi sat up straight and said, "Dad, I scored 440 out of 720; it will be tough for me to get into any government college."

Her dad looked at her angrily, then said, "Why didn't you study properly?"

Sandhi remains silent as everyone gathers in the room—Uncle, Aunt, Auntie, and Mother. All eyes are on Sandhi.

Then Uncle asks, "How do you know you won't get into a government college?"

"Many people apply, and very few get in."

"It's not like that, brother... Remember, in our village, the son of Chachiya Sasur's aunt got into a government college."

It took Sandhi's father a moment to remember, then he said, "I'll find out more," and left the room. Everyone resumed their work while Sandhi remained seated, pondering the harsh realities of a student's life. Succeeding in exams was celebrated, but failure brought only disdain, which seemed even harsher for girls—as if their failures somehow restricted their freedoms more.

When her father returned, he said, "It's difficult to get into a government college; you should have studied harder." The others reentered the room, too.

This time, Sandhi didn't remain silent and replied, "Dad, for a subject I have no interest in, I scored this much just because you asked. You know where my real passion lies."

Her father, angry, retorted, "So, you'd spend your life on the field?"

"Yes, I would have... Better to live out there on the field than suffocating over these books, wondering where I could have been."

Uncle intervened, "Sandhi, don't talk like that... don't answer back."

"Then don't ask such questions."

The room fell silent. Breaking the silence, her father asked, "Do you still want to pursue medical studies?"

"Yes, but only for you, to show you that I'm not weak in studies... My heart was always set on sports and winning our country's medals." This response shocked everyone, as they had never seen this side of Sandhi.

"When did this patriotism arise in you?" her father asked with a slight chuckle.

"It was always there, Dad, but you never tried to know, and I never thought it necessary to tell because I knew I'd have to give it up someday."

"But you can also serve the country by becoming a doctor."

"That's what I thought, Dad, but I've made another decision, too," Sandhi said firmly, more seriously than usual.

"What decision have you made?"

"I will finance my education."

"How will you do that?"

"I will take out an educational loan."

Her father looked at her, realizing he was speaking to the grown-up Sandhi. Aunt remarked, "Do you know how expensive medical studies are?"

"I know, Aunt. I've looked it all up. It will cost at least 70 to 80 lakh in a private college." Uncle asked, "Such a huge loan. Do you think you can repay it?"

"For God's sake, stop doubting me and my capabilities. If you can't trust me, please keep your disbelief to yourselves."

Her father said, "I just called a friend who teaches in coaching centers. He told me it's tough to get into a government college with your marks." Sandhi's heart sank with the mention of her marks again. But then her father continued, "He mentioned another possibility."

"What is it?"

"Many Indian students study medicine in Ukraine, where the fees are much lower—almost half of what is here. You could get admitted based on your NEET scores, and after studying there, you can come back and qualify to practice here."

Sandhi's mother asked, "Where is this Ukraine?"

"Very far, overseas," her father explained.

"Oh God, you would send our daughter so far away!"

"I'm not sending her, just presenting an option," her father clarified.

Uncle protested, "Why even suggest it?"

Her father responded, "Someone paying their way should at least know all her options." He then left for his room.

Sandhi couldn't tell if her father was helping her or forcing her to make a tough decision. She watched him return to his room and kept thinking about his words. Aunt, Uncle, and her mother blamed each other and then turned their frustrations towards her. Sandhi got up, saw them all laughing, and went straight to her father's room.

Entering the room, she sat near her father's feet and asked, "Why haven't you eaten yet?"

"I'll eat soon, the food's not ready yet... Tell me what's on your mind."

"Dad, why did you suggest Ukraine? You want to see what I choose. You know how much I love you, Mom, and this city. If I can leave all this, then I truly want this, right?"

Her father looked at her differently this time, almost as if he were talking to a peer. He said lovingly, "Dear, you have great potential and even greater compassion, and together, they make an incredible combination. You'll be a great doctor and an even greater person."

Sandhi said nothing more. She got up, lightly squeezed her father's hands, and thanked him for his advice and praise. "And yes, now I'm going to sleep because I need to visit the bank in the morning to inquire about the loan." She left the room laughing.

Reaching her room, Sandhi first stood on her desk, tore down her 'I Don't Care' poster, kissed her sports books, and tucked them neatly into her bag. Then, she stood on her balcony, looking at the nearby temple. When her mother came up behind her, she didn't turn around, continuing to stare at the temple. Her mother hugged her from behind, and she remarked, "Jai Shri, you're showing much love today."

"Cheeky, using your mom's name," her mother chided.

"Let me joke... I'll be far away soon."

"I heard what you and your father discussed. It's good you've grown up and become wise. All I'll say is do what I couldn't— become not just 'a big man' as I heard all my life. Be a great woman, not just in terms of money, but integrity too."

Sandhi turned and hugged her mother tightly. "If you hug me this tightly, I'll suffocate."

"Since Dad doesn't hug me, you complete his share," she replied, taking a deep breath and adding, "I'm so happy because it's been a long time since I've seen Dad this happy, and after all my efforts, today I saw not just love but respect in his eyes for me." This moved her mother to tears, and they laughed and cried awhile.

The following day, Sandhi woke up, bathed, got ready, and sat down to read the newspaper in the courtyard until her father woke up. Seeing her, he was delighted and exclaimed, "The sun has come out in my courtyard today."

"Shall we have tea?" Sandhi asked.

"Yes," her father replied.

By then, her mother had brought tea for both of them. Then Sandhi started doing something on her mobile. Her father asked, "What are you doing?"

"I'm looking at how to apply to universities in Ukraine. I'll try to complete the forms in a few days."

"Good job!" he said, and they went for a walk. Sandhi continued gathering information until she left for the bank.

A month later

By around 6 pm, Sandhi hadn't returned, and her father was pacing outside in worry. He kept calling her, but her mobile was off. He checked his watch and asked Jayshri, "Where has she gone? She hasn't come back yet."

"She'll come... Don't worry," her mother reassured him.

"How can I not worry? She's been running to the bank from morning to evening lately. Who knows when this loan will be approved? If a student even wants to study in this country, that's torture. You have to fulfill a thousand laws and then a thousand more... This country is a joke, just a joke. Being poor is a bigger crime than anything else in this country." Just then, they saw Sandhi arriving on her bike.

Her father couldn't contain himself; he opened the gate quickly and made space for her bike. As soon as she got off, he bombarded her with questions. Sandhi listened quietly and parked her bike, saying, "Dad, only a few days are left, then you'll only scold me over the phone."

Her father realized the loan must have been approved. He immediately hugged her. It had been so long since he had hugged Sandhi that she just stood there frozen, closing her eyes. She wanted to keep this feeling with her forever. Uncle, Aunt, and her mother all came outside. It had been long since they had all been happy together without any resentment.

As soon as her father let her go, Sandhi touched his feet, and then she touched her uncle's and aunt's, and finally, her mother's. Her mother gave her money from Grandma's handkerchief, saying, "Buy some sweets." Sandhi smiled and led everyone back inside the house. They all sat down in the courtyard. Sandhi told them, "I need to book tickets for next week because classes will start soon."

Her father immediately asked, "Should I call the travel consultancy?"

"Yes, Dad, we must arrange the tickets, visa, and everything as soon as possible."

Her father signaled to her uncle, and they left for the travel agency. Her mother and aunt went into the kitchen to make sweets for Sandhi. Her aunt started packing her stuff in her room. Sandhi was left alone in the courtyard. She looked around the house calmly, thinking that despite all their disagreements, they were all ultimately one. The specialty of homes is that no matter how different the rooms are when it comes to the house, you can't leave any room behind. She realized she had to leave this home now. Tears welled in her eyes, and she murmured, "Can't everything I need be found around this house, Mahadev?" Then she answered, "No, it can't, I know." She got up and went to her room.

On the day of her departure for Ukraine

Early in the morning, Sandhi's father was up before anyone else, followed by her uncle, aunt, and mother. Everyone was hurrying to finish their tasks as quickly as possible. Sandhi was the last to get up, then she got ready and came downstairs. Everyone was outwardly happy, but inwardly, they were all sad. Sandhi understood this. Her father sat outside, not coming in, agitated about everything. Seeing all this, Sandhi went to her father, placed a chair beside him, and sat down. As soon as she sat, her father asked if she had checked all her belongings. Sandhi reassured, "I have packed everything correctly, but why are you worried, Dad? What's bothering you?"

"What can I tell you... What's there to hide? You know everything. Your uncle does nothing; your aunt has left her home to be here, and all we have is this house, the land in the village, and whatever little my dentistry practice brings in. Nothing has been right in this house for long, so I'm nervous. I couldn't do much for you either; I just managed your ticket and some money."

Sandhi listened patiently and then said, "Have faith in God... Everything will be alright, and you can't imagine how much you have done for me. The determination I have toward my goals today is all because of you. You think you haven't done much but don't understand what you have done for me. I would have been lost all my life, but you showed me what to hold on to. You have guided me; what more could you give?"

Her father couldn't hold back his tears and went inside. Sandhi sat outside longer, staring at her father's name plate until she could only see Vrindavan.

It was time for the flight. Everyone got into the rental car. The airport was close to the house, and they arrived quickly. No one spoke on the way; complete silence prevailed as no one wanted to make the atmosphere more solemn.

At the airport, Sandhi and all the family members got out, unloaded the luggage, and stood to one side. No one knew who would speak first. After a long silence, Sandhi said, "Okay, then. See you."

Just saying this brought tears to everyone's eyes. Her mother took off her glasses and started crying; her father held Sandhi's hand, her uncle put his hand on her shoulder, her aunt held her bag, and her other aunt pulled her cheeks. Sandhi was in the middle of everyone.

After a while, Sandhi hugged everyone, picked up her bag, and started to leave. It seemed she felt that if she stayed any longer, she might not leave. Everyone watched her go, but she didn't look back because she was crying. Once inside the airport, a glass gate separated her from her family. She turned around and waved to everyone, then proceeded towards her destination.

Sitting in the airplane, Sandhi felt very strange. It was her first time leaving home, and she was heading 5,000 kilometers away. While fastening her seatbelt, she felt as if she was leaving her people and city behind, and because of her nervousness, she couldn't fasten her belt at first. After several attempts, she managed to secure it.

The plane started racing down the runway. From the window, she saw everything moving swiftly away in the opposite direction, and as the plane took off, Sandhi felt incredibly light, as if there was no life left in her. Then, she saw a temple and prayed for everyone's well-being. As the plane ascended further, it seemed everything was left below. She felt she had risen above everything or was utterly alone up there. She raised the window shade higher, trying to spot her 100-meter track field, but she had risen so high that she couldn't see her city anymore. Only clouds of hope spread far across the horizon were visible. Life is indeed a battle where only desires die. Who would tell the outcome of my life's battle—how many desires were martyred and how many wishes were wounded? But a sailor who has left the shore must sail on.

"Patriotism is a guardianship, a form of love, both in military and cultural aspects. Nationalism, however, is an aggressive stance, a behavior filled with rage."

Kharkiv

February 24, 2022

Hero barks and begins to move backward in fear. Natasha strokes him, but he doesn't stop and keeps retreating. He seemed to be looking forward but was moving backward. Sandhi tries to stand, but her legs fail her. Helga gives her a slight support, and she manages to get up.

Sandhi tells Natasha, "It seems a large number of Russian troops have entered."

Natasha angrily says, "God knows how many bombs they will drop; it seems they don't intend to spare a single life."

Ivan says, "How can we just end like this? It's not that easy to kill us."

Marco wipes the sweat from his forehead. Vladimir, seeing this, says to him, "What's the matter... sweating even in this cold?"

Marco was about to respond when an explosive hit the upper part of the station, shaking the entire station. Paint and some concrete from right above Sandhi falls. She quietly shifts her position. The doctors also removed the IV since the transfusion was complete. Everyone starts slowly crawling from one place to another. Natasha and Helga moved aside from Julia's stretcher. Her pain was less now... the doctors had given her painkillers.

Ivan says, "Everyone, move inside so that if the Russian army comes here, they find this place empty." Petrovich says, "The metro station is quite big... we should move away from the stairs." Sandhi slowly crawls inward as bullets and shells continue to be fired above. Following her, the others also start to move. Helga initially crawls but then stands up.

Vladimir gestures to her to crawl, but she doesn't understand. A bullet hits a bulb above the stairs, and Vladimir rushes to knock Helga down, and everyone goes quiet. Hero also pulls his panting tongue back in after this incident. Vladimir forcefully pushes Helga down. She quiets down after hearing the bulb shatter just seconds ago. Vladimir quietly asks her, "Don't you cherish your life? These aren't school games, Helga, one bullet, and it's all over."

Seeing the fear in his eyes, Helga gets scared because he looks terrified. She tells him, "Thank you, Vladimir." Vladimir hears her but says nothing and moves on.

Now, complete darkness has settled in front of the stairs, and there is little light inside because so many bombs have fallen on the surface that many bulbs and lights have stopped working. Some lights flicker on and off. It is clear from the sounds above the stairs that a large group is moving there.

Vladimir says, "It seems they are speaking in Russian."

Petrovich tells Vladimir, "Yes, you are right, it is Russian, but I can't understand what they are discussing."

Helga tells Sandhi, "Your story... no, your life is exciting. From India to Ukraine and now here, wow." Sandhi smiles at her and says, "Interesting it is, but also difficult. Perhaps it's hard to be interesting without the difficulty." Helga nods.

"Talking to you reminds me of my parents and my entire home. It's been two days since I spoke to them. They must be worried after hearing the news here."

Gradually, the footsteps above quieted down, but no one dared stand up. After a while, when the environment seemed to return to how it was earlier, where sounds were coming from afar, everyone stood up, but now they all sat facing inward. Sandhi got up and leaned against the wall. Everyone else also sat down, still scared. Sandhi's face wasn't afraid, but she was lost in thoughts.

Petrovich sits beside her and asks, "What's the matter, Sandhi?" Sandhi, looking down, answers, "I'm tired of life. I'm thirsty, have a headache, and I'm missing home. My mother must be in a bad state; my father wouldn't have eaten. I used to talk to them daily, but I haven't spoken in two days... I wonder what they are doing." Saying all this, she starts crying and adds, "I need to talk to them. Are the phones even working here, or is all communication finished?"

Petrovich says, "I think the phones should still be working. I'll see if anyone has a phone around here. Due to being underground, there might be a signal issue."

"Yes, please check. If I can speak to them, it would reduce their worry. I don't understand what this life wants from me. I still have a loan, a year left in my degree, and I am here underground. I don't know how long I will stay. I need to get out of here and go home." After saying all this, Sandhi began to cry.

Sandhi's tears were few; perhaps the shock was too great. Her grief was more burdened with responsibilities than with tears. It seemed like she had been shot the way she was screaming. Petrovich puts his hand over her mouth and tells her, "Sandhi, your screams might draw the Russian squad this way; please cry quietly."

Petrovich, saying this, started thinking that what he said about crying quietly was odd. Petrovich was thinking about the immense distress that not crying might also not allow you to live. Perhaps crying is proof of being human. Thinking this, he, too, had tears, but before Sandhi could notice, he wiped them away.

It was evening. The lighting in the subway was dim; most bulbs barely provided light. The atmosphere itself was very subdued. Life isn't usually this slow, or maybe we aren't used to seeing life so slow. At this moment, everything was happening quickly or slowly. Everyone was tired, hungry, thirsty, and wounded; almost everyone had lost something—either a home, a friend, a family, or peace. Above all, no one had a clear path ahead.

Sandhi couldn't sit comfortably despite wanting to. She was reminiscing about the warmth given by her family. At this moment, she even remembered her bed. Then she remembered her bike, her friend Roshni. All her consciousness wanted to connect with her family. She was also contemplating what she would tell her parents about her whereabouts as she hadn't told them she was going to Kharkiv. She hadn't even mentioned that she had been in love with a boy for two years. She had thought that once she returned to India after finishing her degree and starting her practice there, she would repay her entire loan and tell her father. Many dilemmas and confusions were holding Sandhi. It wasn't easy to escape those dilemmas and confusion. She had understood that there wouldn't be any solution until she talked. She couldn't decide what she would tell them about how she was, where she was, whether she should mention Petrovich or not, etc., etc., etc.

Looking for Petrovich, Sandhi asked Ivan, "Have you seen Petrovich?"

Ivan told her, "Yes, I just saw Petrovich talking to Marco." Sandhi started looking for Marco. After walking a bit, she saw Petrovich talking to Marco. Petrovich and Marco were discussing something, but she interrupted their conversation and started talking to Petrovich, asking, "Did you find out where we can get a phone?"

Petrovich, "I was just discussing that with Marco. Marco lives nearby. He told me there is a telephone booth a little further down the street... it might still be working because the Russian army wouldn't have damaged it." Then Vladimir comes over and asks, "What's up?"

Petrovich ignored him, but Marco said they were talking about a phone. Sandhi wants to contact her home.

Sandhi asked, "Am I the only one who wants to talk to their family? Isn't there anyone else who misses their home?"

Vladimir said, "I also want to talk to my parents to tell them I am safe."

Sandhi asked Ivan, "Don't you want to talk?"

Ivan said, "Yes, I want to talk to my sister."

Sandhi said, "There are quite a few of us. We can all go together to that telephone booth."

Petrovich said, "It will be hazardous; it won't be easy. There's a risk to our lives; Russian troops are all over Kharkiv."

"If there's a risk to our lives, so be it, but I must tell my mother I am okay."

Natasha and Julia also came over, having overheard the conversation from a distance. Natasha said, "If we have to go, three or four in the morning would be the best time; the soldiers will be less active then. They will be more relaxed because they've been causing terror since 4 AM."

Sandhi agreed with her, "You are right."

Petrovich asked Natasha, "How do you know all this? When will they be relaxed, and when will they not? How do you know?"

"I know a lot... my fiancé was in the army."

Sandhi, "Where is he now?"

"He is with the fairies now. He died in 2014 when Russia attacked Crimea. He was in the Crimean army. I don't understand why some nations keep waging wars."

"Yes, Natasha, you are right... some nations keep waging wars, sometimes to wield power, sometimes to preserve it."

"I don't understand why those who wage wars can't see that wars only alter human relationships; they end their permanence, and then these very relationships, due to not being able to take any definitive form, hollow out the fundamental structure of families, communities, and nations. When the fundamental structure is hollowed out, what will the structure built on it achieve?" said Natasha.

"What we need isn't war; we need love and trust. We learned to fight later; first, we learned to love," replied Sandhi.

Ivan says, "In my opinion, war is like a toddler throwing a tantrum. He insists on having his way out of stubbornness, not realizing he could express it differently, do it differently. But he insists and wants to enforce whatever he has decided through war. The people should immediately replace any governments that want war. They should leave behind all their interests linked to those governments and elect someone who talks to the people and discusses issues with them. The more discussion there is, the better the governance will be. Otherwise, a crisis will come."

Marco: "War is a crisis that arises from a lack of discussion. Whenever things aren't progressing from one point to another, a crisis is about to emerge, and this crisis doesn't necessarily have to take the form of war. It can also be unemployment, hunger, crime, and a poor economy."

Petrovich: "The truth about war is entirely something else."

Sandhi: "What is the truth...? Certain groups determine truths, and the truth never arrives without bias. It always nurtures some groups. Just look at this war; President Putin's truth differs from Zelensky's. America's truth is different; the European Union's truth is different. But look here, our truth is different from all their truths. Interests and greed cannot preserve the truth; the truth is impartial and universal. It will appear fair to everyone if it exists, provided those looking for it are not drowned in hatred and greed and want to see the truth. We are suffering through this war, and our families are troubled. What do they care about? They want to become immortal in history. They want to tell stories of their bravery through print media, newspapers, TV, social media, radio, and ordinary people; their truths are different. Yes... but the effort is to unify all these truths. Look how the Russian newspapers will craft a truth for their people and the Ukrainian newspapers for their people."

Marco: "Russia is causing this war because it can't manage its internal situation."

Sandhi: "You are right, but it's not limited to Russia. Nowadays, any country that cannot manage its internal situation well, uses hatred skillfully. They first nurture hatred, then control it, and when their situation weakens, they use it. In this era, hatred is an emotion and a weapon to preserve their power. Rulers hide every problem of the nation behind this hatred and prevent any issues from reaching them."

Petrovich: "But how is this possible? Do people not realize their unholy intentions?"

Natasha: "How would they realize it when everyone's relationship with the state differs? The nature of your relationship with the state is determined by what class you belong to. It means your status in the market defines your relationship, whether you are a producer, trader, intermediary, investor, donor, or merely a consumer, laborer, or farmer. When everyone has a different relationship with the state, why wouldn't the state treat every individual differently? This is why the state can breed hatred. It will support one at the expense of another."

Ivan, stirred by this, says, "So, are we supposed to betray our state, not remain loyal to it?"

Everyone falls silent upon hearing this question, but Sandhi looks at Ivan as if pondering something and then says, "Ivan, listen, there is a big difference between patriotism and nationalism. We all get caught in the trap because we don't understand these two words. By patriotism, I mean faith in a particular place and a different understanding of life, which anyone living there believes is superior. Still, they do not wish to impose it on people of other nations or even on their people who do not share this sentiment. Patriotism is a vigilance, a love, both militarily and culturally. But nationalism is an aggressive attitude, a resentful behavior. Patriotism is a conscious effort to protect against external attacks and cruelties."

Upon hearing this, Ivan falls silent and says, "I understand now who has patriotism and who has nationalism between Russia and Ukraine."

Vladimir, who had been listening all this while, irritably says, "Forget nationalism and patriotism; I am very thirsty; can someone tell me where I can find water?"

Sandhi asks, "What time is it now?" Petrovich says, "It's 2:45 AM."

Sandhi: "We still have plenty of time. Are you ready, Natasha?"

Natasha: "Yes, I'm ready."

Petrovich: "Think again, Sandhi... because of you, everyone's life here might be in danger." Everyone looked at Petrovich, their eyes seeking an explanation.

Petrovich says, "If someone spots you, they might follow you here, and everyone's life will be at risk." Natasha and Sandhi look into each other's eyes. Marco and Ivan also seem worried about this.

Julia says, "Sandhi saved my life; I'll go with her."

Sandhi says, "No, you have a child; you are not going." Julia's words wake the baby, who starts crying loudly.

Julia covers the baby's mouth, but Sandhi tells her, "Don't do that; the child will be scared." Sandhi says, "You are not going anywhere; feed him so he can sleep."

After a long silence, Sandhi says, "I'll go alone." Petrovich and Vladimir try to interrupt, saying, "What if someone follows you or sees you?"

Sandhi firmly says, "Listen to me fully, Vladimir, Petrovich... if someone sees me, I won't return here. I will fight them, or I will go somewhere else. And yes, Petrovich, I won't ask whether you will accompany me after this. I wouldn't have taken you with me anyway; your life has always been significant to me and still is."

Petrovich, hearing this, says, "No, Sandhi, you misunderstood me... I would always go with you. I was saying it for the sake of these people." Sandhi says, "Petrovich, you know me; I neither give explanations nor take them."

Sandhi moves forward and stands there. Natasha approaches her. She glares at Petrovich, stands by Sandhi, and says, "I will still go with you." Ivan also comes forward, saying, "Me too." Natasha says, "We should go now, or it will be light soon."

Sandhi asks Natasha, "Will Hero come with us too?"

Natasha: "Where I go, Hero goes."

Sandhi laughs and hugs her, giving Hero a respectful look. Hero licks Sandhi in response. Sandhi goes back and hugs Petrovich without asking. He tells him, "If I survive, we'll meet again."

Petrovich says, "Shall I come with you if you need me?"

Sandhi: "No, you stay here. It's safer here." Then she goes to Marco and says, "Thank you for being with me."

Marco: "Daughter, I'm scared about life. I don't have the courage like you. Forgive me."

"You have spoken the truth. It's okay to be scared of life, but it's wrong to lie to yourself." Then she goes to Vladimir and says, "Take care of everyone... You are a very straightforward person. People might categorize you as bad, but you show what you are, and that's good." Finally, she goes to Julia, who starts crying upon seeing her and says, "You are a god to me." Sandhi laughs it off, picks up the baby, kisses him, and says, "You are the future of Ukraine, and remember, don't do anything that hurts your mother."

She then hands the baby back to Julia and tells Natasha, "Let's see what happens."

Petrovich calls out to Sandhi from behind. Sandhi thinks he will say to leave, but he asks, "Will you tell your parents about me?"

Sandhi: "Yes, I will... don't think I will forget you just because you are not coming with me. I am a woman. When I leave everything for my father, I can forget your words for you."

Sandhi, Natasha, and Hero move forward. Suddenly, gunfire starts. From below, only minor points of light could be seen moving in both directions, nothing else.

The others were frightened when he grabbed Natasha's throat, but before Petrovich and Ivan could intervene, Hero proved his mettle. They had seized the Russian soldier, attempting to kill him. Ivan, Petrovich, Helga, and Marco tried to beat him. Sandhi exclaimed loudly, "No, we won't contribute to the war either. We need to stop the war, not fuel it." Everyone stopped and looked at her.

Petrovich challenged, "He's Russian; why shouldn't we kill him, and who are you to tell us what we should or shouldn't do?"

Sandhi thought, 'Perhaps this decisive hatred, once settled in hearts, proves to be the most destructive enemy of human civilization, a decision borne out of jealousy.'

Marco angrily said, "They've stolen our peace and turned our homes to ash. Why shouldn't we kill them?"

The Russian soldier was terrified, seeing his fate being debated before him. Only one woman wanted to save him; no one else did. Vladimir said, "Do whatever you want, but speak softly... so the other soldiers might not hear and come here." He paused for a few seconds, then added, "Check his pockets, see what rank he is. If he's high-ranking, other soldiers might come looking for him."

Julia said, "What's the use of searching his pockets, Sandhi? He killed a Ukrainian soldier right in front of you. He's a murderer; he killed our country's soldiers. My condition is because of him; my child is also in danger because of them."

Sandhi replied, "Killing this man won't solve your problems. He's a soldier; if he hadn't been killed, the Ukrainian would have killed him. This conflict arises from two completely opposing discourses; killing him would only strengthen the discourse of hate, and sparing him might let love win and humanity win. Life is important to me, whether his or anyone else's."

Meanwhile, Marco was checking the soldier's pockets and pulled something out. Sandhi was shocked to see it.

Petrovich took it from Marco's hand, and just as Sandhi was saying, "Can I use this to call home?"

Natasha said, "It's hard to say how much the Russians have damaged communication."

Petrovich laughed, stood up while the others still held the Russian soldier, and watched him stand. A kind of pride appeared on his face. He looked around and said, "This is a satellite phone, and with this phone, we can call anyone anywhere. No matter how much the Russians have destroyed communication, this will work because it operates via satellite."

Sandhi was relieved and said, "Now I can speak to my family."

Petrovich suddenly became serious again and said, "If this satellite phone was with him, it means he's a high-ranking Russian officer."

Hearing this, the Russian soldier's condition worsened. He tried to speak, but Marco had covered his mouth. Julia said, "If he's such a high-ranking officer, then it's right to kill him." Sandhi again disagreed more firmly, saying, "No, understand, Julia, this is not our problem; our problem is the war. Killing him will kill humanity; I, too, feel like killing him, but that would mean victory for the ideology that says killing a human solves problems."

Natasha suggested, "If he's a high-ranking officer, he might know much about Russian plans. Why don't we interrogate him and then contact a Ukrainian to pass on all the information? This could solve the current problem and help the country." Everyone liked this suggestion. Vladimir also agreed; he didn't want to kill the Russian soldier; perhaps he didn't care whether he lived or died. He just wanted to stay alive. So, it was decided not to kill him.

Petrovich said, "Then we need to stop his bleeding." He started moving people away from him and instructed Marco, Ivan, and Helga to interrogate him. He tasked Helga because he thought Helga would get agitated quickly and start beating the soldier. Petrovich didn't want the soldier to survive.

When Sandhi saw Petrovich creating such a trio, who would start attacking him first, she said, "Natasha, you interrogate him too." Natasha didn't want him to die either; hence, she deliberately played this move. She didn't want to argue loudly, but she didn't want to let him die either. Marco, Helga, Ivan,

Petrovich, and Natasha dragged him aside, first stopped his bleeding with some available clothes, then began interrogating him.

Before the Russian soldier could be dragged away, Petrovich handed Sandhi the satellite phone and said, "Here, make your call. I brought this for you because you were not afraid to risk your life to speak to your family." He said this in front of everyone, but the truth was that aside from Sandhi, no one else wanted to take the risk of making a call. Only Sandhi had put her parents above herself, adhering to the principle of risk and reward.

She initially looked at the phone as soon as she received it. Then, when Petrovich encouraged her to make the call, she took the phone, stepped forward, and asked Natasha, "Natasha! Would you like to call anyone?" She replied, "Thank you, Sandhi, but I have no one except Hero."

Sandhi wondered why she was delaying the call when she was so eager to speak. She then dialed her father's mobile number and sat down with her head in her hands.

The phone rang. There was no answer at the first or second ring, but on the third, someone picked up. A very subdued voice said, "Hello, who is this?" Sandhi replied with a heavy voice, "Dad." After clearing her throat and tears, she said, "Dad, it's Sandhi."

"Daughter, how are you? We saw on TV that the situation is terrible; you are okay, right?"

Her mother's voice was also heard in the background, and her uncle's, too. Sandhi heard everyone's voices and then closed her eyes. Tears streamed down her cheeks, breaking her smile. She said, "Dad, I'm fine. Don't worry about me. I'm okay."

"How can I not worry? Where are you now?" Just hearing this question, Sandhi broke down but composed herself and said, "Dad, I'm at a friend's place in Kharkiv."

"Kharkiv, where is that?"

"Not too far. We are safe."

Her crying father said, "The government will bring all the students from Ukraine, don't worry."

"Yes, Dad, I'm not worried. How is Mom?"

"Talk to your mom." When Sandhi heard 'mom' on the phone, she started crying again and covered the part of the phone where the voice was coming from. Meanwhile, her mom kept calling, "Sandhi, Sandhi, Sandhi." Sandhi then continued talking, clearing her tears and voice.

"Mom! There's something I wanted to tell you."

"Yes, daughter, tell me."

"Mom! I'm here in Kharkiv with my boyfriend. I've hidden this from you, but I've been with him for two years."

"It's okay, daughter, it happens. You've grown up... take care of everything; talk to your father now."

Before taking the phone, her father asked his wife, "What was Sandhi saying?"

"Nothing, she was just saying she's fine."

Sandhi told her father, "Dad! We'll meet soon."

"Yes, absolutely, come for a longer visit next time. The room upstairs feels empty without you," and he began sobbing heavily.

Sandhi replied, "I understand, Dad. I'll come soon. Take care. Tell Mom and Uncle I'm okay. I'll be back soon," and hung up. After hanging up, she placed the phone on her forehead and began crying, murmuring, 'Dad... Mom.'

You don't like love because it is simple; you prefer war.

Kharkiv

Time: 5 AM

February 25

As everyone was engrossed in the joy of communicating via satellite phones, and some were busy interrogating a Russian soldier, Hero was sniffing around the underground area where the Russian soldier had previously fallen. Then, Hero dashed back to where Natasha, Marco, and Ivan interrogated the soldier; Petrovich was not present. He was at Sandhi's house, listening to her speak, and began talking as soon as Sandhi hung up the phone.

Surrounding the Russian soldier were Natasha, Helga, Ivan, and Marco, among whom Hero kept trying to squeeze in because he wanted to sniff the soldier. Initially, Natasha restrained him and continued the interrogation. Still, when Hero persistently tried to intrude, she suddenly stopped everyone and said, "Wait...wait...why does Hero keep trying to get to him? There must be something here."

Everyone stared at Hero in amazement, and Hero sat looking back at them, still eager to get closer to the soldier. Natasha said, "Let Hero sniff him." Marco retorted, "Oh come on, why do you take this dog's actions so seriously? Sit down and interrogate, or I'll do it myself."

Natasha responded, "Firstly, his name isn't 'dog,' its Hero. And secondly, Marco doesn't do things without reason, just like you don't. To think that animals act without reason reduces us to beasts."

Taken aback by her words, Marco relented, "All right, let him sniff. What harm could it do in two minutes?" Ivan patted Hero, saying, "Go on, Hero, sniff."

Hero began sniffing, but the Russian soldier, who hadn't been as disturbed by the questioning as he was by Hero's sniffing, started panicking. "Get him away... he might bite me."

Natasha retorted, "When we were asking you questions, you couldn't speak, and now you start talking when you're scared."

Hero then pulled a pressed shirt from the soldier's pants and sniffed inside. Seeing this, Natasha reached inside the shirt and felt something; pulling her hand out, she found chocolates. The mention of chocolates reached the ears of Petrovich and Sandhi, who also arrived at the scene.

Natasha informed everyone, "About 12 chocolates were found and a water bottle hidden inside his waistband. These aren't ordinary chocolates... These are specially made for war, packed with energy and nutrients."

Sandhi interjected, "How much water does he have?"

Natasha, laughing, said, "Enough for a sip each."

Everyone was slightly lost in the allure of chocolates, water, and the satellite phone. These items brought a semblance of life to their hungry, thirsty, and isolated existence, though they were still far from everyday life.

Sandhi told Natasha and Petrovich, "These items will be equally shared. And one more thing, they will be shared with the Hero, too."

Vladimir exclaimed, "What's this about sharing with Hero?"

Natasha said, "He found these things. Marco didn't search properly; he only pulled out the satellite phone."

Vladimir argued, "At a time when food and water are crucial, we will share these with animals!"

Sandhi smiled and replied, "Absolutely, Vladimir," adding, "The crisis affects him too, not just you. We will also give food and water to the Russians."

This caused everyone to look at Sandhi differently.

Marco, sitting near the Russian soldier, grew very angry and said, "This woman has lost her mind."

After hearing Marco, Petrovich said, "Sandhi, you are right in your thoughts, but you can't decide who gets food and water and who doesn't."

Sandhi replied, "I haven't denied anyone; I just suggested sharing."

Vladimir added, "Sharing with Hero is fine, but why the Russian soldier?"

Julia also spoke up, "If my share goes to someone who tried to kill my child, I won't tolerate it."

Sandhi responded, "Julia, I understand where you're coming from. You haven't gotten over what happened at the hotel. Wasn't I there with you? You wouldn't be here if I had thought like you're now. Can the world function on such thoughts?" She paused and said, "Yes, maybe it does. But it's a world where wars happen, thefts occur, rapes occur, violence happens, hunger exists, wealth is unevenly distributed, unemployment is rampant, and helplessness prevails."

Sandhi paused momentarily, then continued, "That's why when we talk about justly sharing resources and rights, we are divided by caste, species, color, appearance, clothing, money, fame, province, and nation. Today, we don't want to give food and water to this Russian soldier because he's Russian, and we are in this war because of Russians. But his nationality is overshadowing his humanity. He's human first, then anything else."

Petrovich, after hearing all this, said, "Your intellectual arguments won't change the reality that this man just killed a soldier from my country who was protecting my home and family. How can I give him my share of food and water?"

In response, Sandhi said, "The real tragedy is that, in these times, its intelligence and the intellectual atmosphere that are being mocked the most. This is because the intellectual class has become sycophantic. Most intellectuals don't speak what's right but rather what benefits them. When intellect seeks benefits, what else can we expect from fools but more foolishness, which is prevalent? Intellect migrates to where it finds benefits, strengthens its position, and gains profit. The result is a nation ready for war while everyone else looks after their interests. You and I look for our benefits even in this situation. This pursuit of self-interest will one day harm us all. The creators and harsh painters of human history keep beating the drum to unearth benefits from the idiocy that arises, hidden behind the nobility of those who suffer."

Petrovich said, "You've spoken enough. Now tell me how we decide whether to give him water."

"If you can't understand even after all I've said, then you are truly obstinate and foolish."

"I'm not foolish... I see what you mean, but I'm not entirely convinced."

Helga, sitting next to the Russian, said, "This soldier is writhing in pain and asking for water; give him a sip and a piece of candy; what could go wrong?"

Petrovich replied, "Helga, it's not about just a sip of water or a piece of candy. It's about who gets what resources and how they are distributed. We all have a right to make that decision."

Sandhi, laughing, said, "Could you say the same to the government? When the government gives a portion of our resources to its capitalist friends, often almost snatching it from us and ignoring our needs and shortages, do you say the same to them?"

Petrovich calmly stated, "I can't say it to them, but I can say it here."

Julia, irritated, said, "If these are our resources, then we should all decide together who gets them. We should vote, and whoever gets the most votes will have that decision stand."

Petrovich agreed, "We'll decide by voting."

Sandhi: "No need, I'll give him water and chocolate from my share."

Petrovich:- "Voting is necessary." Marco also chimed in, "Yes, that's the right way." Petrovich continued, "Let's see who thinks he should not get water or food."

Everyone raised their hands except for Helga, Natasha, and Sandhi.

Julia declared, "The decision is made... no food or water for him."

Sandhi politely said, "Then give me my share."

"Absolutely!" Petrovich told Sandhi, "Don't feel bad; I wasn't comfortable giving it to him." Petrovich handed her the share as they spoke and mentioned that Marco had the water.

"You've changed in the last two days, Petrovich, but that's your prerogative." Sandhi then took half of her chocolate for the Russian, approached him, and gave him the piece. The Russian looked at it intently and quietly said 'thank you' in Russian before she walked away.

Marco called out to her, "Take your share of the water."

"Give it to the soldier," Marco muttered, reluctantly keeping the bottle.

Helga, witnessing this, said to Marco, "Give him the water; it's Sandhi's share."

"Keep quiet, Helga!"

"Do you have even a shred of humanity left? You're old and still harboring malice. Don't you fear God? My mother says that God is always watching whether or not someone is watching. Just give him the water."

"You're crazy and talk too much." Marco reluctantly opened the bottle and gave the soldier a drink. The soldier was in lousy shape, spitting blood repeatedly.

Marco said, "Petrovich, we should start interrogating him now."

Petrovich: "Bring the water bottle here."

Petrovich also told Sandhi, "You come to sit where the interrogation is happening."

Sandhi nodded. Petrovich took his share of the chocolate and joined Sandhi, the Russian, to start the interrogation. Natasha and Helga distributed the chocolate and water to everyone else.

Vladimir, taking his share, facilitated calls on the satellite phone for everyone who wanted to talk, but now there was a time limit—everyone got only two minutes.

Petrovich first asked, "Tell us the plan for the war... where will you attack?"

The soldier remained silent. Marco hit him, and although Sandhi was right there and immediately objected, Marco ignored her and threatened, "If he doesn't tell us anything, I'll kill him."

Sandhi said, "I won't let you do that."

Petrovich saw they were arguing and intervened, "I'm talking here... you stop arguing, and Marco, wait."

Marco, grinding his teeth, reluctantly agreed, "Fine."

Petrovich asked again, "Tell us where the attacks will be." This time, Sandhi also told him, "Tell us, otherwise these people won't listen to me." The Russian looked at all four faces and said, "We will attack all over Ukraine and win." Then he fell silent.

Petrovich asked, "What else do you know about the war?"

"I don't know much because the orders change daily." The soldier started coughing. After an hour of interrogation, Petrovich stood up, and Sandhi stayed to tend to his wounds.

Petrovich said, "Kill him, Marco... he has nothing to tell."

Hearing this, Marco's eyes gleamed with the opportunity to turn his hatred into reality.

He grabbed the soldier's neck and began to strangle him. Sandhi struggled to free him from Marco's grip. Helga helped her, but Marco was relentless. Seeing that Marco would kill him, Sandhi called out for Natasha. Natasha also started to intervene, and eventually, they succeeded. The Russian's neck was freed. When he was released, Sandhi called out powerfully, "Petrovich... Petrovich."

Petrovich looked their way as if nothing had happened.

Sandhi: "What kind of cruelty is this? Why did you tell Marco to kill him? Why are you all after his life? What will his death bring?"

Meanwhile, Natasha had grabbed Marco from behind. Petrovich told her, "Let him go." Natasha didn't release Marco. Then Sandhi also said, "Let him go, Natasha." Natasha then finally let go of Marco.

Hero growled at Marco. Petrovich said, "He's told us all he could; what are we supposed to do with him now?"

Sandhi: "Wow! Everyone has one function in your eyes: how consumerist you've become, Petrovich."

"It's not like that Sandhi, but he threatens us. As long as his hands are tied, he's here... the moment they're free, he'll kill us all first."

Marco had squeezed his neck so hard. The Russian was repeatedly spitting blood, and Marco was laughing at the sight.

Having facilitated everyone's calls on the satellite phone, Vladimir left his task and moved towards the ongoing turmoil. Arriving, he angrily exclaimed, "You all are always fighting; that's all you have. I am sick of all of you." He sat down quietly, and after a while, he muttered to himself, "I spoke to my parents today... they were apprehensive. I miss them, and here you are, still fighting. I hate this atmosphere now."

Sandhi approached him, spoke with him, and explained that she, too, wanted to go home. He shared stories about his family and home. After talking to Sandhi, Vladimir felt better and hugged her. Sandhi placed her hand on his head and said, "Don't worry. If there is a problem, there will be a solution. Sometimes, certain situations demand patience and composed behavior from us, which is beneficial for the future."

The Russian soldier's condition worsened. Sandhi went over to him and unzipped his jacket to help him breathe more easily. Then, looking at Marco and Petrovich, she said, "His condition is because of both of you. You two are murderers, escalating this hateful atmosphere in the war."

Marco retorted, "He doesn't deserve to live."

Natasha asked Marco, "How can you decide who lives and who doesn't?"

Petrovich loudly interjected, "Enough, all of you!" He then approached Vladimir and demanded, "Give me the phone."

"Why do you need the phone?" asked Vladimir.

"I need to call my office... to tell them what the Russian soldier has told us, and I need to talk to my family as well." Vladimir handed him the phone.

Petrovich stepped away to make the call, and during the conversation, he became visibly shocked and then angry. He looked at the Russian soldier with fury, pacing back and forth. After about 5 to 10 minutes, he returned to the group, where he saw Sandhi crying and telling Natasha that she wanted to go home and no longer wanted to stay here or continue her medical studies; she just wanted to go home and hug her parents. She wanted to be away from this city, away from this environment, living at home in love with everyone.

Despite seeing all this, Petrovich didn't approach Sandhi and announced, "Do you know what the Russian president has said?"

Marco and Julia eagerly asked, "What did he say? Tell us!"

"The Russian president has said that they have launched a special military operation not to harm the people of Ukraine but to save the Russian-speaking people in the east. The Russian president claims that these people have been persecuted under the Ukrainian government. Thousands have died... This operation is for their rescue," explained Petrovich, growing louder and more agitated. "He also mentioned that NATO has been moving closer to their borders since the end of the Cold War. Russia tried several times to find a solution, but America prevented it. All this is Russia's doing, and we are here talking about saving this soldier."

The Russian soldier tried to speak but initially couldn't; blood pooled in his mouth. After catching his breath, he began, "Our people have suffered greatly in Ukraine; they must be saved; they are our people. This war is because of America and NATO. NATO and America came to our borders, not us to theirs. This war is a creation of America," he said, coughing up blood again.

Suddenly, Vladimir stood up and exclaimed, "What are you repeatedly blaming America for? What have we done? What war have we caused?"

The Russian soldier, groaning in pain, reminded, "Have you forgotten about Iraq, Libya, and Syria?"

Hearing this, Vladimir sat down silently, tears welling in his eyes, pondering whether the games of great powers and the suffering of humanity would ever cease to coexist.

Petrovich declared, "This soldier is teaching us what patriotism is! It's in everyone's best interest that he dies."

Hearing this, Natasha glared at Petrovich but said nothing.

Sandhi, frustrated, responded to Petrovich, "Why do you keep talking about killing him? Don't you understand that this cycle will never stop? You kill, then someone else will, then your children will seek revenge, and then theirs. Once we start hating, our future becomes trapped in an endless cycle of hate. What do you want to pass on to your children, a philosophy of revenge or love? Do you want to teach them to love or to seek revenge? The decision is yours... Tomorrow is yours; what do you want to see, strife or love?"

After that, Sandhi walked away silently, followed by Natasha. Vladimir remained seated, head bowed. Helga sat by the soldier, listening intently to everything.

Petrovich signaled to Marco, who walked away. Ivan was also disturbed and kept glaring at the Russian soldier.

Julia was lying down, holding her child, looking at everything with a sense of suspicion.

Marco suddenly ran back with a piece of glass and, in one swift motion, stabbed the Russian soldier in the throat. By the time everyone's attention turned to him, it was too late; the Russian soldier was dead. Witnessing blood flow, Helga was scared; it flowed like water from a broken faucet. Blood spattered on Helga's face, and she quickly stepped back but couldn't keep her balance and fell.

Seeing the blood, Marco's face was filled with grim joy, as if he had avenged some personal wrongdoing through the Russian soldier. Then suddenly, he sat despondently by the soldier.

Sandhi rushed over to save him, followed by Natasha, who checked his pulse, which had stopped. Natasha told Sandhi, "Don't bother, Sandhi... he's gone. Hate has won."

Sandhi was utterly silent as if someone had stolen her voice. She was crying but soundlessly.

Vladimir remained sitting, slowly shaking his head, murmuring, "The war has affected us all; we are no longer human. Sinking into the fire of revenge and becoming violent beasts only means we are prepared to accept destruction on all levels. This behavior was a primary cause of devastation in the two world wars." Tears started rolling down his cheeks.

Julia, observing this, tucked her child under her gown, her face filled with confusion and doubt.

Helga was still trying to clean the blood off her face, repeatedly asking others, "Is the blood on my face cleaned off?"

Hero, the dog, sniffed the Russian soldier, then walked away, seemingly understanding that the scent of life had left.

Ivan paced faster and faster as if something inside him was moving just as quickly. Sandhi tried to speak but couldn't at first. On her fourth attempt, she finally said, "Marco, why did you do this? Why? I thought you were a better person. Why did you do this?"

Petrovich quickly approached Marco and Sandhi, put his arm around Marco, and tried to explain, "These things happen sometimes. It's the pressure of war."

Sandhi replied, "Under pressure of war! What kind of reason is that to take someone's life?"

"It's not just anyone; he was a Russian soldier. He deserved to die like this."

Marco continued to stare at Petrovich. Sandhi wanted to say more but then looked at Petrovich's face and remained silent. She just sat and stared at a space above the stairs. The sounds of gunfire grew louder. Petrovich took Marco away, telling him that he had informed his office and they would be sending help soon.

He instructed Marco, "Don't tell anyone that I signaled you to kill him, all right?" Marco remained silent, just watching him.

The bleeding had stopped; the soldier's body had been completely drained of blood. Helga was still cleaning her face. Ivan was walking even faster. Almost everyone was stressed by the death that had occurred so close to them. It was a surreal scene. The glass was still embedded in the soldier's neck. Sandhi returned, removed the glass forcefully, and threw it away—the last bit of blood drained from the body.

Sandhi sat beside Natasha and said, "I want to leave here as soon as possible; this place is no longer livable."

"Yes, I think the same," Vladimir said, sitting beside Sandhi.

Petrovich handed the phone to Marco for him to use, but Marco looked at it as if unsure what to do with it and said, "Who would I talk to? I have no one. My son and daughter-in-law don't talk to me. I'm completely alone. Who would I talk to... can I talk to the Russian? I want to talk to the Russian soldier. I don't even know his name, and I killed him. Petrovich, let me talk to him. This is Russian."

Petrovich stepped back from Marco and asked, "Marco, what are you talking about?"

"Yes, I want to talk to him. I want to call him back... I want to talk to him."

"Marco, come to your senses... he's dead."

"Yes, he's dead; I killed him," Marco then calmed down and suddenly said, "I killed him, but you provoked me to do it." When these words left Marco's mouth, everyone started looking at Petrovich.

Petrovich was stunned and exclaimed, "What nonsense are you spouting, Marco?"

"I'm not spouting nonsense... you provoked me before, and you signaled me again. It's not your fault, Petrovich; you took advantage of my hatred. You just provided the spark to the explosive inside me, and as soon as it got the spark, I exploded."

"But what did I gain from his death? Nothing, nothing at all, only the blood spread on the ground that marks me as guilty and the hatred within my mind."

Marco approached the Russian and embraced his corpse, saying, "If I had done this earlier, I wouldn't have regretted it so much. I should have hugged you, Russian; even if you hadn't hugged me back, I could have maintained my respect for you. And even if you had come to my city to harm our people, I shouldn't have killed you. There must have been a way to live; we must find such paths. I didn't want to kill you; I was just troubled by myself... the hatred I received from my wife, my son, and his wife, I wanted to end it, but instead, another layer of hatred piled on."

After looking at the Russian for a while, he says, "Petrovich, you made me commit a great sin."

Seeing this, Sandhi looks at Petrovich, who responds, "He's talking nonsense. His mind has gone mad. I haven't done anything... Sandhi, believe me."

Sandhi says, "Believe what? I've seen many changes in you these last two days. You don't want to support me, you mislead people, and you instigate them to commit murders. What should I call you? What should I say to you... You are not the same, or maybe you never were. Your love was just material; it never really existed. It just disappeared suddenly, perhaps. I read somewhere, Petrovich, that someone shows their true face during a crisis. This is your true face. This face of yours loves nothing but war. You need war; your innermost being craves war; you need competition in the office, even in love, you seek competition; you always told me what you had done for me; you needed competition even in the family; that's why you don't talk to your parents because you earn less than them. You probably like these small forms of war. You don't like love because it's simple; you like war, the tactics of war. You also have a greedy desire to acquire more, nurtured by your parents, society, and a worldly environment. The ultimate result of being taught the importance of love is that you have become a fraud who perceives all this behavior as a struggle. The failure to understand the difference between honest labor and envious struggle due to greed results in social unrest because it inherently involves the ostracism of others. When viewing everything from his perspective, a person only loses the ability to appreciate the beauty created from human labor and creativity."

After saying this, Sandhi said nothing more and turned away to look in another direction, towards the stairs, where the sky was visible above. Looking at the stairs, she kept repeating, "You like war... you like war, you like conflict, you like competition, you don't like being human."

5

"If the love between two people does not reach the deepest conflicts of society and cannot transform the disputes into love, then it is not truly love."

Kharkiv, 01 PM

February 25

Sandhi sat enveloped in deep uncertainty, continuously gazing at the stairs. She was in a terrible state due to hunger. Everyone at the underground metro station was distressed. Hunger, thirst, sleeplessness, the constant sound of gunfire, and the perpetual shadow of fear were having a profound impact on all the people present. Some were becoming better humans under the influence of this restlessness, while others were turning more ruthless. The station had become a remarkable human exposition, a rainbow convergence born from the nutrients, water, air, environment, and values instilled from childhood.

Vladimir approached Sandhi and said, "Why are you continuously looking at the stairs? I've watched you for the past 4 or 5 hours, and you keep staring at them. What's wrong?"

Sandhi said nothing and continued to look. Vladimir called out again, "Sandhi!"

She finally spoke, "What else should I look at, Vladimir... I'm just seeing whether I can go back up these stairs. I came down, but can I go up again? It's strange. No one is stopping us from going up, but we can't because our lives would be in danger. I don't know when I'll leave here or when I'll be able to return home. Where will you go once we get out of here, Vladimir?"

Vladimir looked at the stairs and said, "First thing, as soon as I get out, I'll drink lots of water. Then, if I find something to eat, I'll eat. After that, I'll go straight home to my mom and dad. It's been a long time since I saw them." He paused, then added, "You know, I didn't have the best relationship with my parents, but today, when I spoke to them, I felt I was wrong about them. My dad said they would get me out of here. It felt so good to know how much my dad loves me."

A grief-stricken Sandhi, affected by the death of a Russian soldier, responded to Vladimir in a very calm voice, "In the embrace of love and peace, joy and creative beauty naturally flourish, whereas hatred and envy slowly expand the terrain of destruction and unrest. That's how love is; experiencing it feels unique, and contrary to it is war. Knowing and witnessing war can drive you mad. You cannot tolerate war for long. People change in war; look at Marco."

"Do you think Petrovich might have hinted at something?"

"I don't know, but he might have... People change; he has changed too; who knows what he might have done!"

"The way Marco spoke, I think Petrovich might have done it."

"It's possible; he has changed a lot." As they were discussing this, Petrovich arrived and sat down beside Sandhi.

As soon as Petrovich sat down, Vladimir got up and left. Petrovich stared at Vladimir as he went, but Vladimir, as usual, was lost in his world and didn't notice Petrovich staring.

Petrovich said nothing for a while and just sat next to Sandhi. She, too, remained silent.

After a long silence, Petrovich finally spoke, "Are you angry with me, Sandhi?" She replied, "Why must I be angry with you?"

"I thought you were; that's why I asked."

"It's good that you asked."

"I did not signal Marco to kill that Russian soldier."

"What difference does it make now? He's already dead... his body is starting to smell, and besides, you had once told Marco to kill him. Maybe you would do it again, who knows?"

"Why don't you trust me? Has your love for me ended?"

"The person who could let me go out alone, knowing my life could be at risk, who doesn't respect my ideology—I'm not saying you have to agree with it, but you neither respected it nor cared about it. I've known you for many years, and now it seems that one has to think about how much time it takes to know a person. I don't know how you became like this."

"What have I become?"

"You've become anti-love."

"Anti-love? But I love you."

"Anyone who likes war, who tries to kill people, is anti-love. And don't say you love me... if you did, you wouldn't even think about killing the Russian."

"Understand this: it's war; we are in a war."

"War! What does that mean? If something wrong is happening, would you support it? Does war give you a license to kill or plot against someone? Love, Petrovich, is when you are in it, you just are. It can't be that you are in love with me one moment and hate someone else the next. Love is like blood; it flows everywhere uniformly red. Domination in love leads to corruption of its essence—it won't remain love then but will turn into tainted energy. Just like blood flows uniformly from any cut, so should love if it's truly love."

Petrovich looks at Sandhi. This time, Sandhi also looks into Petrovich's eyes.

Petrovich says, "There's no love for me in your eyes anymore."

"It's still there, but not for you. The love you gave still exists, now taking the form of love for humanity, keeping the tide of blood in check."

"The form of love, I don't understand."

After a long silence, Sandhi laughs and says, "Love, do you understand love? Let me show you what love is today." She lifts her head and looks towards the ceiling. "Do you think I was attracted to you because you look good, your golden hair, your tall stature? No, Petrovich! I felt a revolution whenever I looked at you; something would change in my life and yours. My love isn't just the moments spent with you in bed engulfed in pleasure. If my love doesn't teach me to love others, it's not love. My love leads me from lust to revolution. Selfishness in love makes it burdensome. I see how my generation perceives love... for them, love is just holding hands, being together, sleeping together, and consuming each other—that's all."

"Wow! So you mean to say all this isn't necessary in love?"

"It is necessary, but it's just one aspect of love. Love that reaches only the consumptive dimension will die by itself. If the love between two people doesn't reach the deepest societal conflicts and transform them, then it's not true love. The contraction of love seeking its expansion is hindered by selfishness, leading to its failure. Nowadays, why is love disappearing so quickly? Why do we look for another relationship after one ends and then another until we grow old and die without ever experiencing true love? Love is the solution to every problem, not the problem itself."

Petrovich listens and then, after a deep thought, stands up and asks, "Do you still love me?"

"Yes, I do."

Joy returns to Petrovich's face, but then Sandhi says, "But not in a way that I would stay with you. I love you, which is why I told my mother about you, but now I feel you are so lost in war that you have forgotten love. I cannot watch love get hurt, so I've decided to leave you. I can't bear to see your inner war fighting against my love. Thus, love and war must be separated. If my love is true, you will emerge from war and embrace love, and if your war is a holy war, then future generations will sing its praises, which I doubt. After the two world wars, European people realized they couldn't destroy each other and could only coexist through love. This global interdependence is the basis of the Euro currency, the European Union, and the European Parliament existing there today."

"I love you so much, why can't you see that? I take you to the finest hotels, buy you the best clothes, and do everything for you, yet you leave me."

"No, Petrovich, I'm not leaving you; I'm just holding onto love. You were in love, so you felt you were with me. You are not in love today, so don't feel I am with you. I was with love yesterday, and I am with it today. What you've told me about what you've done for me shows how incapable we are of the market's ideological invasion. The market is defining relationships and meanings, and what you call love, these commercial standards are shaping it, and our generation mistakenly believes it to be love." Maybe Sandhi's intellectual honesty felt too brutal to Petrovich today.

"Petrovich, what you understood as love, I never could."

After hearing all this, Petrovich leaves. After his departure, Sandhi closes her eyes, smiles faintly, and thinks that the expansion of love, based on market profits and losses, will proceed in a commercial direction. In this, both sides will sink into profit, not love.

She then looks at the stairs again.

After a while, Sandhi stood up and walked over to where the others were. Julia was lying down with a child sleeping beside her. Sandhi asked Julia, "How is the child?" Julia replied, "She's okay for now, but if the rescue team doesn't arrive soon, we'll have a problem." Sandhi said, "Keep faith in God. Everything has been alright so far, and it will be alright going forward, too."

Helga was lying with her head in Natasha's lap. Sandhi also sat down there and asked softly, "Is she unwell?"

Natasha said, "No, she's not sick, just exhausted. She hasn't slept well, so she probably just fell asleep, poor thing."

Sandhi remarked, "She is so young, yet this war spares no one. Who knows how many children this war will consume, how many will become orphans, and how many will not receive a proper upbringing because of this war? War devours everything... your present, future, and soul."

Natasha responded, "All I can say is if you want to see people change, start a war. Whatever face someone has, it will surely show itself. What can I say about changing faces? The courage to seek solutions for humanity cannot coexist with selfish, partisan sentiments, and this is why we see people's true faces; their decisions don't rise above their vested interests."

"Just get out of here as soon as possible, or I'll end up mad like Marco."

"Why, what happened to Marco?"

"Look at him trying to lift the Russian soldier. He keeps picking him up and trying to talk to him."

"He's still human, after all. A human swinging between hatred and humanity. He made a mistake, and now his brain is trying to compensate for it by creating illusions."

Natasha hummed in despair.

"Let me tell you something, Natasha. I need to get out of here quickly. Then I'll see how to reach India, but first, I must get out of here."

Natasha asked, "Did something happen between you and Petrovich?"

"What happened? Nothing at all... just those who do not want love, why should they stay together?"

"Can I ask what happened?"

"I won't blame him; this war has changed people. This war has exposed the flaws in our development and the undeveloped aspects of our humanity, which is why we're seeing many inconsistent changes in people today. But how did you think something happened or not?"

"I heard Petrovich telling Ivan that Sandhi is no longer with me."

Sandhi laughed, saying, "The threads haven't even properly broken yet, and they've already impatiently handed everyone an end."

After this, Natasha and Sandhi both started laughing. Hero also began affectionately licking them.

Kharkiv, February 25

Time: 11 PM

Everyone was trying to sleep on an empty stomach; some had already fallen asleep while others were still waiting. Some were disturbed by the stench of the decaying body of the Russian soldier when suddenly someone's voice was heard, speaking vehemently. Everyone suddenly woke up from their sleep to see Petrovich on the phone, saying, "I've been calling continuously but can't get through to anyone."

After listening for a while, he said, "That's more like it. I am proud to be Ukrainian. Our President Zelensky has done wonders. I am proud of him." Then he said, "I am going to hang up now."

As soon as he hung up the phone, Petrovich exclaimed, "Do you guys even realize what happened just a while ago!"

Marco ran over and said, "Tell me, tell me, did you talk to the Russian soldier?"

With a mocking tone, Petrovich said, "You, Marco, go away, sit over there." Marco, hearing this, went and sat at a distance.

Petrovich then began to tell everyone, "Today, our President Zelensky released a videotape, and in it, he said that he is here in Ukraine, the army is here in Ukraine, the common people are here in Ukraine, and he mentioned the female soldiers and said that they are doing a great job as protectors." Petrovich continued, "Everyone thought our president would flee as soon as the attack happened, but he proved he is a true Ukrainian. He hasn't left Ukraine, and I don't think he will leave soon. All my friends are happy; they are stuck in the office, and here I am; this is our victory."

While saying all this, Petrovich started shouting, "Long live Ukraine."

Vladimir, seeing this, said, "Petrovich, calm down... he has just released a video, not won the war."

Petrovich, angered, retorted, "Why are you annoyed?"

"I am not annoyed... I am just saying that you woke everyone up from their sleep. It's hard enough to sleep on an empty stomach, and now you are chanting slogans. I am also happy because this will strengthen our country but doesn't change the situation. There is happiness, but the situation also needs to change."

"How will the situation change when there are people like you? Right now, Ukraine is fighting alone, without America, without NATO, without anyone... understand? You may not feel proud of your country, but I am proud of mine."

Vladimir calmly tried to explain again, "The war has divided us, humans, into two ideological classes: violent and loving, and ignoring the capitalism that is dissolving into ordinary life behind this human defeat is not just. We have turned from civil society into a frenzied crowd of businessmen buying and selling victories and defeats.

"I am proud of my country, and when my country does something wrong, I criticize it."

"You are a traitor... you criticize your country."

Vladimir, laughing, said, "If criticism is wrong and only applause is right, then the country should abolish educational institutions and teach only slavery. I am a free citizen of my country; I criticize when necessary and applaud when needed."

"I am happy, and I will celebrate."

Petrovich's euphoria from the war had taken hold. He was jumping around loudly. Everyone watched him in astonishment.

Vladimir said, "Petrovich, don't make noise, or the soldiers will notice us. Don't put others' lives at risk for your enthusiasm."

"Why are you irritated? Does your Russian blood feel offended?"

"I have American blood too, don't forget."

"I am happy. You will be happy too, then."

Sandhi kept watching. Then, unable to bear Petrovich's noise anymore, she said, "Petrovich, stop this. Why are you putting everyone at risk?"

Petrovich retorted, "Why are you speaking... who are you to me?"

"Why are you bringing our matters up to everyone?"

"I'm not airing anything; I'm just saying. Let me do what I'm doing."

"Do you even realize what you're doing?"

"What I'm doing, you could never do. You're saying this because your country hasn't faced such a crisis."

"Our country! It's funny, Petrovich... now you're dividing everyone by their nationality—first Vladimir, and now me. Regarding situations like war, we have seen many wars, not because of our own decisions but because of the expansionist policies of other nations. Wars have happened in our country, but our people have tried to end them, not escalate them."

"You always state your opinions, considering your ideology superior."

"That's not true, but I prioritize humanity above all. Nothing is greater than human beings for me. I place humanity above caste, religion, gender, color, species, and nationality. If a nation discriminates against some people in the name of religion and divides the nation under the guise of religion, then what kind of nation is that and why should we call it a nation? Just because of its distinct borders, when it has lost its transparent sovereignty by treating its citizens unequally."

Ivan interjected, "Petrovich, let it go... let's calm down. We were so united when we came here; now we're all divided. I don't know why this fragmentation has happened."

Sandhi added, "This fragmentation has happened because we were together out of fear, and we separated because our interests began to diverge."

Pointing towards the body of the Russian soldier (where Marco was still sitting), Sandhi said, "When a murdered person lies next to you, screaming to this underground metro station what happened to humanity, how can you ask how we became separated?"

Saying this, tears came to Sandhi's eyes, and she wiped them away, saying, "One last thing I want to say is that I don't want to be more separated from all of you, nor can I sink further into the madness of war."

Sandhi remained silent for a while, then said, "I've decided to leave this place. I was scared for my life before, but not anymore because staying here is also a kind of death for me; going outside might be the same. But it's better to face physical death than to die internally. I am sad about the Russian's death, and I regret that I couldn't save him. Every time I see him, the human inside me torments me. I can't stay here anymore." Sandhi folded her hands to everyone and started walking towards the stairs.

As she stepped on the first stair, only Natasha called out to her, saying, "I wanted to come with you to the telephone booth, but I had some doubts about my decision at that time, but not anymore because if I stayed, I'd feel like I didn't support a human. All my life, I met doctors, lawyers, engineers, and Christians, but not humans. Today, I met one, so how can I leave her? Let's go, Sandhi, let's go." As Natasha said, 'Let's go,' Hero was ready to leave. Vladimir zipped up his jacket and said, "I don't want to stay here either. It might be the wrong time to leave, but not the wrong decision. I didn't dare to leave her alone, but now that you all are with me, I'm leaving too."

Sandhi turned back and said to Petrovich, "Petrovich, I'm taking this dress with me. Besides this, I have nothing of yours... whatever there is, it's just love that perhaps only I felt." Hearing this, Petrovich said nothing and just shrugged indifferently. Sandhi waved goodbye to him, but Petrovich's hand remained in his mobile pocket.

Marco ran up to Sandhi and asked, "Are you going to get the Russian soldier?" Sandhi replied, "No, he's already gone from this world."

Sandhi, Natasha, and Hero began climbing the stairs, and from below, no one called them back or asked them to stay. Just as they left, Marco started shouting, "We've driven the Russian army out... we've driven the Russian army out," and he began singing the Ukrainian national anthem loudly.

"*Shche ne vmerla Ukrainas, i slava, i volia*" (In Ukrainian) - Ukraine's glory and freedom have not yet perished, luck will still smile on us, Ukrainian brothers.

6

"We become so lost in the sparkle of life that the essential elements of life begin to seem meaningless, and we start gathering things in place of love."

Kharkiv, February 26

Time: 1:00 AM

As she emerged above ground, Sandhi first saw the body of a Ukrainian soldier, the bayonet that had pierced his neck still lodged within. The blood, frozen by the cold, had solidified on the ground, ice encasing the bayonet in his neck. It didn't look like it was embedded in flesh; the blood had broken the skin and veins, kissing the earth as it froze.

Shivering, Sandhi turned back to look at the metro station and wondered if her actions were proper. Should she have left Petrovich? Should she have abandoned everyone in such a state? Were they all her responsibility? Did she do the right thing by getting Natasha and Vladimir out of there? Were they all in danger because of her? Had Natasha and Vladimir come of their own free will? Would she be able to return home? Would she ever meet her family again? Did her mother tell her father that Sandhi had fallen for a boy? Amidst these swirling questions, Natasha suddenly remarked, "It's so cold outside!"

Sandhi said nothing... she was lost in her thoughts. Natasha asked again, "Sandhi, did you hear what I said?" Sandhi didn't respond. This time, Vladimir called out, "Sandhi... Sandhi!" and shook her as they walked. Sandhi replied, "Yes, say it!" but she truly did not comprehend what she had just said to Vladimir.

Sandhi's questions had taken many forms, and she conversed with these apparitions.

Vladimir said, "Natasha is saying it's freezing here."

Sandhi gave a strange response, "The Russian soldier's body was also icy after death."

Natasha said, "Sandhi, you've left that underground metro station in Kharkiv behind; stop thinking about it. You are here now, and we must find a place to stay, understand?" Sandhi nodded.

Gradually, they started walking, and Hero was looking around cautiously.

Sandhi murmured to Natasha, "Two days ago, when I passed here, it was morning, and there was shooting, and people were running. Today, there's only the sound of gunfire, and something is chilling me from inside. My legs are shaking; maybe I am scared. So many things are consuming me; why did I part from Petrovich? Was there no other option?"

"Sandhi, don't overthink... Sometimes, relationships are just there to teach us. You've learned what you needed to learn. Lesson over, relationship over."

Sandhi remained silent, just feeling the cold winds touching her body. Everywhere were dead people, covered with ash and frost, looking as though each person was displayed in a showcase. Perhaps this is how a death exhibition looks at a war council.

Due to the severe cold and frost, transparent ice had formed over the bodies, making their faces appear as if they might speak any moment, perhaps unable to utter their last words, as if not dying for the last time. Maybe they had died several times before due to this entire system. Perhaps this death was their liberation from a life and a system submerged only in pain, their dying a wish for a higher stature. Sandhi kept walking, seeing everything—the trees were without leaves, and the bodies were without heads. Nature can make everything incomplete whenever you are away from love. Perhaps it's nature's silent message.

Suddenly, Vladimir gestured, and everyone stopped. He whispered, "It seems like there is someone alive nearby. I hear something."

Sandhi said, "I hear it too."

Natasha: "I hear it too, but whose voice is it?"

Sandhi: "It seems someone is alive, not dead." Sandhi looked around, but there was no one alive. People had turned into corpses, the frost had placed the bodies into a showcase, and death was laughing all around, either too helpless to stop what had begun or enjoying itself. Sandhi, each time she approached a body, hoped it would be alive and would say something, but death announced itself with a profound silence.

Natasha saw a person and called out to Sandhi, "Sandhi, maybe this one is alive."

Sandhi approached and saw that the person's eyes were open. Vladimir also arrived and shook the person, saying, "Listen... Listen."

Sandhi: "Vladimir, he is not alive."

Natasha: "Look, his eyelids are frozen; maybe he died of the cold."

Vladimir muttered, "His blue eyes were like looking into the sky. Maybe the last thing he saw was the sky."

Natasha said, "Maybe in his last moments, he was thinking of God, or perhaps looking to the sky, hoping someone would come to help him, seeing everyone on earth as dead."

Unable to ignore their conversation, Sandhi softly remarked, "Holding onto hope for life amid a rain of death is not a sin, but amid a violent carnage, such hope might be nothing more than faith in humanity. Look around; there's no one alive."

Hero, sniffing around, found a living person and quietly called everyone over. They all reached the spot where Hero stood. Upon seeing the person, Sandhi started to tremble; she needed a jolt to snap out of the world of her thoughts. Natasha exclaimed, "Oh God," upon seeing him.

As soon as Vladimir saw him, he vomited and fell to the ground. The man was alive, his head split open. From his eyelids upward, his head was exposed entirely; blood was visible, and his brain could be seen. His intestines were hanging out below, and his lower leg was crushed as he moaned in pain. Natasha asked, "Can he be saved?"

With a trembling voice, Sandhi replied, "It's tough."

Vladimir, getting up after vomiting, said, "Let's get out of here... I can't look at this." The man's groaning slowly quieted and then suddenly stopped. Natasha shook him, but he said nothing, clearly indicating he had died.

Sandhi said, "The agony of life is terrible; perhaps he just needed to be seen by someone. He wanted to see a living person one last time in this battle of life."

Sandhi shivered more... Natasha said, "Vladimir, give your jacket to Sandhi if it's alright with you."

Vladimir first looked at his jacket and then at the trembling Sandhi. He took off his jacket and gave it to Sandhi. Sandhi initially refused the jacket, but Vladimir said, "I'm okay; my condition isn't as bad as yours, Sandhi."

The three of them and Hero slowly moved on with heavy steps, now just searching for a place to stay. Sandhi was inwardly cursing herself, wondering why she had come here. She had been refined in Varanasi... Whatever it was, why did she need to go here to become a doctor? She had left everything to come here and now had to leave everything again. How long would she keep losing, and what more would end within her? What more would continue to drain away in this life?

Sandhi was feeling slightly better, but as soon as she did, her mind bombarded her with a thousand questions. Everyone had been walking for a long time and were exhausted, constantly frightened by the sound of gunfire; they just needed to stop somewhere so they could rest, but stopping wasn't so easy that night as the Russian soldiers were incited after President Zelensky's speech.

Suddenly, Natasha said, "It seems like a heavy vehicle is coming from ahead with a deafening noise." All they could see from the front was the barrel of a tank, and they were terrified. The fog was dense. Due to the cold and smoke, they first saw the barrel, the front wheels, and the entire tank. They ran scared into a nearby apartment. By the time the whole tank emerged from the fog, they had already entered the apartment. The sound of the tank broke the silence spread across the street, and the soldiers seated on the tank looked around. Sandhi, Natasha, Vladimir, and Hero all went upstairs.

From the window, Natasha saw the tank moving forward. The three looked at each other, and Hero looked at them. Then they all started shivering with fear, holding onto each other and hiding against the wall. Vladimir then said, "Should we go upstairs?"

Natasha said, "No, it's not safe upstairs... Tanks are roaming the streets; staying up there won't be safe."

"We can stay on the first floor," Sandhi suggested.

Vladimir asked, "Will we be safe there?"

They became silent as the tank passed right in front of their apartment. There was no immediate danger, but the fear remained, so they stayed quiet. The sound of the tank intensified their fear, the rumble hitting their ears and hearts, increasing their shivering. Fear was mounting, sweat appeared on their foreheads, and the tank gradually passed.

They went to the ground floor and tried to open the door there. Sandhi looked outside once; then her gaze swept from outside to inside. Upon entering, to the right, there was a large white door with "Mr. and Mrs. Andrew" written in red. Near the door, there was a dried-up plant. In front of the door was a trash can with bloodstains on it—likely from fingers soaked in blood. Ukraine seemed painted into an entirely different kind of fresco.

Sandhi's eyes returned to the door again. Together, they tried to open it but failed. Then Natasha suggested, "Let's all push together with full force." They pushed together, but still, the door wouldn't budge. Vladimir started swearing, stopped, realized he was cursing in front of the two women, and scolded himself instead. In frustration, he kicked at the door, then turned around and sat down. Sandhi said, "Don't worry... we'll go somewhere else."

Vladimir responded, "You know there are tanks outside, Russian soldiers. It's perilous to go outside now."

Suddenly, Natasha remarked, "Vladimir, remember the sound when you kicked the door?"

"What about the sound? It sounded like it always does when you kick something."

"It sounded hollow like it does with hollow things."

"So what?"

Sandhi looked at Natasha and said, "It means there's an underground space beneath where we're standing."

Vladimir dismissed them, "What nonsense are you both talking about?"

Natasha countered, "It's not nonsense. Remember, back in 2014, during the crisis, many people made collective underground shelters in their homes and apartments."

Hearing this, Vladimir lay down and began tapping on the wood, finding another reason to keep going. He readily accepted this because, deep down, he knew how important it was to have a place to stay. When he tapped, he, too, felt the hollowness in the wood. He pulled back the carpet in a frenzy as if hurrying to discover something.

Sandhi was still shivering, and now the cold was getting to Vladimir and Natasha. When Vladimir removed the carpet, he noticed one of the wooden panels was slightly different. He lifted the panel, which came off quickly, revealing a downward ladder. Vladimir looked at the others and said, "I'll go down first, then set up the ladder, and you all can come down."

Hero seemed to understand that they had found a new home, wagging his tail in agreement. Vladimir peeked into the underground room from above, then jumped down—it wasn't too high, so he landed comfortably. Once down, he set up the ladder, and then Natasha told Sandhi, "You go down first."

Sandhi didn't object. She descended slowly. After her, Natasha helped Hero down; Hero jumped without needing the ladder and barked as if to say, "Come down, Natasha." Natasha followed and gently replaced the wooden panel from below. All four looked at each other, immensely relieved and happy to have found a new place to stay.

Sandhi was happy, too, but her joy was soon tinged with memories of those she had left behind. Vladimir exclaimed, "Look at this!" With his call, Sandhi returned to the underground room, where her friends and a dog were with her.

Vladimir was pacing the room joyfully, saying, "This room is great!"

Natasha corrected him, "Not a room, Vladimir, this is a hall."

"Yes, a hall," Vladimir agreed, "but it's much better than where we were."

Sandhi was observing everything very carefully, feeling everything around her. She ran her hand over a bed, and then Natasha said, "Sandhi, tonight you'll get to sleep on a bed."

"Yes, but I was thinking of something else," Sandhi replied.

"What else were you thinking about?" Vladimir asked.

"I was thinking, all these beds are set up here, there's a fridge, there's gas, everything is here, but the people who own all this are not here."

Hearing this, Natasha also fell silent. She said, "Who knows where they are if they're alive!"

"I accept all this is here," Vladimir added, "but we mustn't forget that we can't do anything about those things. We are helpless. We can only survive and make it back home, nothing more. We are nothing against the Russian forces."

"Is that all we can do?"

"Let's forget all this; I'll see what else is in the fridge."

Vladimir opened the fridge enthusiastically but found only a packet of bread and four eggs. He said, "Just a packet of bread and four eggs, that's all in the fridge." He then looked around and found a large water filter filled with water. Seeing the water, he became pleased and exclaimed, "Wow! Sandhi, Natasha, we found water... we have water!"

Sandhi remarked, "Look how our circumstances have become like the Stone Age. Today, even the smallest things bring us joy. Everything has changed so much. Did we ever imagine that we would be so happy just seeing water? Perhaps we should always live life with this much enthusiasm. Only then will we begin to truly utilize essential resources properly."

Vladimir asked, "But how do we bring about such enthusiasm?"

Natasha replied, "By living daily as if it's a battle. Every moment could be the last; we don't know what will happen next."

Sandhi added, "Yes, that would make life more enjoyable, and our love for people will either remain, or we might become detached."

Natasha wondered, "How would detachment come?"

Sandhi explained, "When you know you could die at any moment, don't you think everything will start to seem very stark?"

Natasha responded, "It might feel a bit stark, but in those things where we need to find joy, we surely will find the essence of life."

Vladimir said, "What essence are you talking about? I don't understand."

Sandhi explained, "War teaches you the value of things. But why do we only learn during war? Why can't we learn these ordinary things on normal days? Do we always need shocks to understand life, or do we get so lost in the sparkle of life that the essential elements of life begin to seem meaningless, and we start gathering things other than love—things that might have value in the market but no value for the happiness of life, turning into empty shells with no gunpowder left. Life slowly becomes a burdened machine, collecting spent shells whose gunpowder has run out."

Natasha asked, "So, you mean to say that the gunpowder of life is love, maintaining relationships, communicating with each other, and not living life thinking we are important but recognizing that society and the environment are important?"

Vladimir interjected, "If society is important, does the individual disappear if we only think about society?"

Sandhi said, "No, as far as freedom is concerned, I am a staunch supporter of individual freedom. But what kind of freedom do you need that society cannot give an individual? As a citizen within a society, you should have the freedom to eat what you want, wear the clothes you desire, marry where you wish, follow any religion, or not follow any at all. Individual freedom is fine; society should allow it if it does not disturb society or another individual. Meaning, if you're thinking of waging a war like the ongoing one, your freedom should be curtailed because it could cause the deaths of millions."

Vladimir skeptically asked, "So, will society ever be effective enough to stop wars?"

Sandhi said, "I can't say whether it will happen, but if you want freedom as an individual, then every person should collectively boycott wrong actions. Society can be that influential, but I'm afraid that before society becomes that effective, it might witness endless wars because, without destruction and death, society won't realize that it needs to take concrete steps for change."

Vladimir said, "Let's drop this... drink some water."

Sandhi laughed at Vladimir's remark, and Natasha picked up a glass placed below. They all drank a glass of water one by one. While they were drinking, Hero was watching them intently. Vladimir said, "Hey, Hero, are you thirsty too?"

Natasha said, "Yes, he hasn't had a good drink in two days."

Sandhi started looking around the room and found a small bowl. Natasha asked, "What will you do with that bowl, Sandhi?" Sandhi replied, "Hero will drink water from it."

Hero understood that Sandhi was talking about him. He came over and started playing with Sandhi. Sandhi filled the bowl with water as evenly as everyone had drunk. As soon as Natasha said, "Hero, drink the water!" Hero quickly lapped up all the water.

The three were delighted to see Hero drinking like that and showered him affectionately. Sandhi was the first to fall into a deep sleep. Natasha lay down next to Sandhi, looking up at the ceiling with her eyes open. Vladimir was also about to lie down when suddenly a sound made him get up. He moved the mattress and found a half-bottle of wine underneath.

As soon as he saw the bottle, he said to Natasha, "Look what I found."

Still looking at the ceiling, Natasha asked, "What did you find?"

"I found a bottle of wine."

Startled, Natasha exclaimed, "What, a bottle of wine?" She took the bottle from him and looked at it intriguingly.

Vladimir jokes, "It seems like, for Natasha, this bottle is not just a bottle but a magic lamp."

"It is a lamp; now I will ask it to sleep."

Vladimir laughed, and Natasha said, "Let's wake Sandhi up."

"But she's already asleep."

"Should we wake her up or not?"

"Let's wake her; she was the one who said to treat everything as if it's the last."

Natasha remarked, "Really... I didn't know when I would get to drink wine again."

Vladimir quickly went to Sandhi and woke her up, "Sandhi... Sandhi!" Sandhi suddenly woke up and started saying, "My blood is flowing, I'm dying... I'm dying..."

Vladimir shook her firmly, not wanting Sandhi to linger in such a bad dream. Sandhi woke up frightened, took deep breaths upon waking, and asked, "Where am I?"

Natasha said, "We're all in an underground bunker."

"Yes, yes, I remember everything, but I was asleep. Why did you wake me?"

Vladimir said, "We thought we would share this bottle with you, but it seems we disturbed you by waking you up. Sorry,

Sandhi, we didn't mean to scare you. We just wanted to celebrate our new home."

"Where did you find this bottle?" Sandhi asked.

Vladimir explained that he found it under the mattress. Sandhi quickly took the bottle from Natasha's hand and gently felt it.

Then, with a sense of wonder, Sandhi said, "Our story started here. Let's claim this wine as our own and drink it." She asked the others, "May I open this bottle?"

Natasha and Vladimir laughed because Sandhi stood up, lifted her nightdress with decorum, and asked the question—it seemed pretty amusing. Then Sandhi opened the bottle and started drinking. After taking a sip, she passed the bottle to Natasha. Natasha also took a sip and then handed the bottle to Vladimir. This sequence continued until only three sips were left, and the bottle returned to Sandhi. She said, "Hero, I can't share this with you."

She raised the bottle and said, before sipping, "This sip is for peace."

Natasha also declared before her sip, "This sip is for peace."

Vladimir added, "This sip for peace." Then Vladimir rolled the bottle to a corner and started laughing.

All three stood, looking at each other, with Hero among them. They grabbed each other's hands, formed a circle, and began to spin around. Hero, too, started to circle with them. Then, swaying gently, Sandhi said, "I don't know what tomorrow holds, but today I want to celebrate life." Vladimir and Natasha also said, "Yes, me too!" They kept spinning, and tears slowly fell from their eyes. It seemed like they were the only ones celebrating the remnants of life in all of Ukraine, and the way they held onto each other while dancing stated that in the dance of life, we must hold onto our loved ones, not letting them fall, waver, or falter. Life deems this vibrancy unnecessary at every step and is progressing towards decline.

7

You cannot harvest wheat by wielding a cactus.

Kharkiv

Time: 10 AM

The sound of gunfire is deafening. At least 50-60 bullets are fired in rapid succession, along with tank shells raining down. The cries of people are also overwhelmingly loud. Hero starts barking furiously as the sounds of bullets and bombs begin suddenly. Hero and the others suddenly stand up, trying to listen in all directions.

Vladimir asks, "What's happening?"

Sandhi says, "I have no idea." Just then, another bomb drops, and their underground room starts shaking again.

Natasha pulled Hero closer to her, and it was the first time all three of them had heard such loud explosions. Sounds were coming from the floor above— a new peak of fear for everyone.

Sandhi says, "I think there's someone upstairs."

Anticipating the worst, Natasha says, "Could it be Russian soldiers?"

Sandhi asks, "What should we do?"

Vladimir, frightened, says, "I don't know who it is, but anything could happen." Then, for a while, the sounds of bullets and bombs lessen. Vladimir gathers some courage, climbs the stairs, and tries to listen. Sandhi quickly grabs the ladder to support him. Natasha is pacing the room rapidly.

Vladimir returns and says, "There are several people upstairs shouting." Natasha becomes scared by Vladimir's words, then climbs and tries to listen, but she hears nothing.

"There's no sound, Vladimir... You're imagining things."

Vladimir: "I heard something."

"I'll try listening too." She climbs up, but she also hears nothing. They look at each other with eyes full of distress and then sit down, disappointed and sad.

Sandhi: "I don't know what will happen now."

Natasha: "I am terrified."

Vladimir asks, "If I'm not wrong, we are all scared." Sandhi and Natasha nod in agreement.

Natasha thinks momentarily and says, "We need to go upstairs."

Vladimir, startled, says, "Why go upstairs? Who will go? I'm not going."

Natasha: "Vladimir, if they are Russian soldiers and they want to kill us, they will just blow up the whole building, and we will die trapped in the debris. They will find us eventually. We should get out and understand what's happening."

"How will we face them? They have weapons."

Sandhi: "Facing them isn't even a question."

Natasha: "Maybe they haven't found us, and they've gone."

Vladimir: "We don't know if they've left, but going upstairs is risky." They all sit down again, and Natasha suddenly stands up and asks, "How long has it been, Vladimir?"

"It's 11 AM."

Sandhi: "I don't know when we slept last night."

Vladimir takes a deep breath and says, "As good as the night was, so dangerous is the morning." Natasha hears something this time and says, "Vladimir, you were right; there is someone upstairs." She stands, holding the ladder.

Vladimir: "What are you doing, Natasha?"

Natasha says, "I'm going upstairs, mentally preparing myself."

Vladimir: "Sandhi, explain to her how she can go upstairs if those people kill her and then come down here."

"It's dangerous, Natasha, don't go upstairs."

Natasha: "You don't understand what happens in a war, Sandhi."

"What do you mean, what happens?"

"I've seen 2014. I've seen how ten people barbarically rape a woman. It's a very insecure time; you could consider it the death of humanity. I'm afraid it might be a group of such people."

Sandhi: "What kind of people are they? Even in such a dire time, they want to celebrate their animalistic victories by trampling a woman's body. It's not even lusting; it's grotesque lust, or perhaps they want to flaunt their victory over another country, religion, by crushing the women, but in reality, they are diverting attention from the real issues."

Natasha says, "You're right, they are more scared than us."

"Even if they are all there, why are you going?"

"Someone has to confront them eventually."

"If you go, I will go with you."

Vladimir says, "You two have gone mad."

Natasha and Sandhi look at him, then say, "Stay here with Hero. We will go and check."

"I'm begging you, don't go... listen to me."

Trying to reassure Vladimir, Sandhi says, "There's no noise now; they are not up there." Sandhi looks upwards. "Look, the cover isn't bearing any weight, meaning no one is standing on it."

"Wait a minute," he climbs up again and peers through the cracks in the cover to see that no one is there.

Vladimir returns and says, "Yeah, no one is above us. We can go up."

Sandhi says, "I'll go first."

Natasha says, "Okay. I'll follow you." Looking at Vladimir, she asks, "Will you stay here or come with us?"

"I'll stay here with Hero."

"Alright!" Sandhi starts climbing the ladder, gently removes the wooden cover, peeks her head out to look around, and then moves onto the ground floor. Following Sandhi, Natasha does the same. Then, looking down at Vladimir and Hero, Natasha says, "See you soon."

Vladimir watches them and doesn't say anything, but his eyes reveal a fear of being alone more than parting. Natasha and Sandhi creep, cautiously looking around as they go up.

Sandhi whispers, "It looks like they have left."

"Perhaps!" Suddenly, both focus on noises coming from the upper floor. They look at each other, then Natasha ascends the first few steps... then suddenly retreats.

Sandhi asks her, "Why did you come back? What happened?"

"What if there is a soldier with a gun? How will we face them?"

"I don't know."

Natasha looks around and only sees a pot with a dried plant. She picks up the pot. Sandhi asks, "What are you doing?"

"If something goes wrong, I'll smash this pot on their head," Natasha says so determinedly that Sandhi becomes genuinely frightened and believes she will do it. Then, they both advance towards the stairs, each step quickening their breath. Just before opening the door for the final time, Sandhi says, "Whatever happens, we face it together... we will see it through."

Natasha looks at Sandhi... a girl in a nightdress, thin and frail but filled with resolve. She responds, "Absolutely." Sandhi slowly pushes the door from behind. The door is also pushed hard, and all this happens in silence.

Sandhi applies all her strength, but the door does not open. Then she says, "It feels like someone is pushing from the other side too."

"Maybe." Then Natasha pushes again with her foot and Sandhi with both hands, yet it doesn't open. Natasha looks at Sandhi and says, "It seems there are at least four or five people on the other side."

"Or even more." They were scared, but now they were committed to opening the door. While pushing, suddenly Sandhi stops and says, "Wait, wait."

"What now?"

"So far, no gunshots have come from that side. No threats either, which means they probably don't have weapons either."

Natasha thinks about this momentarily and then quickly agrees, "Yes, you are right." Then, in Ukrainian, she calls out, "Who are you people?" Only whispers come back.

Natasha says, "You heard that, right? They are talking too."

"Ask what they want."

In Ukrainian, Natasha asks again, "What do you want?" Still, no clear response comes.

Frustrated, Sandhi shouts, "Who are you people?" From inside, a voice comes, "You are Indian; we are also from India."

Sandhi looks at Natasha and says, "They are just girls." She pushes again, but the door still doesn't open.

Sandhi: "What happened now... Why don't you open the door?"

From inside, a voice comes, "Who is that girl with you who speaks Russian?"

"She is my friend; don't be afraid of her." The reply from inside was, "Not afraid! How can we not be scared? Fear is natural."

"Don't panic, open the door." A voice from inside responds, "We will open the door, trusting you."

Natasha cautions Sandhi, "Be careful." Sandhi nods and waits. Soon, sounds of something moving inside are heard. After a while, the door opens, and Sandhi sees three frightened girls—one holding a broom, another holding a thick book, and one with a knife. When Sandhi sees they are just three girls, she says, "Natasha, put down the pot; it's unnecessary."

Natasha sets the pot down. The three girls step back, and Sandhi and Natasha enter. Once inside, everyone looks at each other, and silence fills the room.

Natasha asks in English, "Why were you guys screaming earlier?"

The girls replied that it was because of the sounds of bombs.

Sandhi says, "Don't you know? Screaming can increase the danger."

"We know, but this is Nida, who will explain it to her!" one of the girls, who was holding the knife, says.

Sandhi asks, "Which one of you is Nida?"

The girl with the knife points and says, "The one standing in the middle." Sandhi and Natasha look at her. She was very slim, short-haired, and dressed in a salwar suit.

Sandhi - "From now on, don't do that again, okay?"

Natasha: "Hey, we haven't even asked each other's names because of the situation here."

"My name is Natasha."

The girl with the knife says, "My name is Tamanna."

The girl holding the book says, "My name is Geeta."

Looking at everyone, Sandhi said, "My name is Sandhi."

Natasha asks, "Why are you guys staying on the first floor? It's more dangerous here because of the bombs."

Nida says, "Where is it not dangerous? Destruction is everywhere."

Tamanna: "We have been here since yesterday. Before that, we were in our hostel."

Natasha asks: "What were you guys doing here?"

Geeta explains, "We had come out of the hostel, and then suddenly the shooting started, so we got scared and entered this apartment."

Sandhi: "Let's go downstairs!" Looking at Natasha, she says this.

Natasha says, "Yes... yes, let's go."

Tamanna, with uncertainty, said, "Downstairs... why?"

Sandhi: "We are staying in an underground room downstairs."

All three girls exclaimed, "An underground room... where is it?"

Natasha: "Just downstairs."

The three girls were astonished to hear about the underground room. Natasha asks, "How were you managing your food and drinks here?" The girls say, "There isn't much here. We have a packet of bread and a bottle of water."

Sandhi: "Bring all that downstairs."

Natasha: "We are outside, you guys come quickly."

Sandhi and Natasha emerge, and the rest climb over a sizable downstairs cupboard. When Tamanna comes down, Sandhi asks, "Why did you drop this cupboard?"

"It was Nida who dropped it; I just helped her because we thought if someone comes, they will push, and if they are more in number, how will we stop them... so we dropped the cupboard."

Sandhi laughed, and Natasha said, "You guys thought well." Then, all three girls, Natasha and Sandhi, descended the stairs. After coming down the stairs, the three girls stood still, and then Sandhi gently lifted the cover, and the cover lifted easily. As soon as the cover was lifted, Sandhi saw Vladimir hugging Hero. When Vladimir saw Sandhi and Natasha, he jumped joyfully, saying, "Come in, come in, welcome both of you."

After a while, he saw Sandhi descending, then three more girls and Natasha gently putting the cover back in place. Vladimir felt a bit uneasy seeing so many girls and stood back. Natasha, coming down, said, "This is Vladimir."

Vladimir looks at everyone and says, 'Hello'. All the girls also greet him with a 'hello.' Then Natasha introduces, "This is Hero." Hero sniffs all the new girls.

Nida asks, "He won't bite, will he?"

Sandhi: "He's not like people; he only understands and gives love."

Vladimir: "Yes, he's a true companion... he doesn't harm."

Sandhi: "Sit down, you guys."

Everyone starts to set down their belongings on their shoulders.

Then Tamanna asks - "Are you guys friends?"

Natasha: "How we met is an interesting story. We all met in an underground metro; Sandhi had saved a woman's life there."

Sandhi said, "And she had helped me save that life."

"I came here with Sandhi and Natasha; I was also at that metro station," Vladimir added.

Sandhi and Natasha say, "Not just you, only you came with us, no one else came with us, only Vladimir came with us."

Natasha explains, "Everyone else had left us."

Sandhi: "Leave those things; why entangle them in all that."

"Right, you are, Sandhi."

Looking at Sandhi, Geeta says, "Your dress has a lot of blood on it."

"It's from the woman she helped."

Tamanna - "What happened to her?"

"She had given birth to a baby; I had helped her during the birth."

Tamanna: "Are you a doctor?"

"No, I am not a doctor yet, but I still have a year to complete my medical degree. I am studying for my medical degree in Kyiv."

The three girls look at each other and say, "We are also studying medicine here in Kharkiv."

Natasha laughed, "Now this room is full of doctors."

Nida, "No, we are far from becoming doctors; it's only been a year for all of us."

"Ah, so then you guys are my juniors."

Everyone starts laughing.

Geeta asks, "You're getting your degree from Kyiv, so how did you end up here?"

"Don't even ask about all that."

Tamanna insists, "Please tell us... we've got nothing but conversations!"

"I came here to meet someone I loved; he had a meeting here. That very night, the Russian soldiers attacked, and we got trapped."

"Is your boyfriend Vladimir?" Nida asks shyly.

"No, he didn't come with me; we're not together anymore." As she says this, tears begin to form in Sandhi's eyes. Natasha places her hand on Sandhi's shoulder. Then Sandhi wipes her tears and says, "Now the three of us are together." Vladimir and Natasha echo her, "Yes, now we three are together."

Vladimir suddenly interjects, "No, no... all four of us are together now."

Natasha exclaims, "Oh yes, Hero is here too, my Hero," hugging Hero as she speaks.

Sandhi declares, "I just need to get out of here; I want to go home."

Tamanna agrees, "We all want to go home; our families are worried. The Indian government will try to evacuate us soon. We need to stay in touch with the Indian embassy."

Natasha asks, "Where do you guys make calls from?"

Nida replies, "There's a phone in the room upstairs; we use that."

Sandhi inquires, "Is the phone working?"

Tamanna confirms, "Yes, it's working."

Natasha exclaims, "That's great!"

Sandhi asks, "Did the Indian embassy tell you this?"

Geeta confirms, "Yes, they told us."

"That's excellent news," says Sandhi, standing up and adding, "I don't know when I'll be able to leave."

The three girls watched Sandhi intently as she spoke. Vladimir says, "I'll also talk to my embassy to see what they say."

Natasha takes a deep breath, "I need to see if my home is still there or if Russian tanks have destroyed it."

Geeta says, "We call every day; we'll try again tomorrow and see what happens."

Sandhi adds, "Yes, let's see what happens," and starts thinking.

Natasha asks, "Where is your passport, Sandhi?"

"It's still in the hotel; what will happen now? How will I get it? I don't know. Why do all these troubles come to me? Oh God! What will I do?"

"Don't worry, Sandhi, everything will be alright."

"I don't know how I'll get there. Everything depends on papers; where we can go and where we can't depend on papers. A person is nothing outside of papers. Systems always establish rules and regulations to control human actions: nationality, passports, visas, and stamps. A person is nothing beyond these paper rules. A person may win one battle and lose another. First, it was paper; now it's the computer. Outside here, there are Russian soldiers, bullets, guns, tanks."

Thinking this through, Vladimir lowers his head and asks, "How will the passport come?"

Natasha responds, "Sandhi, if I am with you, I am with you."

Vladimir asks, "What does that mean?"

"It means I will go with her if she wants me to."

"Yes, I must go because how can I go home without it?"

"So, when are we leaving, Captain?" Sandhi says, looking at him and starting to laugh.

The three girls also start laughing at Natasha's comment. Natasha says, "It would be better to leave at night."

"Yes, we can leave at night." Suddenly, Vladimir asks, "Okay, who's hungry? Tell me. We have a lot of food, pasta, macaroni, pastries, and red wine."

Natasha laughs, "Vladimir, you've made a fortune for these dry breads, calling them by such fancy names." Tamanna, surprised, says, "I started to believe that there would be so much, but there isn't, which is a bit sad. It's been ages since we had a good meal."

Sandhi says, "It's been ages since we had a full meal."

Natasha says, "I was hungry yesterday but didn't say anything because we only had a packet of bread. Who knows what will happen next, so I thought I'd skip eating for another day. At least the bread will last another day."

Vladimir brings the bread and opens it, saying, "There are 18 pieces of bread in this." Tamanna says, "We also have bread, one packet."

Vladimir says, "So, we have 36 pieces, and there are 8 of us, including Hero."

Nida says, "Hero will eat with us too."

Tamanna asks, "Won't he be hungry?"

Vladimir says, "That means we will get one piece of bread daily for four days, then half a piece each."

Geeta says, "Hopefully, God willing, we'll have left here by then."

Vladimir states, "God doesn't do anything; he only gives us the strength to act... the rest is up to us."

Natasha says, "Like we're going to the hotel tonight." Then she adds, "May God give us strength and courage and protect us."

In a subdued tone, Geeta says, "May God also give us good food."

Nida says, "May God also get us home."

Vladimir adds, "God, get me to America so I can live peacefully there."

Tamanna says, "May God keep us well."

Sandhi looks at everyone and says, "God has kept us alive; what more can we ask for? He has given us life; what more can we want? He has given us the strength to endure all this and the ability to cope with the loss of our loved ones. I think we don't need to ask for more from God. We should be grateful for whatever he has given us. However, he has given it. We should thank God more than we ask him for what he gives us."

Natasha jokingly asks, "Should I also thank him for the war?"

"Yes, perhaps you should."

Everyone looks at Sandhi in surprise.

Sandhi continues, "Look, a different character is being forged. We are becoming tougher than we ever were. We can now manage our emotions, hunger, thirst, and ourselves. This better version of ourselves is here, and perhaps God has shown us this war to introduce us to our better selves. This is the test God is giving, giving you different paths. In this war, you can either help others or harm them. The choice is yours. You can harbor hatred or empathy, and it's up to you to understand that whatever you choose, the consequences will follow. You cannot sow cacti and harvest wheat. What do you want the world to have, cacti or wheat grains in the future? Human making lasts from childhood to death, and deeply ingrained unpleasant and pleasant influences can offer much to the world. Gandhi and Hitler are significant examples that can be seen and understood as examples of dealing with human circumstances and problems with empathetic or aggressive approaches."

Listening to this, everyone is touched by Sandhi's words.

While eating her bread, Sandhi adds, "Life only teaches you; you will receive good or bad lessons based on your judgment and patience. Thank God for every lesson. Life is a journey of progressive development. Celebrate your existence; we make happiness and sadness."

Sandhi laughs as she eats her bread, and her mind drifts to Petrovich, remembering how he had taught her to understand love. Sandhi becomes teary-eyed but then starts laughing again. Perhaps Sandhi had overcome Petrovich's selfish behavior.

8

Lenin said, "Can any nation become free by oppressing other nations? It cannot.

Kharkiv

Time: 9 PM

February 26, 2023

Sandhi was pacing back and forth in the room, muttering to herself. Vladimir's gaze followed her constant movement. Natasha was sitting with Hero, telling him they would go home soon and play in the garden while Hero gently pawed at her affectionately. Tamanna had wanted to speak to Sandhi for a while, but Sandhi was lost in her thoughts, so Tamanna waited for the right moment. Geeta and Nida discussed how they would call the Indian Embassy the next day.

Tamanna finally attempts to start a conversation with Sandhi, asking, "Can I ask you something, Sandhi?"

Sandhi, while still pacing, responds, "Ask."

"Why aren't you sitting down? You've been walking continuously. I've been watching you for nearly two hours now. You're neither talking nor stopping, just walking."

"I'm just thinking about how I'm going to leave tonight, what will happen and what won't. Times aren't like before, where you could step out and go wherever you wanted to. Times and circumstances have changed so much that I don't know what I'll encounter outside. And it's not just about me; Natasha will be with me too. If it were just me, I wouldn't think so much. But the lives of those connected to me are as important as my own, yet I consider theirs more critical because if someone is taking a risk for you now, it means they are putting their life on the line for you. Times have changed, and so have the rules of relationships."

"You're right, Sandhi," agrees Tamanna.

Natasha chimes in, "Don't stress too much about these things, Sandhi. I'm coming with you to share some of your burdens, not so you can worry about me."

"I understand," Sandhi replies.

Geeta says sadly, "We are the reason you're stressed, aren't we? You wouldn't have had to go for the passport if I hadn't said anything."

"Oh no, I'm glad I got home because of you, but trouble is inevitable; life doesn't let you live that easily."

Everyone laughs at Sandhi's remark.

Sandhi then asks, "Tell me how you all like Ukraine?"

Nida responds, "Do you need to ask that now?"

"Why do you say that?" Sandhi asks.

"Ever since we arrived, it's been nothing but trouble. First, we struggled with the cold weather, then it took time to adjust, and just when we started to settle in, this war broke out."

"Yes, it takes time to adjust, but once you do, it's all peace," Sandhi muses.

Tamanna says, "Where's the peace? Our parents told us to study medicine, so we did. Now here we are, listening to bombs, and our parents are back home worrying about us, wondering how they manage their days."

"Yes, I often don't understand why we are all here—it's because the fees here are lower. If our government reduced the fees back home and increased the number of seats, then why would we come here? I don't know whether to question the government about why they haven't done this or to thank them for letting us evacuate from here."

Nida lets out a deep sigh, "Don't ask questions; questioning is forbidden in these times. You're supposed to endure pain and remain silent. If you do, you're right; otherwise, you're a rebel. And I'm not just talking about the government. Everywhere, it's the same. Everyone expects you to endure everything; only those in power can make mistakes. When you make a mistake, they won't understand."

Tamanna exclaims, "What's gotten into you? Why are you talking like this?"

"I've been here for two days and don't know what to do. We can't go outside, and how long can we stay inside? Everything is uncertain: whether we should go out or stay in when the government will let us go home. Nothing is certain except that the war won't stop anytime soon."

Vladimir says, "Why would they stop? The narrative being set up is that any nation can attack another if it doesn't care about the repercussions. If this narrative takes hold, the survival and existence of humanity will be challenging. Colonialism might have ended in history books, but its form has changed. It still exists and probably always will."

Geeta asks, "How is colonialism still around? I don't understand."

"What else is going on? Any nation attacks another and takes control of any state. There must be some way to stop this."

Natasha adds, "I don't know of any method right now; we live without methods."

"I'm talking about those very methods. Sometimes, I laugh when people worry about what others will say about small things. If people can speak up about small matters, why can't they all unite and say war is wrong? I learned about the Renaissance in school, the Age of Enlightenment, and thought society had become very logical. After the Renaissance, everything would be logical, but then countless wars happened that were either pointless or only meaningful to a select few."

Sandhi agrees, "You're right, Vladimir; war is for a few—earn money from making weapons, then earn when people get hurt."

"From the Renaissance to now, many changes have happened and wars have happened, but now I feel like we need another intellectual revolution that talks about the basics, about the future of humanity. Monarchy is gone, but dictatorship, monopolism, and military rule are still going on."

Natasha asks, "What would be the theme of this revolution?"

"I don't know what the theme would be." Everyone falls silent, thinking.

Releasing the shackles of doubts, Sandhi says, "Humanity... it will only be about humanity."

Geeta asks, "Won't religion be a part of it?"

Vladimir replies, "No, not a religion because humanity encompasses the essence of religion. A strong human community in defense of humanity is the true bearer of any duty or religious flag, making real-time decisions based on their circumstances and experiences, aiming for the universal desire for love, peace, and welfare."

After listening attentively to Vladimir, Sandhi says, "Your idea will always face one problem because we rarely live with conscious awareness."

"What's the problem?"

"The spiritual aspect of religion aims at the continuous improvement and advancement of human life, but a society entangled in worldly illusions and circumstances doesn't get the chance to wander in knowledge and experiences. It's because its inspirations are the people, society, and families entangled in gains and losses, whose footsteps it follows, drowning even the partially existing ideas of good and evil in the mire of those gains and losses. The lack of a persistent thirst for knowledge or awareness leads to a society on the brink of decline, where establishing true life values without knowledge becomes a mere fantasy."

Natasha says, "Both you, Sandhi, and Vladimir are correct. Vladimir, I'm Christian, Sandhi is Hindu, and there might be Muslims and Sikhs, too."

Nida interrupts, "I'm Muslim."

Tamanna looks at Nida and adds, "I'm Sikh."

Natasha said, "Yes, it's good that there are followers of so many religions here. Tell me, does any religion speak against humanity?"

Everyone together responds, "No, it doesn't." Natasha continues, "Humanity itself is the true religion, and if it were practiced, there would be no wars."

Vladimir says, "I've read, and it astonishes me that the French army went to help during the American Revolution. When they returned, they realized that they had established a rule for the people in America, where the voices of the people would be heard, and they would be free. But back home, we still had a monarchy. This realization by the soldiers was also one of the causes of the French Revolution. They spread the consciousness of the American Revolution."

Tamanna asks, "Why are you telling us all this history?"

With his characteristic sly smile, Vladimir explains, "When the French soldiers realized the importance of liberty, equality, fraternity, and justice, why haven't we understood till today that war isn't right? These ideas were all meant for the betterment and future freedom of people. We haven't understood yet, but perhaps we will after the war."

Sandhi comments, "Vladimir, it seems you have studied history deeply."

Vladimir laughs more heartily this time and says, "Being wealthy has this advantage, though it comes with many disadvantages. The rich and powerful do not want change because they fear it will alter their status, but I am not like that... I desire change. A time will come when everyone will want change and will yearn for humanity. I keep seeing this vision of humanity's vastness in my future."

"Vladimir, I've never seen you speak so openly; why don't you speak up?"

"I'm afraid of myself because I truly believe in what I say. I don't speak without belief."

Sandhi laughs and says, "Oh, Vladimir!"

Natasha asks, "How much time has passed, Vladimir?"

Looking at Natasha, Sandhi says, "I know why you're asking the time."

"It's 11 PM."

"We should leave now... What do you say, Natasha?"

"I'm ready."

Natasha swiftly gets up and says, "Let's go." She bends down to kiss Hero and says, "I'll see you soon."

Tamanna tells Sandhi, "Change your clothes; it's freezing outside." Sandhi replies, "I don't have any clothes."

The three girls together say, "We have them." They stand up, grab their bags, and place them before Sandhi.

Sandhi laughs and says, "There was a time when I had no clothes, and now I have three bags full of them."

Sandhi takes pants from Tamanna's bag, a shirt from Geeta's bag, and a fur jacket from Nida's bag. "I have taken something from all three of you; that's fine."

Sandhi stands with the clothes as everyone watches and then she says, "I need to change; everyone look that way."

Everyone laughs and turns away, but Hero keeps looking at Sandhi. Sandhi says, "Aren't you going to look away, Hero?" Hero keeps looking her way. After changing, Sandhi says, "Now everyone can look here." Everyone turns back to look at her.

Vladimir, seeing Sandhi, remarks, "I have been seeing you in night dresses all these days... you look good in these clothes."

Sandhi, laughing, says, "This is change, Vladimir... change."

Natasha interrupts, "Sandhi, we really should go now."

"Yes, I'm ready."

Sandhi takes a deep breath and moves forward.

Natasha asks, "What was the name of your hotel?"

"Oriental Palace Hotel."

Natasha notes, "It's not far from here, but every inch is fraught with danger."

Tamanna tells Sandhi, "I want to go with you, but I don't have the courage."

"Courage isn't always needed to fight battles; some battles instill courage within us. I didn't have it either; perhaps I still don't, but I have more than before. You will also gradually embrace courage. No one becomes non-violent in a day."

Sandhi then looks at the stairs, grabs the rail, and climbs to open the hatch. Once at the top, she looks back at everyone and says, "See you soon." After she goes up, Natasha follows and closes the hatch behind them. Both start walking.

Sandhi cautions Natasha, "Be careful, Natasha. I hear more gunfire and tanks today."

"I'll be watching every step," Natasha replies. They leave the apartment, stepping into complete darkness and silence. Natasha adds, "It seems air raids have started or are about to start."

"How can you tell?" asks Sandhi.

"Because it's pitch black." Only the frost on the roadside and the vapor from their breaths, common in winter, were visible. Natasha starts walking faster, driven by the darkness-induced fear. Sandhi keeps pace. They couldn't see much around them—perhaps they couldn't see at all due to the intense darkness. Only a few streetlights that had survived tanks and bullets were lit. Like the few remaining humans, these lights were sparse. They keep moving forward, contemplating what will happen once they reach the hotel. The streets are empty, split by the sound of gunfire. Natasha and Sandhi walk down a straight path. Ahead, a vast statue appears, and from it, four roads branch off. The statue is wholly covered with sandbags to protect it from Russian bullets.

Sandhi asks Natasha, "Whose statue is this?"

"It's the great Lenin."

"Oh, Lenin's statue..." Sandhi says with despair, "Oh! In this condition."

Looking at Sandhi, Natasha says, "Lenin had said, 'Can any nation become free by oppressing other nations?' No, it cannot. This one sentence is enough for his immortality."

"What a time it is when great people's statues and words are being covered up, and massacres are ongoing on the streets. Natasha, will we be enslaved again by arms and capital?"

"Maybe," Natasha says as they hurry along, "Today, the courage and morality to speak and act rightly are at their lowest ebb. Here, people aren't eating each other, that's about it. Nothing stops them from devouring each other's social and economic aspects, even rendering their ability to demand justice powerless due to their economic and social vulnerabilities."

"I think being eaten by another human wouldn't feel as bad as being ruthlessly crushed and exploited by another," Sandhi muses.

"Perhaps you are right," Natasha agrees. They fall silent again, walking on amid the explosions, pondering when this cycle of failing to recognize the humanity in others will end.

Sandhi sees a glimmer of light in the distance. "That light might be from the hotel," she suggests.

"Yes, you're right, that's the hotel," confirms Natasha.

They continue walking and pause a short distance from the hotel.

Sandhi looks around, "See any Russian soldiers?"

"I don't see any."

"Let's get a bit closer and then check again." Near the gate, Natasha tells Sandhi, "Look at the gate. That's a Russian soldier."

"What now?"

Looking at the hotel, Natasha insists, "We've come this far; we won't go back without the passports."

Sandhi gives Natasha a piercing look, her eyes conveying that she wants Natasha to understand what she is. Natasha says, "We need to find another gate. Such a large hotel can't have just one."

"Maybe I know another door."

"Maybe... What kind of answer is that? You said you know, yet you say 'maybe.'"

"The last time...

Just then, a Russian soldier looks their way, and they quickly lie down."

The Russian soldier starts looking the other way again, but they continue to speak while lying down. Sandhi resumes her story: "The Last time I escaped from here, I was leaving through the front gate, but many people were also escaping from the back. So, I think there must be another gate there."

"Okay... let's get out of here first." They then move slowly, half-crouched, so the soldier cannot see them at the main gate.

"Natasha, it's tough to move like this; I won't be able to keep it up for long."

"You can do it. Walk for your life, yourself, and your family; keep going."

"Yes, I'm trying." They eventually reach the back gate via a slightly larger path. Sandhi pulls on a heavy steel door with a large handle, but it doesn't budge. Natasha tries as well, to no avail.

Sandhi looks down the alley and says to Natasha, "If someone comes from the front or the side alley, we won't see them. One of us should stand there to signal if we see the Russian soldier." They agree on this, and Natasha starts to go to keep watch but then returns halfway and says, "No one has opened it yet; if someone who only speaks Ukrainian or Russian comes, how will you communicate?"

"Yes, you're right... I'll go stand watch." Sandhi takes her place. Natasha continues to knock on the back door. Suddenly, a voice in Ukrainian from inside asks, 'Who are you?' Just then, Sandhi signals—a signal that a Russian soldier is approaching.

"I am Natasha. My friend's passport was left here in a part of your hotel when a bomb fell. She couldn't take it with her in the panic and chaos. She's of Indian origin. Her government is sending her home, but she needs it..." Sandhi starts signaling more urgently, and she runs to Natasha.

"Russian soldiers are coming from the other alley; our lives are now in your hands."

The voice from inside responds, "I can't open it. How can I trust you?"

"I'm not going anywhere; we'll see what happens. You're Ukrainian and still not ready to help us."

Sandhi adds, "Open up. They could be here any second." The Russian soldiers were just a couple of steps away from the alley when suddenly the door opened. They rush inside just as it closes, seconds before the soldiers reach the alley.

Inside, they face a tall, broad man holding an iron rod. Seeing the rod, Sandhi and Natasha look at each other, and Natasha says, "We are not enemies; we are your friends." The man with the rod gives them a stern look and then sets the rod down.

Natasha explains in Ukrainian, "This is my friend Sandhi. She was here two days ago when your hotel was bombed." She then asks Sandhi, "Which room were you in?"

"105."

Natasha continues to explain to the man, "She was in room 105 when the explosion happened, and in the chaos, she left her passport here. She needs to go back now, so she needs her passport."

The man looks at Sandhi, then says to Natasha, "Okay, you can go to the room to look for the passport, but hurry because the Russian soldiers are coming to stay here."

Natasha asks him, "Which way should we go?"

He responds, "I'll lead the way." Both say, "Okay, let's go." As the man starts climbing the stairs, Natasha asks, "Why not take the elevator?"

He replies, "No, the elevator is too dangerous. If there's an attack, the elevator could get stuck, and we're unlikely to find someone to repair it right now."

Sandhi and Natasha follow him up. As they walk, Natasha signals to Sandhi to be ready for anything suspicious. Sandhi acknowledges with a nod, prepared for anything. As they reach the first floor, Sandhi notices hair stuck to the hallway carpet and spots of blood here and there. There were no people, but signs of their distress were evident. Memories of that dreadful morning flood back to Sandhi, causing her to feel dizzy, but she steadies herself by grabbing onto a door. Natasha, seeing her standing still, asks, "What happened?"

"Nothing... just felt a bit strange for a moment."

The man asks why Natasha isn't following. She replies, "She got a shock... coming here brought back all the memories of that morning."

He bluntly says there's no time for that, "Do what you need to do quickly."

Sandhi gathers her strength again and prepares to enter the room. The man opens the door, which is unlocked, and steps inside. Natasha follows, then Sandhi. As Sandhi enters, she feels as though she and Petrovich are still sitting on the bed talking. She shakes her head to dispel the illusion, knowing it's unreal. The man's stern voice rings, "Hurry up, I don't have much time." Sandhi's daydream is shattered, and she begins searching for her passport. She first checks the wardrobe, but it's not there. Watching her, Natasha starts searching through the drawers. No luck.

The man says, "If it's not here, then leave. Since then, many people have come and gone; someone might have taken it."

Sandhi thinks about what she'll do if it's not found. Will she ever be able to go home? Will she die here in Ukraine? Will she never see her mother's face again? These thoughts race through her mind as she looks out the broken window, remembering how it had cut her. The pain is still there; she touches her wound to feel its freshness. Suddenly, Natasha calls from under the bed, "Sandhi, I found it."

Sandhi snaps out of her reverie and looks at Natasha, who is about to hand her the passport when the man snatches it.

"Getting the passport won't be easy," he says. Sandhi and Natasha look at each other.

"Why won't it be easy? It's her passport; why can't she have it easily?"

"It won't be easy because it's now in my hands. You'll have to give something in return, money or something else."

Natasha retorts, "Even when everything ends, you're worried about money."

He replies, "Money is needed most now. Please don't waste my time. If you take too long, the Russian soldiers will come, and then who knows what they'll demand."

"We are both far from our homes; we have nothing."

He looks Natasha up and down and says, "I want that chain around your neck."

"Please don't take that; it was given to me by my mother."

"Is your mother alive or dead?"

"She's no longer in this world."

"So, she's dead. What will you do with her keepsake now?"

"I'm Ukrainian, and so are you... you won't spare me either."

"What's wrong with exchanging one thing for another? What do you know about what happens in war... I'm only asking for your gold chain in exchange for the passport." Sandhi also pleads with him, but he refuses and leaves the room. He says, "If you don't want to give it, leave empty-handed."

"Wait!" Natasha kisses the chain and says, "You always said money isn't more important than people; I'm just following your words." She takes off the chain and hands it to him.

Then the man turns to Sandhi and says, "Take off that ring from your finger."

Sandhi smiles at him and then removes the ring. The man looks at the ring and the chain and hands over the passport. When Sandhi holds the passport, she touches it as if it's not just a passport but a sense of home. Perhaps she's recalling her arrival in Kharkiv, which brought her closer to Petrovich, at least in her thoughts.

The man says, "Now, both of you leave here as quickly as possible." They turned to leave when suddenly his phone rang. He picks up and starts speaking in Ukrainian. Both women hurry downstairs, open the steel door, and enter the alley.

As soon as they are outside, Natasha asks Sandhi, "What kind of people are these, looking for profit even in war?"

Their greed wasn't satisfied even after taking our chain and ring. Sandhi asks, "What happened suddenly?"

Natasha responds, "When we were descending, his phone rang, and he said he would give the room only if he got three times the money. Morality has fallen so low that what he was doing seemed right to him; in fact, he considered himself better and more honest than others."

"Perhaps this is an era of comparative decline in morality; yes, someone's calamity is an opportunity for others to increase their wealth." Natasha gets disturbed hearing Sandhi's comment and starts pondering why humans are so attached to money. Why can't they prioritize humanity? Then, she thinks about why humans created money and why society remained transactional. Lost in thought, she suddenly realizes that money is the perfect tool to test humans. If humans hadn't created money, they could never honestly assess one another. With this thought, she starts laughing, realizing that humans have made their means to test themselves. Sandhi, seeing her laughing, feels odd.

Then Sandhi finally asks, "Why are you laughing?"

"People are not as clever as you think."

Sandhi doesn't fully understand but nods in agreement.

"Why were you laughing when you took off the ring?"

"I was watching, unable to see beyond money, oblivious to how horrific the war will be. She finds comfort solely in money."

"Her comfort might be short-lived; ours and yours will last longer."

"She has taken everything from us; now there's less to lose."

They found themselves in front of Lenin's statue as they walked again. This time, both instinctively bowed before the statue. Perhaps, as they saw the different faces of humanity in this war, their faith in those who thought for the society grew stronger. They looked at each other as they bowed but did not ask why the other did so. Lost in these thoughts, they discreetly made their way to the apartment. Upon arriving home, Sandhi removed the covering and peeked inside, finding everyone's eyes filled with joy. Sandhi came down, followed by Natasha. As Sandhi descended, Hero licked her and started licking Natasha after she arrived.

Tamanna asked, "How was your journey?"

Both said in unison, "We saw Lenin today." Then Natasha looked at Sandhi, who continued, "Covered with sacks at the crossroads, it was suffocating. They must be suffocating inside. I felt like removing the sacks and sitting with his statue and seeing if they would also pierce the great hero of Russia. They could... they have already pierced his thoughts."

9

"My victory will still not be mine. I will be glad that my nation wins but will remain defeated.

Kharkiv

Time: 11:00 AM

February 27th

Sandhi was sitting comfortably, a pen in her hand and a dirty page she might have found on the street, stained with some marks, writing something on it. Natasha was lying on the bed, watching everyone, touching her neck where her necklace had been. Perhaps the necklace reminded her of her mother's touch; there's nothing one can do about human nature. Vladimir had found a book in the room and was engrossed in it. Tamanna, Geeta, and Nida were discussing that they would contact the embassy in a little while. Hero was lying down, probably missing the outside world more than anyone else, but who would consider his desires when even human wishes were barely grasped here?

Natasha asked Sandhi, "What were you writing?"

"Not writing, really." Sandhi replied, "Just transferring what's already written in my mind onto these pages to lighten the load. Otherwise, my brain will burst."

Natasha said nothing, just continued to watch Sandhi from behind. Watching her, Natasha began to cry, perhaps being close to Sandhi's pain. Feeling someone's pain is a difficult task, and Natasha had possibly managed that difficult task. Having noticed or guessed this, Tamanna tried to give hope, saying, "Sandhi, we will call the embassy again today."

"When will you do it?"

"Very shortly."

Geeta asked, "Should we all go upstairs and come back down? I've been sitting here all day, and I'm bored. I thought maybe everyone else was bored, too."

Vladimir closed his book by saying, "Yes, I want to feel water on my face. This war has stifled even the smallest feelings."

Natasha laughed at Vladimir's words and said, "Every day, I have to ask myself if we are still alive."

Looking worriedly at Natasha, Nida said, "I only feel alive when I cry; otherwise, it feels like life is in someone else's hands, as if I am living a life given by someone else."

With her head bowed, Sandhi quietly said, "We are all living a life given by someone else. Our freedom is dependent on their agenda. If they want war, then there's war. The day they decide to end it, life will resume. Life is gripped by war, whether with bullets flying or the battle of life where there are no bullets but the formalities of life, your dreams, what you want to become, beliefs, and dreams. Life will always be gripped."

Natasha responded, "How unnecessary burdens are placed on a person. Life should liberate a person, but instead, life dies under the weight of controls set to manage us."

Vladimir, standing up, added, "Nothing happens by itself in this society; that's why it feels like a burden. Everything is artificial, thought out by someone. It might be right for him, but it will feel like a burden to your psyche."

Sandhi, looking up, remarked, "That's why Mahatma Gandhi spoke of participation, upliftment, and non-possession. These aren't just words; they are a way of living."

Vladimir, surprised, asked, "Sandhi, you're a medical student. How come you've read so much about Gandhi?"

"My father," she replied. "He has always been a follower of Gandhian philosophy."

Vladimir continued, "Mahatma Gandhi strongly believed in non-possession, and this belief is even more relevant now when the environment is polluted with weapons and tanks. I have never managed to live a life of non-possession, but I want to."

Natasha said, "When I saw Lenin's statue at the square yesterday, I felt this war isn't just consuming people; it's consuming our heritage and nature. I fear because there are nuclear plants like Chernobyl on our land; if something happens there, it will affect fifty generations."

Vladimir's voice revealed his fear, "Like what happened in Hiroshima and Nagasaki... perhaps even worse."

Nida, frightened, exclaimed, "Don't talk about such things; I'm starting to get scared."

Natasha concluded, "Yeah, let's stop this talk; it's useless."

"Why are you being so pessimistic, Natasha?" asked Sandhi.

"What should I do if I don't talk about these things? It's getting difficult to live. I can't change this system," Natasha lamented.

Sandhi reassured, "That's not true. We can change things. We need to unite and truly consider human welfare and our future. We must consolidate everything else and pause, think, and move forward thoughtfully."

Geeta, listening intently, finally said, "My priority is to get out of here first."

Sandhi nodded and agreed, "That's my priority too."

Natasha added, "Someone has to prioritize this country too."

Vladimir said, "Not just this country, but the protection of humanity must be made a priority."

As they talked, Tamanna suggested, "Let's go upstairs... let's make the call." They all looked at each other, perhaps finding courage in each other, and started to move forward.

First, Geeta grabbed the stair railing and started heading up, followed by Tamanna, then Nida. Vladimir grabbed the railing next, and Sandhi noticed Vladimir was a bit scared. She told him, "Vladimir, we're all going; come on."

Vladimir climbed up slowly after her, followed by Natasha, carrying Hero in her arms. Finally, they closed the wooden hatch from above, and Sandhi laid the carpet over it. Then Geeta gently opened the door upstairs. As soon as the door opened, a rat darted out quickly. All the girls got scared. Nida started screaming, and Tamanna covered her mouth with her hand. They all went inside and closed the door from the inside.

Tamanna laughed, saying, "Even these rats are surviving the war and scaring us."

Sandhi remarked, "It's strange... Here we are, observing everything on our own, managing ourselves, fighting the stress of the war, and yet we're scared of a rat."

Natasha said, "It's natural to be afraid. You realize your strength when your life is truly at risk. If that rat had attacked you, you would have torn it apart with your fingers. We're scared because we know it's just a rat, and it will quietly leave if we scream."

All the girls and Vladimir accepted Natasha's words without objection.

Vladimir announced, "I'm going to the bathroom."

Geeta said, "I'll make the call."

Sandhi replied, "Yes, yes, make it." Geeta motioned for everyone to come to another room. Natasha decided to stay where she was to keep an ear on any noises from downstairs. Geeta went into another room filled with scattered books. A photo frame was also there, showing a woman with her children. Sandhi picked up the photo and started looking at the children and their mother, saying, "When someone is in love, it shows on their face. The mother's face has so much contentment and affection for her children. I wonder where these people are now."

The three women sat down, and Geeta picked up the phone and dialed the Indian embassy. The phone rang, but no one answered, so Geeta put the phone down. Nida urged her to "Try calling again."

"I'll try again in two minutes."

With a hint of doubt, Tamanna said, "What if they don't plan to evacuate us?"

Sandhi placed the photo down and reassured, "Don't lose hope; everything will be alright."

Geeta picked up the phone again and called; this time, someone answered as soon as the ring went.

She blurted out in one breath, "There are four of us stuck in an apartment in Kharkiv. Please get us out and send us back to India." Sandhi went to Natasha and asked, "What's the exact address of this place?"

Natasha replied, "It's A Square Apartment."

Sandhi went back. Meanwhile, Geeta continued talking on the phone.

After a while, Geeta hung up the phone with a joyful expression and looked at everyone, announcing, "We are going home soon."

Joy spread across everyone's faces. Vladimir came out of the bathroom and asked, "What happened?"

Everyone began to tell him that their government would soon repatriate them. Vladimir said, "I will also call my embassy now." Smiling, he went to make the call.

Sandhi's face also lit up with happiness. All the women hugged each other. Sandhi went to tell Natasha, "Geeta just spoke to the Indian embassy... They will get us out of here and send us back to India."

Natasha hugged Sandhi and asked, "Are you happy now?"

"Yes, I am thrilled."

"That's good; I am happy in your happiness."

Vladimir made his call and was also very happy afterward. He said, "I will also be going home." Everyone started moving downstairs. They gently closed the door of the first-floor room and lifted the hatch after removing the carpet, descending the stairs one by one, then closing the hatch again. Once downstairs, everyone began to congratulate each other.

Sandhi asked Vladimir, "When are you leaving?"

Vladimir explained that he would leave the next day. He said, "I must go to Pysochyn first; they will take me from there."

Geeta said, "We also need to go to Pysochyn; from there, we will leave too."

Sandhi asked Natasha, "How far is Pysochyn from here?"

"At least 12 kilometers away."

Geeta confirmed, "Yes, that's what the embassy told us. Some Ukrainian soldiers will come to pick us up, and they will take us."

Vladimir added, "I was told the same thing; they gave me a time of 10 AM."

Geeta nodded, "Me too."

"I've given them our current address... they will send someone," she said. Everyone sat down very happily and started chatting.

Natasha told Sandhi, "You are leaving tomorrow; I am happy for you, but I will miss you a lot."

"I will miss you too, Natasha. You've been a great support everywhere, caring for me; I will never forget your kindness."

"There's no kindness in it... I supported you because I felt you were doing the right thing then, so I helped you. I felt good helping Julia; she needed blood."

"Yes, you are right."

Tamanna said, "Tomorrow, no one is to be late... understand, everyone is ready on time."

Vladimir commented, "If we're late tomorrow, then we might have to stay here, which I don't want." Then he started laughing.

Nida asked, "Why are Ukrainian soldiers coming with us to Pysochyn? Who asked them to come with us?"

Geeta responds, "Nida! My naive girl... The embassy told me that the Government of India is conducting 'Operation Ganga' to evacuate Indian students from here, and Ukraine is cooperating with us."

Vladimir said, "There's no such operation from America, but they are helping evacuate as many people as possible because America stands with Ukraine in this war. America and India favor peace, and that's why Ukraine is assisting so much in evacuating students."

Sandhi added, "Yes, you're right. Governments taking sides will not do anything. The people of our country, people from all countries, must stand against war. Everyone must understand that this problem could arise with any country, and thus everyone should oppose it, or else the war will never end."

Natasha said, "The way the war is escalating, one thing is certain: it's not going to end anytime soon."

Geeta replied with great despair, "The war must end; otherwise, how will we complete our medical degrees?"

Tamanna added, "I don't know how it will happen, but I know this much: once the war ends, we'll have to come back because the college authorities were still saying there are no holidays, but my father told me to come back because the situation there is not safe."

Geeta said, "When will society be safe for us girls? It feels like a war even on ordinary days."

"You're right; for us, the war never seems to end," Sandhi said.

Nida added, "What a strange university; I don't know why they're doing this."

"It might also be the same situation in our university." Sandhi said.

Vladimir says happily, "Tomorrow, I'll go home and meet my mom and dad."

Everyone is happy. Sandhi is sitting next to Hero, stroking his hair. Natasha sits at a distance, watching Sandhi. Vladimir observes everyone from a corner and smiles, which is the essence of all smiles. Vladimir sits beside Natasha and says, "I will miss the time spent with you. You never get scared, Natasha. I am proud of you. The less you fear, the more I fear."

"You're as sharp-minded as I am quick-hearted," and they laugh.

Vladimir hugs Natasha, and Natasha hugs him back. Suddenly, Vladimir moves away from Natasha and starts rereading a book. Natasha realizes that Vladimir is crying. Natasha signals to Sandhi. Sandhi quietly stands up, and Natasha does too. They go to Vladimir, take his book from him, and say, "Vladimir, you can cry in front of us."

"I know, but I don't want to cry because if I start, I won't be able to stop."

Natasha, Vladimir, and Sandhi hug and hold each other. The three girls also notice everyone getting emotional and hug the trio.

Vladimir says, "Wow, today everyone feels love for everyone." The people hug each other in a big circle.

Sandhi emotionally says, "I wish every country and its citizens could hug each other like this and live only with love, without any conflict or misunderstanding. This beautiful dream could spread happiness in every street, every corner of every country, if only we kept yearning for each other's happiness every moment."

Kharkiv

February 28

9:30 AM

Everyone had been ready to leave for Pysochyn since morning except Natasha, who was unprepared to go.

Natasha tells Sandhi, "I won't come to see you off, Sandhi. It would be dangerous for me to come alone, and I don't want to leave Hero alone."

Sandhi laughs and says, "The Natasha I know doesn't get scared, nor will she ever. Tell me what's going on."

"That's just it."

Sandhi looks into Natasha's eyes and says, "Tell me what's happening."

Tears fall from Natasha's eyes, and she says, "When I first supported you, I didn't know we would come this far; I didn't know that when you leave, I would feel so weak. All I have in my mind is that I'll be alone when you go; how will I live here alone? Sandhi, you were alone when I met you on the underground metro. I wasn't there with you. I understand you must go, but how do I convince my mind?"

"Come with me to India," Sandhi says, taking Natasha's hand.

Natasha laughs and says, "No, I can't leave my country now. Everything I have is here, and my mother was from here. I will rebuild her house and keep busy with little things like that. My heart will eventually understand, just as it has endured the sorrow of losing my mother, my father, and our house turning to ashes."

Sandhi hugs her and starts crying.

Vladimir looks away, perhaps trying to strengthen himself.

Trying to lighten the mood, Tamanna says, "Has everyone packed their stuff?"

Everyone responds, "Yes, we've packed."

"Slice the bread and share it among yourselves." Everyone takes two slices each.

Tamanna said, "It's 10 o'clock... They haven't arrived yet."

Geeta suggests, "Why don't we sit on the ground level? How will they know we are in an underground place?" Everyone agrees, "Okay."

Sandhi hugs Natasha again and, embracing her, says, "I'll return after the war... We'll meet again. I've remembered your home address."

Natasha responds, "I'll stay here for a few more days, then I'll see." Then Vladimir hugs Natasha and says, "Come to America sometime... I'll take you around."

"I'll come."

"I've put my home number under your bed. The paper is tiny; take good care of it."

"I've kept your paper and your laughter safe," Natasha replies.

Sandhi caresses Hero's forehead and tells him, "Take care of Natasha."

Hero emits a strange, choked sound.

Natasha says, "He understands that you're leaving."

Vladimir also meets Hero and says, "Thank you, Hero, for getting me through much stress many times."

Then, each of the three girls takes turns meeting Natasha. Nida tells her, "Take care of yourself. When we come back, we'll have lots of fun." Natasha laughs and agrees.

Gradually, everyone comes up, and Natasha remains below with Hero. The last sound heard from below was Hero crying.

Everyone reaches the ground level, hides, and begins to wait.

Vladimir notes, "It's 10:30, and no one has arrived yet."

Geeta says, "I wonder if they will come at all."

Nida says, "Don't say that; they will come."

Tamanna stands with her eyes closed. Geeta asks her, "Why are your eyes closed?"

"If I don't close them, I'll get angry. I closed them to forget the anger, so I only hear the sound of the Ukrainian army's vehicle and nothing else." Everyone stands silently, just waiting.

Vladimir says, "It's now 11, and they still haven't arrived." After a while, everyone gets tired of standing and sits down. Soon, the sound of a vehicle is heard. Vladimir stands up and says, "Maybe the vehicle has arrived."

Everyone stands up. Then Sandhi asks, "How will we know if this vehicle is from the Ukrainian army?"

Vladimir asks, "Who will take the risk?" Everyone looks at each other.

Sandhi says, "Wait, I'll do something." Sandhi peeks so that those in the vehicle do not notice her. She sees four soldiers looking at their watches, seemingly waiting for someone.

Gathering all her courage, Sandhi asks in English, "Are you looking for someone? Are you looking for Indian students?"

One Ukrainian soldier replies, "Yes, we are looking for them." Meanwhile, two more soldiers join and ask another soldier, "Have you seen any American citizens?" They ask Sandhi the same question.

Sandhi replies, "He is with us."

Sandhi calls everyone, "Come out... they've come for us." Everyone comes out and stands. The Ukrainian soldier steps out of the vehicle and signals the driver to move the vehicle. The vehicle leaves, and only four soldiers remain. Vladimir asks, "How will we go?"

The soldier answers, "We will walk. The sound of the vehicle could attract danger, so we walk."

Sandhi exclaims, "12 kilometers on foot!"

"Yes, on foot... there is no other option, let's go."

All the girls look at each other in fear. Vladimir says, "You will walk with us, right?"

"Yes, we will walk with you, and other Indian students will join us, too."

As they walk, Sandhi asks, "How many other students are there?"

"About 30-40 more."

Sandhi looks around at everyone in astonishment.

Nida remarks, "Wow! So many people will walk together, and they say the vehicle would attract danger."

The soldier overhears Nida and says, "The Prime Minister of India might have spoken to the Russian President, and he promised a safe passage." He adds, "I don't know much more than that... I have to fight."

Sandhi looks at him attentively, her perception deepened by his remark, suggesting he, too, is bound by the duty to fight. She observes him from head to toe. He wore a large helmet-like green cap under which some items were strapped. Below that, he wore a bulletproof vest over a thick green fabric shirt. He had gloves on his hands, which provided a good grip; only his eyes were visible, and his nose and mouth were covered with a black mask. A belt with many pockets, probably for ammunition, was around his waist. He wore thick light green pants and heavy black boots. From top to bottom, he was fully covered.

A soldier walked beside Sandhi, one in front, one in the back, and one who changed positions frequently.

They formed a line and moved in it. The cold was severe, and everyone's breath was visible except for the soldiers. Sandhi turned her head back and said to Tamanna, "These soldiers don't even have the freedom to breathe. Or maybe they are wearing these masks to protect themselves from the smoke from bullets and tanks."

Tamanna responds, "It's both."

Vladimir was at the front, followed by Sandhi, Tamanna, Nida, and Geeta at the back. As they walked, Sandhi looked around, observing how every person was engulfed in fear amidst the war. Dead bodies were scattered everywhere, being devoured by eagles. The sight of blood on the streets had become common, and death was omnipresent—not just on the roads but on home balconies and tree branches as well. Witnessing this macabre dance of death, it felt as though the soul itself had died. After walking some distance, the soldier beside Sandhi instructed everyone to stop, and they all halted. Sandhi looked around and asked, "Why have we stopped here?"

"We are waiting for more students to join," he replied. Sandhi and the others remained standing. Above, rockets were visible in the sky, making Nida shiver and Geeta cry. As Sandhi moved to console them, the soldier ordered, "Don't move; stay in line." Sandhi communicated with him through gestures from behind. Geeta grabbed Nida's hand from behind, reassuring her, "Don't worry... we'll reach Pisochyn soon."

Vladimir was also looking up, mesmerized by the glow of the rockets. The cold air muted the light, which made the glowing trails appear even more mesmerizing. Overwhelmed by the sight, Vladimir murmured, "Death can be so beautiful, I never realized," then added, "Only capitalism can do this."

Surprised by his words, Sandhi responded, "Vladimir, you are so wealthy, and yet you criticize capitalism."

"War changes your perspective. At home, you can afford to embrace capitalist ideologies from the comfort of a soft bed, but when you're trapped in a war, you begin to understand what's wrong and what's right." Vladimir was visibly upset, frustrated by his circumstances and his class, and in a moment of anger, he burst out, "Sitting high up and partaking in the plunder of public wealth is one system where everything seems easily accessible, but when you are caught in the throes of its fluctuations and find yourself on a battlefield, the shame and ignorance you wore fall away, and the truth emerges effortlessly. People's greed, ignorance, and acceptance of truth fluctuate and change with circumstances. This is the typical story of a capitalist mindset steeped in extreme individualism."

Suddenly, a truck arrives noisily, and a man opens its gate as it stops. As soon as the gate opens, many students begin to emerge.

The students kept coming out and lined up behind each other. Then, a soldier ahead signaled everyone to start moving, and they all began to march. Sandhi, observing the people on either side and behind her in the line, thought about the hopes people in her country had for their children, and in this country where she stood, there was only one hope: a peaceful life. What a fundamental difference between countries and their changing circumstances. She thought this disparity bred uneven development. As she walked, contemplating and listening to the footsteps of others, she noticed children's bodies along the path and murmured to herself how these children had neither grown old nor reached youth; their lives had remained incomplete. She wondered if it was even appropriate to call their existence a 'life.'

In this morning hour, the setting of their sun was not just their defeat but a defeat for all humanity. The world would remember those who waged wars and those who remained silent.

Sandhi's mind was tangled. She wondered if she could ever count how many had died. Could there even be a count for those annihilated by massive bombs capable of vaporizing a person? Would some corpses even be excluded from the death toll? Such was the extent of this brutality. Sandhi saw not just civilians but also soldiers dead along the way; nothing here was permanent... everything seemed eager to die. Nothing was comforting to think about. Everywhere there was harsh death, standing and laughing... staring at life. You couldn't turn away from it; if you tried, it would tap on your shoulder and force you to look its way. It was a gathering of the deaf... they couldn't hear the wails of children nor the cries of mothers; they only wanted to hear of their victory, and we were to listen to the sounds of their missiles, which would strike us incessantly without actually hitting. We all would keep waiting for death.

"Her eyes cannot see tears, neither those of the people of Ukraine nor her own. She was only born to rule. She does not know what it feels like to die without identity, lying by the roadside, unrecognizable after seeing dead bodies because they only have faces—a layer of faces. A layer of breaking, a layer of trauma, a layer of distrust, a layer of blood. Sandhi thinks there is no light in this eternal valley of death, only the sound of guns. On one hand, a person carries an AK-47, while on the other hand, another lies dead from a bullet of the same AK-47. This is our world human community, which we want to bind in brotherhood.

Suddenly, Sandhi stops talking to herself and tries to talk to the soldier walking beside her. She asks, 'What is your name?'

The soldier stares at her.

Sandhi asks again, 'What's your name?'

The soldier says, 'My name is Paolo.'

Sandhi says, 'My name is Sandhi.'

Paolo nods.

Sandhi asks, 'Is your home in Ukraine?'

'Yes, my home is in Ukraine, but there's nothing left. It was on the eastern end, all gone.'

'I'm sorry to hear that.'

'I've stopped feeling sorry. I don't feel sad anymore, not at all. Perhaps the person inside me has died; now only the soldier remains.'

'You guys are fighting well; victory will be yours.'

'Victory, my victory? I've lost my home and haven't seen my wife and children for days; I'm losing every day. I see dead bodies from morning till evening, and in the evening, I bury them. Even so, my victory won't happen... I'd be happy that my nation wins, but I will still be a loser.'

'Because of you people, people like us can go home.'

The soldier says nothing, but Sandhi keeps looking at him. Seeing this, he says, "People like you don't consider Ukraine your home. As soon as trouble came, you returned to your homes and had trouble in your studies, so you came here. We protect you and transport you from here to there. What will people like you do, tell me? Just change places and eat the bread of comfort, earn money. Visit our country, study, and talk about our problems. You won't do anything substantial."

Sandhi hears this and says nothing; she lowers her head and begins to walk. Around her, she starts to see the huts of refugees. Various colored tarps and people laying underneath them whose eyes search for a home. Their children continue to play there… neither health nor education, just on the brink of life and death. They wait from morning to evening for the situation to calm so they can be resettled. Children play with aluminum pots as if they were toys, and governments take sympathy that they have kept them within their borders. The disabled old, who was crippled in the war by a bomb, no longer call anyone son; they see everyone's relation with bombs. Either you will be dead in this war, or you will be displaced, or your home has been or will be destroyed; in all three cases, you will be very close to distrust. Wives aren't busy caring for children; they count the days until the situation changes. Everything seems irregular. Ropes tied around, which keep the refugees' homes grounded, are the only permanence in their lives. Countless beds are laid out, and on those beds lay myriad people, just waiting for the war to end, staring at the sky, thinking change will come. Some might not even return home; their homes have been sacrificed at the start of the war. Diseases enter their tarp homes and don't leave. They also need weak people. Many children, not their mothers, have dirty faces, but they wipe with their torn sleeves. Their tables aren't set, their food is dropped from airplanes, and they run to grab food. Or a vehicle comes and distributes food to them. Everything is war for them… everything is war. Sandhi, tired of thinking, tries to observe nature, but even nature is absorbed in thought and facing death. Sandhi's thought is interrupted by a nearby soldier who says, 'Look, Pisochyn has come.'

As Vladimir hears that Pisochyn has arrived, he becomes happy, starts shouting in joy, and begins to run. Everyone walking around becomes happy, but Vladimir runs freely. Soldiers try to stop Vladimir, but he runs free. Vladimir approaches the students and asks everyone to clap to greet the Ukrainian soldiers. Suddenly, a rocket appears in the sky. The Ukrainian soldiers shout, 'Get down, get down!' Sandhi also screams, 'Vladimir!' but to no avail. There's an explosion, and an American traveler and three Ukrainian soldiers die. Blood splatters in the smoke, and it is impossible to distinguish whose is whose. Vladimir disappears in the fierce heat of the war along with his thousands of thoughts about the world. In the end, only his smiling face remains in Sandhi's eyes.

Sandhi runs to the spot but finds nothing except the empty air where Vladimir is standing; perhaps the tears were the air's regret, unable to save Vladimir. Sandhi feels like the Earth has sped up its rotation; everything around her seems to be spinning... Vladimir's bag, hands, legs, and laughter just with his lips. His face, Sandhi cannot think of. Perhaps there was also smoke from the rocket on her mental slate. The soldiers were in a flurry to save the other students. But Sandhi stood still, like a mountain, unable to move or cry... just standing. Perhaps she wanted to end herself with another rocket, but death isn't so easy for everyone.

Sandhi sees Vladimir's severed hand in the distance, still twitching, still alive... She goes and picks it up and holds his hand in hers. Inside, she howls for the hand to become whole again and for Vladimir to embrace her, but none of it could happen. She holds Vladimir's hand with her fingers, but the twitching does not stop. With every twitch of the hand, Sandhi becomes more disturbed. She feels Vladimir's agony, his desire to go home, to meet his loved ones. Finally defeated, she places Vladimir's severed hand on her face. Vladimir's fingers feel her eyes, possibly sensing Sandhi's dreams and tears, and the twitching stops. Perhaps his fingers find another dream in Sandhi's eyes, allowing his spirit to rest, to live another dream.

10

"I have lived in Gandhi's country and read Dante; how can I take up arms? And yes, Dante said that the darkest places in hell are reserved for those who maintain their neutrality in times of moral crisis."

Pisochyn

Time: 2 PM

The air was filled with the scent of burning flesh. The soldiers had surrounded all the students and removed them from the scene. A soldier was holding Sandhi from behind, trying to move her from where Vladimir stood. Sandhi was resisting with all her might to stay put. She thought that perhaps Vladimir had just gotten lost; she was looking for him everywhere. The soldier had lifted her into the air from behind, yet she refused to relent, continuing her struggle to stay put. Tamanna, Geeta, and Nida shouted, "Sandhi, move away from there; please listen."

The soldier's grip loosened slightly, and Sandhi moved forward. She was bent over more, and the soldier still held her from behind. Sandhi was digging her hands into the ground; she grasped some soil and began to cry, bringing it to her nose.

Gradually, after smelling the soil, she began to relax. Her arms and legs stopped moving. She had surrendered herself to the soldier's hold. For the first time in this ordeal, Sandhi heard someone's voice. The soldier said to her, "Why are you putting your life in danger? There could be another attack."

Sandhi turned her neck to see the soldier's face and said, "The one who just died was my friend, and before that, he was a person. Who swallowed him up—the air, the ground, or the smoke? Where did he go?"

The soldier said, "Forget what happened... Protect your life; there could be more rocket attacks."

"You might be accustomed to death, but I am not, nor do I ever want to be. I will react this way every time to death, feel this much grief every time, and something inside me dies every time someone I know leaves."

"I was just doing my job," the soldier replied.

"My conscience was also doing its job. I can't bear death in my soul."

The soldier moved Sandhi to the side without saying anything. All the students were watching Sandhi, but she was only looking at the spot where Vladimir had stood. Suddenly, with all her strength and emotion, Sandhi called, 'Vladimir'... The soldier quickly covered her mouth, but she tried to shout again. The soldier told her, "No, don't do that... It could endanger everyone's lives."

Sandhi's scream was stifled within her, turning into a suffocated cry, followed by sobs. She said nothing; she just continued crying. The moments of intimacy she had shared with Vladimir were now flowing out as tears of separation.

Tamanna came over and hugged her... then she, too, started crying. Some children were shivering, some had tears in their eyes, and some sat gravely watching Sandhi. Tamanna said, "We will go home now, don't worry." Tamanna was still holding Sandhi and talking to her, but Sandhi just kept staring at where Vladimir had stood. Sandhi's neck was straight. Tamanna, Nida, and Geeta hugged her from all sides, but Sandhi only looked at that spot. She wasn't saying anything, just crying... She couldn't hear anything; she was completely mute. All she had in her mind was the sound of that bomb, nothing else.

The sound of the bomb—Vladimir's laughter—the sound of the bomb—was all. After Sandhi's long silence, Tamanna shook her face and said, "Say something, Sandhi. Are you all right?"

After being asked multiple times, Sandhi said, "Vladimir evaporated into steam; the war took him."

Geeta said, "We will go to our homes... don't worry."

"I can't go home!" And she was still looking at that spot.

Tamanna, Nida, and Geeta looked at her and said, "Why can't you go home? Your home is in India."

"My home is also here; I have lived here, too. You guys have lived here, too. We are all here now. What is home?"

The three girls looked at each other and tried to explain to her, "Home is where dad is, where mom is, where brothers and sisters are, that's what home is."

"Home is not a place; it's a feeling where dreams are nurtured, memories exist. Home is the space surrounded by human emotions where others' pains and sorrows shake us, compelling us to alleviate their suffering and do whatever we can for them. I want to do that for my friends here, home, society, and the world. I will go to Kashi, but right now, my home is burning; there is a war going on here, and I must try to stop it. Even if I can't, I still have to try. I can't bear to see another Vladimir die."

Tamanna still didn't quite understand what Sandhi was saying. She asked again, "So, Sandhi, you are not going home?"

"No. First, I need to think about the home I'm in; Kashi is still safe."

Nida said, "You were so happy, you wanted to go home... what happened suddenly?"

"Don't you know what happened? The person who dreamed of going home couldn't make it; I know I shouldn't think about his dreams like everyone else and should cherish only my dreams, but I can't do that. Someone has to feel the pain of unfulfilled dreams, understand the agony of lives becoming desolate, and be prepared to end this war so that the remaining dreams don't shatter."

Geeta interjected, "Stop talking nonsense; how can you end a war?"

"That's what I thought when I didn't want to leave home. I thought then, how could I live alone outside? Then, I met Petrovich. When his love changed, I kept thinking it was okay and that it would get better soon. It's the effect of the war. But he remained the same, yet I couldn't leave him, allowing my emotions to be crushed. One day, I moved on from him, too. Every time I do something different, I feel how I will manage, but it happens."

For the first time, Sandhi took her eyes off the spot where Vladimir had stood and said, "I know it's hard to think what will happen to our dreams; I also want to become a doctor. I left Kashi because I thought my father's philosophy of serving others was a greater purpose, so I gave up my dream of running

100 meters. But today, I feel the war is killing countless people, and who knows how many more will die? Nobody knows. The war should end and never happen again, anywhere; now, this goal seems bigger to me than my old purpose. I've given up my dream of becoming a doctor, now do what is easy for you. Fulfill your dreams. My dream is now just this. Only this."

"Your father must be waiting for you. Mom must be hoping her daughter is coming. This isn't right," Nida says a bit angrily.

"Everyone is waiting for someone; some will reach, and some won't. Someone must stay here and consider it their home; plant new sunflower seeds here."

The three girls were stunned and said nothing... They got up and walked away.

Nida asked a soldier, "How long before we leave?"

The soldier said, "We won't leave just yet; it will take some time."

Geeta asked, "Where are we going from here?"

"We are going to Moldova."

"Moldova! That's very far," Geeta said.

"Yes, I know. You will go by bus and then by plane to India from there."

Nida sat down quietly.

Sandhi's gaze remained fixed where Vladimir had stood. This time, she also saw the setting sun behind him, and in her mind, she pictured Vladimir standing in the center of the sun, wearing a black jacket, arms spread wide. Sandhi closed her eyes, unsure if she wanted to embed this image in her mind or escape from it.

Exhausted, Sandhi stood up and asked a soldier, "What if someone doesn't want to go home on this bus?"

The soldier kept looking at her, then went to another soldier and mentioned that the girl was saying something like that. The other soldier came and said to Sandhi with surprise, "You don't want to go home. That can't be."

"Paolo, I don't want to go home. My mother used to say that I handle things very neatly; this is my home, and I will leave it well-organized."

"You are doing all this because I said those things to you."

"No..." As she was speaking, she found a hair on her jacket. She showed the hair to the soldier and said, "Do you know whose hair this is?" Paolo looked at her but did not understand. She said, "It's Hero's. Hero is a dog trapped in an underground room with Natasha, and who knows how many more 'Heroes' and people are trapped in underground rooms? When everyone returns to their homes, the markets will be bustling, everyone will drink cake and wine together at Christmas, and life's celebration will begin, and then I will return to India. And yes, in our culture, once we eat someone's salt, we never betray them. I can't just leave Ukraine like this."

Paolo listened to her and said, "I understand... so you will join the civilian army and fight."

"No, I have lived in Gandhi's country and read Dante, how can I take up arms? And yes, Dante said that the darkest places in hell are reserved for those who maintain neutrality in times of moral crisis. I cannot remain neutral; I will try to stop this war but through nonviolent means so that you can go home and meet your children."

Paolo smiled and said, "We don't have such orders. If you don't want to go, I cannot send you. I only ask that if you are going, you should leave now while it is still light, as it will be dark soon."

Paolo took a toffee from his pocket, gave it to Sandhi, and said, "Keep this. I am from the 22nd Motorized Infantry."

"Thank you for the toffee!" She waved goodbye to Tamanna, Nida, and Geeta from afar.

She then turned and started walking down the road towards Kharkiv. All the students and the three girls were amazed. Most people sitting there would think her foolish or naive, but what she understood, no one else could grasp, that was certain. Her steps were heading towards Kharkiv, and occasionally, her fists would brush against the wheat stalks on the roadside.

Sandhi kept walking. She was slightly dejected, but that despondency was tinged with purpose. She kept thinking about what she would say to her mother, what she would tell her father, and how she would explain to them that she wanted to stay here and try to stop the war. How she would stop the war, how she would convince others, and how she would ensure her safety because those who wanted the war might also want to kill her. She was carrying the burden of numerous questions. There was no fatigue in her legs, but her mind was exhausted, perhaps also despairing over losing Vladimir.

Thinking of Vladimir, she became very stressed. She watched the waving wheat stalks and kept walking. Sandhi held the toffee given by Paolo tightly in her hand. The increasing pressure on the toffee amidst the turmoil in her mind was altering its shape. The shape of life's toffee also changes amidst the blows of time. The sunset was hastening, and the night was about to fall.

Her shoes had become heavy with layers of snow and mud. Her pants were also covered in mud, and the soil she had picked up from the place of Vladimir's death was slowly trickling into the wheat fields. She knew this, perhaps, but it was her way of allowing Vladimir to flow into the living wheat fields. Sandhi's stride had a resolve that was becoming firmer and cooked during this 12-kilometer walk. Perhaps blisters had formed and burst on her feet, but there was no wrinkle on her face. Planes flew above the sky, but she never looked up; she just kept looking straight ahead, dropping the soil.

Sandhi's hair was completely tangled, her face was cracked from the cold, her lips were dry from dehydration, and they had turned dark from lack of food. But no one could tell from her pace that she had been hungry for a long time. A strange flow inside her was faster than all other sufferings, covering everything else.

Suddenly, a Ukrainian soldier stopped Sandhi and nudged her slightly with the barrel of his gun, asking, "Where are you going?" Instead of looking at him, Sandhi started looking at the sky, where stars and a little smoke were visible. The Ukrainian soldier asked again, "Where are you going?"

Sandhi gave the address of the underground room, and the soldier said, "All right, go, but don't wander alone at this time. There could be Russian soldiers around."

Sandhi walked on without fully listening to him and stopped right in front of that house. After deep breathing, she climbed the stairs and reached the ground floor. Then, holding the toffee, she moved the carpet and lifted the hatch. As soon as she did, Natasha looked alert, thinking someone else had come. But when Natasha saw Sandhi, both she and Hero looked happy. Sandhi closed the hatch and descended the stairs. Natasha started questioning her from the stairs, "What happened, Sandhi? How are you here at this time? What happened? Didn't you guys leave? Where are the others? Where is Vladimir?"

After this question, Sandhi, whose fist still contained the soil that had trickled away but was stuck to the dampness of her palm, opened it. Natasha couldn't understand seeing the soil stuck in Sandhi's palm. Sandhi's eyes were only looking at Natasha. Even after repeated questions, Sandhi said nothing; she just sat with the soil in her fist. Natasha realized that Vladimir was no more and started crying uncontrollably. The sound of her crying echoed louder in the underground room.

Initially happy about Sandhi's arrival and licking her, Hero became distressed seeing Natasha cry. He ran away and started barking from afar. Hero's barking and Natasha's crying echoed throughout the room. Natasha touched the soil stuck to Sandhi's open palm and cried even more. Sandhi remained sitting on her knees, and the soil slowly fell from her palm. Natasha carefully collected the soil back into Sandhi's hands and told her, "Close your fist, let Vladimir rest."

Hearing this from Natasha, Sandhi quickly clenched her fist so tightly that her nails bent and dug into her palm, mixing a little blood with the soil. Natasha kept crying, but Sandhi didn't tell her to stop or hug her; she just sat in front of her, watching. After a long silence, when Natasha finally stopped, she asked Sandhi, "Why didn't you go home?"

"My home is here, Natasha. I'll fix this home with you first, then do something else."

"Fix, what do you mean?"

"How can I just leave this war that has almost taken everything from me and you, from everyone? This war took Vladimir from us; how can we leave it like this?"

"What can you do about this war?"

"The power of war is in the shedding of blood, in the death of people. I will stop the bleeding and prevent people from turning into corpses. I will stop the war."

Natasha looked into Sandhi's eyes, the same eyes she had seen when Sandhi was saving Julia. Natasha hugged her, but Sandhi just sat there. Natasha's gaze fell on Sandhi's feet, where blood was flowing... the blisters had burst, and Sandhi had kept walking, which had deepened the wounds, and blood was leaking. Natasha dropped everything and said, "Take off your shoes."

"Wait." Then Sandhi got up and started looking for something in the room. She found a piece of paper and preserved the soil in it. Then she looked at Natasha and said, "Now tell me what you were saying."

"Blood is coming from your feet; take off your shoes... I'll clean the wounds."

Sandhi took off her shoes. There were three to four wounds on both feet, which Natasha slowly cleaned. Sandhi told Natasha, "Don't use too much water."

"Yes, all right."

As Natasha was cleaning her feet, Sandhi felt no pain. Instead, she was intently watching Hero. Natasha tried to understand Sandhi's mind without asking anything; she didn't want to pose any questions. When Natasha had finished cleaning the wounds, she gently told Sandhi, "The wounds are clean now."

Sandhi got up, lay beside Hero, and stared at the ceiling. She then lay down on the bed, turning off the light. They both remained silent yet were awake, not wanting to let the room's darkness overshadow their thoughts of the future. For hours, they didn't speak to each other. Then Natasha softly called out to Sandhi to see if she was awake—she would speak if she were, and it wouldn't matter if she weren't. Softly, Natasha said, "Sandhi." Sandhi turned and replied, "Yes, Natasha?"

"What next?"

Sandhi responded, "I don't know anything for certain, but one thing I do know: this war needs to end by any means necessary.

I need to awaken the people, the whole world. War cannot benefit anyone."

Natasha replied, "It's not an easy task. We'll have to fight those who are much more powerful than us. Those who appear as friends of the people in public and maintain power with the populace's support, but, in reality, many of these people work behind the scenes to benefit capitalists, manufacturers, and business people. War is a game for the makers of arms and ammunition, a game of mineral wealth, oil, gas, and diesel. It's about manipulating and maintaining the power of capital, played with the support of capitalist politicians. This is a disgusting aspect of modern capitalism and totalitarianism, where ordinary citizens, engulfed in emotions, are the victims."

Sandhi said, "Let them do what they do. I only need to clarify that war is wrong, and no political argument they make can ever justify the good in war. I need to get this simple message across to people."

Natasha said, "You're right, but as long as the world doesn't understand that war is wrong, wars will continue. Let's start here, in Ukraine. We'll convince the Ukrainian people that war is wrong and it needs to end. We'll convince the Russian people, too."

Sandhi declared, "The real saviors of a nation are not its prime ministers and presidents sitting in the highest offices, but its people. The people will decide what war is; those in refugee camps will decide; those fighting as soldiers will decide, and those whose husbands and mothers have lost their beloved to the nation will decide. How can those sitting in luxurious buildings, causing the common folk to die, decide whether there will be war or not?"

Natasha expressed her hope, "I want to see Ukraine drenched in love again. I want to run fast across grassy fields, shouting with joy."

Sandhi reflected, "Vladimir wanted the same. He has already sounded the trumpet against the narrow-mindedness and servitude of war. We must fight this battle nonviolently, bearing witness to Vladimir's laughter."

11

"Heroic tales are pleasing to hear, but I believe that before or after every heroic saga, we should also acknowledge how many perished for these few to become immortal, whom we call victors."

Kharkiv,

6 AM, March 1, 2022

Sandhi is abruptly woken by the blaring siren signaling an air raid. The siren's grating sound also woke Natasha, though she was already alert.

Sandhi tells Natasha, "War always catches you off guard and confuses you."

Natasha replies, "You're talking about the siren, right?"

"Yes, but every time this siren sounds, I remember my father, who mostly used to wake me up by calling out."

"My mother used to wake me the same way," says Natasha. "Then she would tell me to move around a bit and exercise, and I would always respond, 'It's not like I'm going to wrestle anyone.' Then she'd say, 'One must always be prepared for trouble.'"

Sandhi laments, "We've created these boundaries for no reason. Everything is the same in Ukraine and India. What's the difference between countries and their people? Emotions are the same everywhere... unless, of course, you decide to differentiate between emotions."

Natasha agrees, "Like the feelings of love and the feelings of war, everything else is nearly the same. No nation's people like war."

Sandhi observes, "Heroic tales sound good, but I think it should also be mandatory to mention how many have died for these few who become immortal, whom we call victors."

Standing up and tying her hair back, Natasha says, "Politics hides so much from society, never letting us realize how being a hero is different from being a victor in war. The victory in war is tainted by oppression and dominance, and this sentiment is plagued by the arrogance of making others feel defeated. We worship the historical characters that have turned these stories into horrors."

"Indeed, there will always be wars because we have revered war more than love. We only see things in terms of fighting and winning; conflict is in our nature, life, and reality, so we keep fighting."

Suddenly, the sound of a bomb dropping shakes everything; Natasha falls back onto the bed. "It seems the bomb fell very close. What a terrifying shock; my heart is still pounding in fear. They... they want to win everything."

Sandhi, sitting with her head down between her knees like an ostrich, then says, "The word 'victory' reeks of domination."

"These people are only thinking about dominating Ukraine. Some even say about God and humanity, 'I will attain Him, I will conquer.' It seems to me that no one can truly possess another, and if they do, then there's no room for love," Natasha angrily adds.

With a choked voice, Sandhi reflects, "Look at me; even Petrovich wanted to 'have' me and thought he owned me."

"It's good that you got away from him."

Sandhi smiles and replies, "Whether I have moved on or not, only my soul knows, or perhaps my mind. Nothing that starts, whether love or any series of events, ever truly ends because it continues to influence our thoughts and actions."

Agreeing with her, Natasha adds, "Marriage is such a strange process."

Curious, Sandhi asks, "Why are you bringing up marriage all of a sudden, Natasha? What happened?"

"It's just that my mind started to wander, thinking if you and Petrovich had gotten married, you would have been brought together in one house, but even living together, you wouldn't have been together mentally," Natasha explained.

"If you had said that a few days ago, I would have fought with you, but today, I would say that marriage is like being with nature, observing it. In nature, there are rivers, mountains, trees, and leaves. There will be leafless trees, too, and storms and thunder, but these events are not to be witnessed alone. I don't just believe in seeing the green leaves; in any relationship, there will be disagreements, and leaves will also turn yellow, but to observe all these happenings, there should just be two people together. Petrovich started seeing events separately, and there's nothing wrong with that. People change, but it's better to leave if you cannot stay with someone who can't peer into your soul during a gentle sunset. Not every day will the sun be harsh, not everything will always be clear, nor will the exuberance always be at its peak."

"Yes, you are right; love is like war, but the war is not to be fought among ourselves but against external circumstances. We should not fear the yellowing leaves but wait for spring again.

Together, we must end the war outside. I'm not saying we should defeat it."

Sandhi and Natasha laugh as they hold each other's hands. Natasha, still holding Sandhi's hand, asks, "Have you thought about what to do and how we can create awareness among people to stop the war?" The sounds of fighter jets start to overpower even the siren's blare. Hero, their dog, comes close and sits by them. The noise quiets down, and a hush falls over the room; both women fall silent.

After a while, Natasha asks Sandhi, "What are you writing? You were writing something the other day and today, too."

"I want change."

"You're not wrong in what you're doing, but you're going about it the wrong way. War is wrong; this message needs to reach many, and while we can keep it alive on these pages, to make a broad impact today, we'll need to use the internet and computers."

"I understand what you're saying, but sometimes I feel a great urgency to change the circumstances."

"We all need a normal atmosphere, but we must be patient; things won't happen so quickly. We'll start and see how it goes."

Calmed by Natasha's explanation, Sandhi asks, "Where can we find a computer?"

"I'll handle everything, don't worry," Natasha says with a confident smile.

"Then make the arrangements."

"Let's go upstairs."

"Upstairs!" Sandhi asks in surprise, "What's upstairs?"

"I'll show you the fighter jets," Natasha laughs.

"Tell me!"

"When you were engrossed in that picture upstairs, the one with a mother and her children, I was standing guard outside. I came in for a moment and saw that there was a computer in the other room; the door was open, so I took a look."

Sandhi hugs her joyfully, "Wow, my Sherlock Holmes!"

"We can go up, but what about the air raids?"

"Whenever the siren sounds, we either lie down or come back here; just remember that."

"Yes, I know, but still." Sandhi pauses, then says, "I was thinking of calling home to let them know I'm not coming."

"Yeah, see for yourself."

"Why shouldn't I call?"

"You can, but telling them you're not coming might be more painful for them. If you say you can't come now, they'll think you'll come eventually, maybe not today, but someday."

"Dad must have seen on TV that the Indian government has started 'Operation Ganga.' He'll definitely say that other students have arrived; why haven't you? And this task of ours, trying to stop the war, won't be over quickly, so it's better to be clear."

"Hmm, all right."

Both hold the railing and head upstairs. Reaching the upper floor, they look out the window. Outside, there is smoke, and some soldiers are patrolling. Natasha sees that the building opposite has completely collapsed, with a massive hole in the middle large enough for two tanks to pass through side by side.

Natasha asks, "Why would they blow up that building... What threat did it pose to them?"

"What was there?"

"There was a college there where students studied fashion, beauty, and physical health."

Stunned, Sandhi says, "What could they possibly have against students?"

"They have enmity with the nation; they are weakening it by destroying educational institutions, killing common people. This will happen; we will have to endure seeing our people die."

Sandhi and Natasha continue to watch as the college disappears into the ground. After a while, they stop looking and close the window. Then they go to the next room. Inside, Sandhi asks, "Now tell me, where is the computer?"

Natasha leads her to the room. The door is still slightly open. As they enter, they see the computer on the desk. The room is adorned with posters of rock stars with guitars and drums.

Sandhi remarks, "It seems the kids liked this artist."

"That's Okan Elji. I really like one of his songs."

"You're thinking of a song now?"

"Yes, I'm trying to bring life back to life," Natasha starts humming the song and Sandhi listens as she turns on the computer.

Natasha sings, looking out the window in Ukrainian, "One day, that day will come, and the war will end. I've lost myself, hold me... hold me... hold me. Never let me go so gently... hold me. Let my spring come.... hold me."

Tears begin to flow as Natasha sings. The computer is now on, and its light falls on both their faces. Natasha's streaming tears and the hidden tears in Sandhi's eyes are clearly visible.

Sandhi asks Natasha, "What now with this computer? I was thinking of taking it downstairs; what do you think?"

"Yes, that would be safer because there's too much danger up here. Seeing the building across tells us they can drop bombs anywhere; they don't care about death."

"All right." Sandhi picks up the computer, and Natasha begins disconnecting the cords. When all the cables are unplugged, Sandhi suddenly sets down the computer.

"Why did you put down the computer?"

"I need to call home."

"Go ahead, tell them that you belong to them and Ukraine now." Sandhi nods and picks up the phone. As Natasha leaves the room, Sandhi dials the phone, hesitates, and puts it down. She picks up the phone again, this time dialing more slowly. After one ring, she hangs up again. Seeing the building outside merged with the ground, she picks up the phone again, pressing the numbers quickly. Natasha's song softly plays in her mind as the ring goes through.

The phone is answered, and Sandhi says, "Dad, it's Sandhi."

Her happy and anxious father responds, "Sandhi, how are you? When are you coming back?"

"Dad, I..."

"We saw on TV that the government has started Operation Ganga. When are you coming back?"

"Dad, I..."

"Yes, tell me, dear."

"Dad, I'm not coming back."

"Don't worry about your studies; come back here, and when things settle down, you can go back."

Speaking very softly, Sandhi says, "Dad, I'm not staying away because of my studies; I'm staying because of the war."

"Because of the war... I don't understand, dear!"

"Dad, I can't leave this country in such a state of war; it's become my country too. I've lived here; I have friends here."

"You can't just leave? What do you mean? You have everyone here; this is your country."

"Yes, India is my country; it is today and will be tomorrow. And if something like this happened in India, I would do what I'm about to do here."

"What are you going to do, Sandhi!"

"Dad, I'm going to try to stop the war." This time, her voice wasn't quiet.

"Stop the war... Sandhi, what's gotten into you? How can you stop a war? You're talking nonsense!" In the background, her mother's voice is heard, "Come back, don't be stubborn."

"Sandhi, are you all right?"

"Yes, Dad, I've finally come to my senses. Until yesterday, I was worried about my goals, not the world. I used to think, why should I think about the world? My goals and my family are enough to live for. But yesterday, I realized we are the most selfish. You used to tell me about Gandhi, Patel, Nelson Mandela, and Martin Luther King, how they faced problems without fear and turned them into something beneficial for the public. Dad, I see the welfare of the general public. I don't know if I can do it, but I can't bear the situation without trying because this tolerance is what every young person suffers from; I was suffering, too. This goal seemed bigger to me than becoming a doctor. It results from slowly listening, reading, thinking, and understanding. I've taken on the responsibility to end this violent atmosphere, to end this war... Now, whether the war ends or I end in trying to stop it, I don't know."

Her father starts crying, and her mother also cries. Sandhi still manages to keep her emotions in check. Her father passes the phone to her mother and, as he leaves, says, "Tell her to take care of herself."

Her mother, holding the phone and surprised, looks at her husband and says, "Sandhi, have you decided this is what you want to do?"

"Yes, Mom, it's decided."

Her mother continues crying, saying, "You're not doing anything wrong, just that we're parents. May God protect you."

Sandhi hangs up the phone. After putting the phone down, a tear escapes Sandhi's eye, and she quietly calls out to Natasha. Natasha comes in and, without asking about the phone conversation, silently picks up the computer cords while Sandhi lifts the computer. They both head downstairs. Reaching the room below, they set the laptop on the desk and connected the cables. Sandhi turns it on to check, and the computer boots up.

Natasha says, "There, it's started; now write what you need to."

"Yes, I will."

"But along with writing, we need to make contacts with ordinary people and bring this message to them that war is not right; it only brings deaths and nothing else."

"We should go to refugee camps, hospitals, and wherever people gather in large numbers so we can spread this message to as many people as possible," Sandhi asks Natasha, "Where can we find refugee camps here?"

"Maybe in the suburban areas of the city."

"Yes, we'll go there, and at night, I can write whatever I need to about peace. We have to do both tasks simultaneously for maximum impact and to reach people as quickly as possible."

"Yes, that's exactly right."

"Can we go to the refugee camp today, right now?"

"Yes, we can. The sooner we start, the better. In fact, it's best to go now since we can talk to more people."

Sandhi quickly gets ready, slipping Vladimir's pouch of soil into her pocket. Natasha also prepares and suggests, "Why not take Hero with us?"

"Absolutely."

Natasha, Sandhi, and Hero all get ready and reach the ground floor. There, Sandhi quietly opens the window and looks at the college in front, then says to Natasha, "Let's go."

"Let's go." They step outside. The environment had grown more menacing. The educational institution had turned into ruins, resembling a mound where eagles were picking at the debris, a stark reminder of the intellectual graves being dug alongside the physical ones.

"Should we go there for 2 minutes?"

"Going there will upset you even more."

"My mind is already in turmoil. How long can I hide from reality? Reality, circumstances, and pain — I don't want to hide from them. I need to face them to make a difference."

Sandhi starts walking towards the rubble, which contains a mix of soil, cement, stones, sand, books, cosmetics, iron beds, and human bones. She touched everything, seemingly lost in thought. Sandhi noticed eagles above and dogs roaming below, and suddenly, she began throwing bricks at them, trying to drive them away frantically.

Then Natasha calls out, "Sandhi, come here."

Sandhi walks over, and Natasha shows her a large piece of metal. "Do you know what this is?"

"No, what is it?"

"It's a piece of a missile."

"All this rubble before me... I don't understand what threat they saw here that they had to explode it."

"It's incredibly destructive, all of it. They are disintegrating everything; it's terrifying, excruciating."

"Let's move on with our mission, Natasha." And they headed towards the refugee camp, which was quite far from the city. They walked, witnessing how the city had been ravaged by bombs, bullets, and tanks. The city's soul — its vibrant life of children going to school, people reading newspapers in the morning, women and elders walking in parks — had been disrupted. Now, only obstacles remained. The city that was once bustling with life was now fleeing to save it. People were heading to the refugee camp, a crowd of desperate individuals who knew only to leave this place, this city, without knowing where they would go next. They did not know why these bombs were falling on them, why their people were dying, why they could no longer live in their homes or take their children to the park. Suddenly, one morning, a declaration was made, both by those attacking and those defending; both governments were just sending out their messages, oblivious to the public. The public was left to carry the burden of representing their country and its decisions. What fault did the innocent public have for the situation that had suddenly arisen? Would any wise leader explain this to them?

In the future, is any leader ready to tell them when their misery will end? After the end of human dignity, pushed into an inhuman situation, why are they being punished? Has anyone ever asked the public about any such decision while they carry their belongings and their children in their arms? All they knew was that they had to save their lives and nothing else. Sandhi thought about all this as she walked. Along the way, a child in the group starts insisting on visiting a house where his friend lives, wanting to play there. His parents explain that he can't go. "Why can't I go? What's happened? Why are we running, and when will we go back home?" The father tries to explain, but the child persists, "Okay, then take me to the park." The father looks at the park, now desolate with large holes likely from grenades or tank bombs.

"Why have there been holes in the park since yesterday, father?" The father, trying to avoid the questions, says, "Son, this is a running game we're all playing; everyone has to run." The son says, "Dad, why are you behind that lady in the blue sweater? You should pass her; don't you also want to win?" The father's eyes meet Sandhi's, conveying a story of grief, and the child asks his father more questions. Sandhi saw that everything that was there before was now diminishing. Now, there was only a rubble of happiness, fear, pain, terror, and revenge. How could the idea of peace survive in this rubble? After the terrible destruction of two world wars, will the global citizenry not express concern over the dire consequences of a progressing third world war? Is there any other option besides peace after the honest process of thought has ended? Extremism is an indicator of destruction, and this is the first thing the civic community must understand. Without devastating devastations, will the global society and leaders realize that love and peace are the only ways out of this rubble?

Everything else, under various pretexts, serves the interests of selfish individuals to keep war and gunpowder alive in society. Sandhi sees a restlessness in people's eyes; when she first arrived here, people were very assured about everything. Now, there is only restlessness and a cloud of anger. Some, who have been troubled for days, have seen their anger eroded. They had also realized that they were just puppets to political overlords. Their only role was to go from home to the refugee camp and weep over their circumstances. We all, the ordinary people, play tiny roles compared to those who are powerful and can determine events. Some of us might be supporting actors, some extras, and the rest are just nothing, mere remnants. From the fields, from the land, from property, and most importantly, from love... we have been dispossessed. We are part of a civilized society where war has become commonplace, and the society remains civilized. Wars between two countries, sometimes more, and sometimes within our own country, and the fantastic part is that despite complete silence, the society still remains civilized. After so many bombs, so many corpses, and so many tears, are we still civilized, or are people like Hitler or those who desire war not just names but a dictatorial civilization that continuously warns humanity of its dangerous intentions? In homes where fathers, sons, daughters, wives, grandfathers, and grandmothers lived, now lies the demonic offspring of capitalists' factories, pulled from beneath the earth, eager to burn and incite burning—known by various names like missiles, rockets, bombs, etc., raining down incessantly.

Sandhi is attracted to various colored wrappers and a bunch of similar-looking white arrangements. Natasha then says, "Sandhi, we've arrived."

A sign reads, "Hope Refugee Camp." Sandhi says, "This is where the remaining people of Kharkiv live. Let's go inside and talk."

Children play outside while some adults sit and talk, and some women clean dishes. Aside from the children, the entire atmosphere is completely still... silent. The noise is intense because many families live in a small area. Sandhi tells Natasha, "When we were coming, it didn't feel like we were alone; so many people were coming from where we started, and they are still arriving."

"That's why it's so noisy here: everyone is in a rush."

Sandhi observes someone gasping for breath, searching for a place to set down their belongings, while another has lost their bed. One is troubled by the long delay from one end of the camp to the other, and yet another, even amidst the crowded chaos, yearns for the comfort of home.

Natasha says, "Look at those children wandering around where they should be at school, consider the displacement of such a population during the war, and what dynamics exist for the war to end or escalate."

"I just heard a child swearing," Sandhi responds. Swear words have replaced stories because everyone is desperate, and this is no one's home. No one can tell anyone what they should or shouldn't learn. It's all left to this uncertain and conflicted crowd to decide."

Finding a quieter place where they can talk to people proves challenging for Natasha and Sandhi. Natasha comments, "Who will listen to us in this environment?"

"The most crucial step in our struggle to end the war is finding out who will listen to us."

"This is where people can hear and understand us."

Sandhi moves among the people and spots an elderly woman sitting in a wheelchair. She approaches her, sits down at her feet, and Natasha joins her. Sandhi greets the woman, "Hello, grandma, my name is Sandhi."

The grandma doesn't say anything and nods her head. Sandhi continues, "I'm from India; I was studying for my medical degree here when the war started. I am against this war and believe that we all should unite to oppose it so that it may end as soon as possible."

The grandmother listens silently as Sandhi has to almost speak into her ear due to the background noise. After finishing, the grandma asks, "You're from India?"

"Yes."

"Why are you here?"

"I didn't go back home because I consider Ukraine my home, too, and I won't leave until the war here ends." The grandmother looked her up and down and said, "You are very brave and passionate, but do you think you can do this, bring peace?"

"I've been living in Ukraine for almost five years... I've learned a lot here. There's a saying here I like: 'A hungry wolf is stronger than a satisfied dog.'"

The grandmother laughs heartily, pats Sandhi on the head, and says, "You are a hungry wolf, not satisfied. Good."

"Yes, I live for change; I'm hungry for it. My eyes dream of an enlightened, thoughtful civil society."

"My name is Sherin. Let me know if there's anything I can do. Everyone here listens to me." She laughs again. "Now, all I have is my old age, but I still want change. Who knows who has cursed our Ukraine?"

Natasha stands and hugs the grandmother, who remains in the embrace for a while before Natasha steps back. The grandmother removes her glasses and wipes them, and her eyes are moist. She resumes speaking, "People are leaving this city; the government is telling women and children to leave; only those fit to fight should stay. They've turned this city into a battlefield. I raised my neighbors' children. We all had dinner together last night; they went out, and I stayed home. When I woke up, their bodies were outside in the car. I closed their eyes with my hands while crying. People told me that Russian soldiers shot them because they were too scared to open the car door."

The grandmother becomes serious and continues, "I don't want revenge, but I don't want war either. I want peace and tranquility, to be able to go to church and to go for walks. I want to meet my walking friends; that's all I want."

Natasha says, "We also want the war to end and peace to be established." The grandmother nods.

"What can I do? Tell me," the grandmother asks Sandhi, "I don't think anyone will listen to or understand you, but I will try."

"I need to talk to as many people as possible so that I can share our message."

The grandmother half-heartedly stops a running child, then gestures for him to come. The child approaches and asks what Sherin needs. The grandmother tells Natasha, "See, he calls me by name... very naughty," and instructs the boy, "Go fetch my son."

"Okay, I'll bring Alex." The grandmother says, "This child's name is Martin. He's a real rascal, lived three houses down from mine."

As Natasha talks with the grandmother, Sandhi waits to speak with Alex. About 20 minutes later, Alex arrives in a red tank top and immediately asks his mother, "What happened, Mom?"

Sherin introduces him, "This is Sandhi. What was your name again, dear?" Natasha introduces herself, "My name is Natasha." "Yes, Natasha," the grandmother nods and points to Sandhi, telling Alex, "This girl is very nice. She is from India. She stayed here just to help people and to end the war in any way possible. You need to help her."

Busy and dismissive, Alex laughs sarcastically, "I have a lot to do, wiring outside and gathering the boys to assign tasks. We all need to keep watch in shifts tonight. I really don't have time (laughs sarcastically) to end this war."

Sandhi, ignoring his mockery, calmly says, "Natasha and I will help with the wiring. Can you help us afterward if you think it is right?"

Caught off guard by her humble approach, Alex replies, "Alright." The grandmother adds, "Sometimes it's good to help others, Alex."

"What else am I doing?" Alex responds gruffly.

"Go on, you all do the wiring... I'll just sit and take a nap here."

Sandhi, Natasha, and Alex head outside, and Hero, Natasha's dog, approaches them. "Sorry, Hero, to keep you waiting."

"Is this dog yours?" Alex asks.

"Yes, his name is Hero," Sandhi answers as Alex bends to greet him.

"Tell us where you need the wiring done."

"We have to wire this whole compound. We've already put up the rebars; just need to install the barbed wires now."

Alex calls, "Gohen, Gohen," and explains, "This is Gohen, my close friend. This is Sandhi from India... she's staying here to help us, and this is Natasha."

"I'm from Kharkiv, my village is on the eastern border."

"That means it's probably gone," Gohen remarks.

"Yes, I haven't been back, but the news is that almost everything is destroyed."

"Alex explains, "They'll help us with the wiring, then we need to help them."

"What kind of help do they need?" Gohen asks.

"They'll explain later," Alex says.

"Alright! I'll call the others. We can only install the wires with everyone's help; it's a large area."

"Hurry up and get everyone," Alex urges.

Gohen leaves, and Alex asks, "What help do you need after that?"

Sandhi explains, "I was studying for my medical degree in Kyiv, came to Kharkiv, and got trapped when the war started. I didn't go home because Ukraine feels like my home, too. All I've seen of the war is destruction, and all the pain and suffering are because of this war. If we manage to stop the war, we can restart our lives as before."

"Putin said the war would end in three days; it's been so long, and the war hasn't ended, and I don't think it will," Alex states.

"We want to try, and in trying, we have nothing to lose... just to spread the word to as many people as possible that this war will ruin us; the devastation from this war will make us weep for years; it must be stopped at all costs." Natasha asserts.

"We need to spread this idea in Ukraine first, then to the neighboring areas. Gradually a dialogue will form, then pressure will start to build."

A woman, having overheard Sandhi's entire conversation, suddenly speaks up: "She's right; this approach is good. The war will end, and then everything will get better; otherwise, everything will be destroyed."

Sandhi greets her with a "Hello," and the woman walks over to her. "My name is Amber; I also live here. This war consumed my husband and my son; I'm just wandering with my corpse."

Sandhi and Natasha introduce themselves, and Sandhi gently pats Amber's hands, which are held in hers. Alex remarks, "What you're thinking isn't easy and will take time."

"If you have any other suggestions for ending the war quickly... tell us."

Alex looks distracted, but then Gohen arrives with about 10-12 boys. Sandhi grabs one end of a wire lying on the ground, and Natasha follows suit behind her, gripping the wire, too. The rest of the boys also line up behind them.

Alex warns Sandhi, "Don't let the wire cut your hands."

Amber also takes hold of the wire.

Now, Gohen asks Sandhi, "So what help do you need?"

As Sandhi pulls on the wire, she explains the whole situation to Gohen, who responds, "I get your point, but how is this going to happen?"

"Why are you laying this wire?" Sandhi asks while tugging on it.

"For security," replies Gohen.

"The greatest security is peace," Sandhi asserts. "In a peaceful environment, nothing poses a threat. Everything is organized."

Gohen nods, "Understood... bring peace and drive out war."

With a wry smile, Sandhi responds, "Yes, exactly."

Together, they finish laying the wire. Sandhi concludes, "We need to talk to as many people as possible."

Alex looks at Gohen, who says, "If this girl didn't go back to her own home and considers our home hers, helping us, then we must do something for her."

Alex agrees, "Let's try to bring people together and spread her message."

Amber speaks softly, "I'll tell the women and girls about you... let's see what happens."

"I'm going to the hospital tomorrow to discuss all this and then to other camps. I'll be back in 5-6 days. Until then, you all should also talk to more people."

"Yes, of course," Amber replies.

Sandhi and Natasha say their goodbyes, and everyone promises to do their best to turn more people against the war. Sandhi walks out of the camp, and after walking some distance, she looks back to see the wire she had tied shimmering in the light, with the people standing behind it, watching.

12

"Let every soldier hold a bouquet, and with each bouquet given to another, honor the compassionate human within."

Kharkiv

March 2, 2022

Time: 10 AM

Sandhi is typing something on the computer. Natasha gets up and asks Sandhi, "Did you sleep last night, or were you writing all night?"

"I did sleep a little, then started writing early in the morning."

"What are you writing about today?"

"I'm writing about the dire conditions of people in the refugee camp."

"Home doesn't seem essential until you don't have one, then life becomes unbearable."

"The most vital need of a human is their emotional nourishment."

"Emotional nourishment?"

"It's crucial what a person emotionally consumes. The relationship between nature and masculinity is significant. They have always interacted with each other since the beginning of time. Nature is everything around us, and masculinity represents the physical effect of consciousness. Both are responsible for the virtues and vices within a human. Hence, we become what we are surrounded by. Look around, Natasha. There is nothing that can make us happy just by thinking about it. Imagine those who have been enduring this since 2014, since the annexation of Crimea. They have heard the sounds of guns and tanks for eight years. What must their lives be like, enduring the vices of fear and distrust? They trust no component of society anymore. What they see is the only truth they believe; perhaps they don't fully trust it. Internally, they are shattered, not declared dead, but their souls have died. Women who gave birth during this war must be cursing why such times fell upon them. The natural process from birth to death is disrupted. Some people are controlling all this on their terms."

Stunned by Sandhi's words, Natasha says, "I don't know what to say. There's so much division that the person is already broken, and then there's societal division... like we are Ukrainians, they are Russians, some are Polish, some are Indian. Where does a person go with their wounded soul and body? Wherever they go, different people are divided in some way, which separates them from others. That's why you have to become a refugee, because where you go, you aren't what you are. These distinctions, divisions, regions, and territories all create separation within a human. How can someone approach another with their pain when everyone is focused on fulfilling their desires?"

"Perhaps all this exists because some people don't want humans to share their pain. They want to turn humans into tormentors, not joyful beings."

"Think about the time before the war... we all were on our TVs, mobiles, Facebook, Instagram, Snapchat, and Twitter. We checked our smartwatches to see how many steps we walked, but no matter how smart the watch is, it doesn't tell you where you're going, just how many steps you've walked. Measuring steps, walking for ourselves, and playing with these machines, we have become directionless. We are now on the threshold of this loneliness, which is physical and mental. Who holds our pulse when we've strapped an expensive watch over it? Our desires are limited to cars, mansions, clothes, fragrant soaps, creams, and a luxurious life. A long time ago, we might have wished that someone would stay with us throughout our lives. Even in that wish, we imagined a luxurious home together. To live together, you need two living beings who hold each other's pulse. Besides being male and female, there should be no other distinction, and they should not be divided. This division is fatal."

Both remain silent for a while. Sandhi starts typing on the computer again, and Natasha gets ready. As Natasha gets ready, she asks, "Are we going to the hospital today?"

"Yes... absolutely."

"You explained things very well to people yesterday." Natasha continues, "Have you ever addressed so many people at once?"

"No... never."

"Then perhaps you participated in a debate competition?"

"No... I haven't done that either."

"How do you do all this?"

"I could never do it before. Even in college, I would sweat profusely when I had to speak in front of everyone. Before your question, I hadn't thought about how to do this now." Then Sandhi becomes quiet, lost in thought. Natasha doesn't say anything to her, and she falls silent.

Then suddenly, Sandhi says, "I think I never believed in what I used to say before, which is why I was scared to speak. But now, whatever I say, I believe in it; I live it. That's the only difference."

"Yes, maybe that's what happened. Let's go."

Sandhi stands up and puts on her jacket and shoes. They both exit the house via the staircase. As they leave, they see the ruins of the building again, with more vultures sitting on it. Sandhi chases the vultures away again.

Natasha, watching this, asks Sandhi, "Why do you chase those vultures?"

"If these vultures are pecking and eating someone, it's wrong. There should at least be some human dignity even in this war."

Natasha looks at Sandhi and then goes back to the road. After a while, she says, "Sandhi, you are outstanding."

"What happened all of a sudden?"

"The amount of love you have for others in your heart."

"I love myself a lot, so I love others too." They both smile and continue walking to the hospital.

Sandhi thought while walking that today would be more challenging than yesterday—blood, corpses, moans. How would she handle all this? Would she break down and start crying there, or would she be able to do something for them, make some change at this life's juncture? Sandhi thought about how many people are killing each other every day without any significant reason, without any solution to this situation. How does one human kill another? This question has always puzzled her. From Marco to this war, she's been tangled in this query. Does the one who kills have no other option, or is a human so helpless before circumstances that they must do it, they must kill another human?

Why are circumstances so harsh that they break a human, or are they made so harsh that no option remains for a human? In war, the possibilities are always limited and stand against your dignity, whereas in love, they are unlimited. Maybe in love, the options are also few; you can only love and nothing else. Then how are we free? Love also binds, or does love free us? Freedom is having the most options. I could have gone home, but I chose to stay here to try to stop the war. I could remain hidden in an underground room here and not go anywhere. I have options; I am free. But what about soldiers? Are they free? Ukrainian soldiers didn't go anywhere; they were in Ukraine. Russian soldiers came to their territory. They must protect their land. Who instilled this feeling that they must defend their land or nation? Sandhi says to herself, "Sometimes I don't understand anything. How can every situation be so complicated?"

Sandhi suddenly stops. A large white vehicle was there, along with a green one, and from both vehicles, many injured people were being taken out, and blood was dripping down. Natasha suddenly reads the board above and informs Sandhi, saying, "This is Kharkiv City Hospital." The hospital building was large, carved with bullets, and the board with the hospital's name was pretty large but broken. One end of the board was attached, and the other end was stuck in a window of the building. The window was holding the weight of the board.

The people coming out of those vehicles were screaming in pain, moaning. Seeing all this, Sandhi stood frozen... unable to move or say anything.

A soldier saw Sandhi and gestured for her to help him bring another soldier inside. Sandhi couldn't move from her spot. Then the soldier and Natasha shouted. Only then did Sandhi break out of her stupor. She ran, and the soldier said, "Hold the stretcher, and on my count of three, we'll transfer this soldier to another stretcher."

Sandhi nodded, as she couldn't understand anything. Everything happened so quickly as soon as she entered the hospital. Her life seemed paused and felt like it was running at high speed.

The soldier counted, "One, two, three." Sandhi and the soldier lifted the injured soldier and transferred him to another stretcher.

The soldier said, "Now we need to take him inside." Natasha was doing the same with another soldier. Sandhi nodded again. The soldier said, "Let's go."

Sandhi and the soldier started moving the injured soldier inside. There were stairs ahead. Sandhi put a lot of effort into climbing the stairs, and the slightly injured soldier's leg moved, making him scream even louder. Frightened, Sandhi said, "Sorry...sorry." The soldier continued to cry. Sandhi saw his wound and felt nauseous, but since she was moving the soldier inside, she clenched her mouth tightly and took a gulp of air through her nose. The soldier accompanying Sandhi realized that Sandhi was terrified and probably had vomit in her mouth. Sandhi couldn't stop thinking about the injured soldier's wound. His flesh was torn, blood was flowing from his arteries, and his bone was broken. The wounded soldier's boots were soaked with blood. The stretcher was covered in blood. The stairs Sandhi was climbing up to the hospital were splattered with blood. In some places, the blood had thickened and coagulated. Sandhi felt her shoes sticking and noticed that in some areas.

Sandhi enters with the stretcher and sees a large hall filled with many beds, only screams echoing through the space. The soldier tells Sandhi, "Let's take it inside and put it down." All the beds are occupied. Sandhi, with vomit in her mouth, nods her head. Sandhi and the soldier lay another soldier down. As soon as Sandhi places the soldier on the floor, she runs to a nearby window, opens it, and vomits out, then starts coughing. She composes herself.

For a moment, the soldier looks at Sandhi and then calls for the doctor when Sandhi returns to where they had placed the stretcher. The soldier who had helped put the injured one leaves as soon as Sandhi arrives. In that brief moment, the wounded soldier grabs Sandhi's hand and says, "Give me a painkiller injection; I am dying from the pain." A doctor rushes over with cotton and medicine. She immediately tells Sandhi, "Get the morphine injection quickly." Now, Sandhi's scientific mind kicks in. Until now, she had been seeing things only as a human and was scared. She is still frightened, but now she has been given responsibility, and this new role momentarily lessens her fear.

Sandhi asks another nurse, "Where is the morphine kept?" The other nurse points it out. Sandhi grabs the morphine injection and syringe and dashes back to the injured soldier. By the time the doctor cleaned the wound, Sandhi had filled the syringe with medicine. Seeing this, the doctor asks, "Are you a doctor?"

"Not yet... I still have one year to go, but I know quite a bit, I guess."

Hearing this, the doctor tells Sandhi, "Go ahead and administer it." And she continues cleaning the wound. Sandhi administers the injection. She reflects that in everyday life, having a degree is very important, but in this war, no one cares whether you have a degree or not. Here, it is only necessary not to be afraid and to work without panicking. The doctor then tells Sandhi, "Bring the bandage." As Sandhi goes to fetch it, she sees that two nurses have wrapped a man from head to toe in a sheet and laid him down, placing another patient in his bed and starting treatment on the new patient, ignoring the one who had died.

As Sandhi heads back, she sees the body lying in her path, and the nurse on the other side asks her, "What do you need?"

"I asked for a bandage."

"Take it from here." She also focuses on treating the patient who has replaced the deceased. Sandhi stands and stares at the corpse, wondering how to step over it. Then the nurse looks at Sandhi again and says, "Quickly take it and go."

Sandhi immediately steps over the corpse, picks up the bandage, and leaves. She thinks that life is just beyond the corpse, and she did the right thing. Sandhi returns with the bandage and hands it to the doctor. The doctor then says, "Help me with the bandaging." Just then, a woman in a Ukrainian military uniform, who seems to be pregnant, comes in on a stretcher. She has a large gun on her chest and is accompanied by another soldier. The woman tells the soldier, "You can leave now; I'll manage from here." When Sandhi finishes tying the bandage, the doctor asks her, "What is your specialty?"

"In obstetrics."

"Come with me."

Sandhi doesn't say anything but follows the doctor. The doctor takes Sandhi to the woman in the Ukrainian uniform. The doctor asks her, "Are you in pain?" The woman replies, "Yes, but I can't tell if it's from the gunshot or labor pains."

Sandhi asks, "Where were you shot?"

"In the shoulder."

Sandhi quickly unbuttons the woman's shirt and asks her to place her gun down on the stretcher. The woman complies. Sandhi almost opens her shirt and says, "Now you can breathe properly." She gently lifts her and examines her shoulder, which is bleeding, the shirt soaked with blood. Sandhi cleans the wound and asks, "Where do you feel the pain now?"

"Now, I feel it in my stomach."

"What month is it?" The woman couldn't hear because of the noise. She said, "I can't hear anything." Meanwhile, another doctor shouts, "Quickly bring the oxygen cylinder." Sandhi noticed that only his white coat collar was white; the rest was red from top to bottom.

The woman, groaning in pain, asks Sandhi, "You don't seem to be from here."

"No, I'm not. I'm from India... I came here to study medicine."

The woman asks, "What is your name?"

"Sandhi," she says as she begins to unbutton the pants of the woman lying on the stretcher.

The woman on the stretcher says, "My name is Stella. I'm a sniper shooter."

Sandhi looks carefully at her rifle. When the woman mentions she is a sniper, Sandhi pulls down her pants and asks, "How do you feel about your job?"

"It's just my job... I don't feel good or bad, but I don't think about it. My mentor told me that if you think about the person you are shooting, you'll never shoot accurately because you'll start shaking inside. So don't think, do your job."

By then, a doctor who had previously been with Sandhi returns, unaware that the doctor has left. She puts a medical gown down.

Sandhi remarks, "This war has trapped everyone."

Stella asks, "Why didn't you return to your country?"

"I didn't return because I feel this is also my country. I'll return when the war ends," Sandhi replies as she helps her into the medical gown. "I came here to talk to everyone, to tell them that war isn't right and that we can only stop it."

"I don't want war either. I joined the army after February 24th when a major told me they needed me. I was at the top of the university level in rifle competitions. So, after the war started, one day, I was told the army needed me. I asked if they needed me, and the army said yes. So, I packed my bag in 15 minutes and left my home for the border in my car."

"What did you do before?"

"I was a model. From walking the ramps to here I am now, lying on this stretcher, being treated by an Indian woman. It feels like I've seen it all now."

"Do you not want war?"

"Who wants war? I certainly don't. I was happy cooking at home and walking on ramps. You are a warrior like me. I fight with weapons, and you with ideas. Both of us will win."

"If I win, you won't need to use weapons."

"Then I hope you win." Just then, a doctor rushes in and takes Stella to another ward for surgery. Stella waves goodbye to Sandhi with a smile. Sandhi then remembers Natasha and starts looking for her. She sees a doctor in military clothes giving instructions to other doctors. Natasha is standing nearby. Sandhi approaches Natasha and asks, "Who is this?"

"This is a war surgeon; they are stationed just a short distance from the border."

"They must be under a lot of pressure."

"Yes, a lot... They have to dodge bullets and treat wounds." The war surgeon is stuffing a packet of cotton into a wound, yet the blood doesn't stop. He holds the cotton inside the wound with one hand and asks for another packet, stuffing it into the wound. The injured soldier begins to hit his hand against the stretcher in pain.

"We have to keep applying cotton until the bleeding stops. We must stop the bleeding because we don't have many units of blood left. Quickly, bring the anesthesia." A doctor runs to fetch the anesthesia among many injections. "It's a race against time," the war surgeon explains. "If time wins, you lose a soldier; if you win, your chances of winning the war increase. We need to act quickly to control the situation." The doctor works remarkably, like a machine without emotions, just doing his job. "Don't panic. We must keep our minds active but switch off our emotions like a mobile phone to treat them better. You need to become a robot." After a while, the war surgeon says, "In the last week alone, I've seen about 1000 severely injured people and treated them. Before, in peacetime, I'd see maybe 100-200 serious cases in a year."

The other doctors around him agree, "Yes, it's the same with us." One doctor adds, "Talking a bit helps distract the mind and makes you feel lighter... otherwise, working 20 hours a day would be very difficult."

"Why do you think I'm talking?" the war surgeon says. Sandhi notices a trash can nearby filled with blood-soaked bandages. After a while, she starts to smell the blood and medicines. Suddenly, three soldiers bring in another soldier and lay him down. The war surgeon approaches and asks, "What happened to him?"

The soldier responds, "He's Russian... treat him, then we'll take him prisoner."

Sandhi initially thinks she misheard, but then the surgeon says, "In my entire civilian career, I haven't seen as severe and dangerous wounds as you Russians have shown me this week."

The Ukrainian soldiers react angrily, saying, "I've asked my commander several times to kill him, but he didn't listen. He said first he's a wounded soldier, then a Russian. We need to treat him, then take him prisoner."

"Yes, that's correct... I also hate them. I used to despair seeing all this, but now my despair turns into hatred," the war surgeon tells the Russian. "Did you join the army just for the money?"

The Russian says nothing. Then the surgeon continues, "Because of you, I'm working day and night, and you're just busy committing murders."

The Russian soldier responds, "I don't want to kill anyone either, but if we refuse to serve, they throw us in jail. We are forced to serve in the army."

"Yes, of course, you would work... your government pays you so much."

"We don't get paid much. Contract soldiers get more; they are the ones who kill more people. We try more to save ourselves."

Listening to all this, Sandhi tells Natasha, "It's easy to say that the war is happening outside. Coming here, I've realized what war is. Bodies torn open by bullets, men killing men, some driven by their circumstances to take up arms and others to support their families. Some are filled with national pride, and others want to earn money, but they seem alike when they are on the battlefield. We call them all soldiers, collectively, but they are so different from each other, driven and motivated by different emotions and fighting for their various causes." The surgeon asks the Russian, "What happened to you?"

The Russian soldier explains, "A Ukrainian soldier's machine gunpowder hit my eye. After that, I fell, and the Ukrainian soldier shot my leg four times."

Looking at the wounds, the surgeon says, "Yes, I can see that."

"Just excluding nuclear weapons, all kinds of weapons are being used here. Every country is sending its weapons here. Often, it feels like this war is a testing ground for their weapons," the doctor says as he removes bullets from the Russian soldier and bandages him, then administers an injection. He calls a ward boy and instructs, "Don't put him with the Ukrainian soldiers; they might kill him... Keep him somewhere separate."

The ward boy takes the Russian soldier away. Then, the war doctor removes his surgical gloves and throws them into the trash bin next to Sandhi. Standing by the window, he lights a cigarette and begins to smoke. It's clear from his face that he hasn't slept in days. Sandhi watches him, trying to understand what he's going through. He was exhaling his despair, fear, and the turbulence in his consciousness that comes with each wound he sees.

A human can never become a machine; it will always remain human—perhaps just more mechanized. The result is that the machine breaks down, needing a burst of love that is impossible to find in this war. The doctor notices that Sandhi has been watching him continuously. He calls Sandhi and Natasha over, and they both stand by him. The doctor's patience, which he tries hard not to lose, prevents Sandhi and Natasha from asking anything.

The doctor asks, "Do you want to talk to me about something?"

Sandhi says, "Yes, we do."

"Alright, but I can't give you much time because injured soldiers are coming and going, and we are short on doctors."

"We only need a little bit of your time," Sandhi tells him everything about herself and her mission. After listening to her, the doctor says, "I don't know when the war will end. The Russian soldiers won't stop fighting. The Russians send their troops, and they fight with us. They call that army 'peacekeepers'. That army kills our people, we find their bodies decomposed, and they call it a peacekeeping force. Tell me, what unrest was there that they were quelling with their bullets? You've also been in Kyiv; did you feel any unrest there that they are silencing with their gunfire? No matter how much someone argues that we need to kill the Russians, we don't want war internally. We are fighting because if we don't, they will come into our cities and kill our families. We are fighting for what's behind us and those ahead; the war will end if they return. Spread the consciousness you are promoting to the Russians. They, especially Mr. Putin, need it the most."

Sandhi thanked the doctor and said, "You are right; I will do just that."

The doctor finishes his cigarette and returns to work, putting on his gloves again. Sandhi and Natasha leave the hospital. By the time they reach home, it's evening. When they open the tap in the bathroom to wash their hands, Sandhi sees the water turn red. Hesitant to touch it, Natasha nudges her, reminding her not to waste water and to wash her hands quickly. Sandhi squints and then opens her eyes. The water now looks just like water, and she wishes everything could be that simple.

She wishes that closing and opening her eyes could end the war, heal all the wounded, bring back all the sons who have died to their mothers' wombs, transform all the gunpowder smoke into spring flowers, wash all the blood into the Dnieper River, have the fish consume it, and have the river flow abundantly again, fragrant with the scent of spring flowers. She wishes all fathers could teach their children to ride bicycles; all husbands who left their wives for the war could love their wives again and not run towards Russians with guns. She wishes all soldiers had bouquets in their hands and each soldier would honor another with a bouquet, acknowledging their compassionate humanity. She hopes that just closing and opening her eyes could make all this happen!

13

This war will further divide human society into more and more classes, and all forms of exploitation by man against man and nation against nation will continue for a long time, which is exactly the opposite of Russia's socialist thought.

Kharkiv,

Time: 9:00 AM, March 9, 2022

Sandhi was typing on a computer, a cigarette in one hand. Suddenly, she wrote something on a page with a pen, put the pen down, and it rolled off the table. Hero barked in fright, awakening Natasha. Natasha looked at Sandhi and asked, "Did you stay up all night again?"

Sandhi smiled and responded, "Sorry... the pen fell, and Hero barked."

"Yes, Hero has been a bit scared lately because all day, it's either sirens blaring or bombs dropping."

Sandhi resumed her work, but Natasha persisted, "It seems you didn't hear me, or you don't want to answer."

Laughing, Sandhi replied, "Yes, dear, I didn't sleep."

"I knew it because you were smoking. You only smoke when you're awake."

"You keep such a close watch on me, grandma."

"If I don't watch you, you'd never rest. You keep working and working."

"Natasha, we've left everything behind. If we don't do something for society now, the war will never end, and we will all remain incomplete. If the war continues, more people will die. Just in these few days of war, so many people have been destroyed, so many have lost their loved ones, and so much of nature has been ruined. How can we ever compensate for all these losses? Every day, this war wages another war inside me, a battle between my soul and heart. They both condemn me. We must stop this war by any means."

"We're constantly talking with all the nearby refugee camps, hospitals, and people."

"Do you think the sentiment against the war has awakened among the people?"

"There's a significant impact. Those who initially wanted the war, saying they lost their people and wanted revenge, are now the ones saying we will lose more people to the war, and it shouldn't happen."

"Then there's a change. I met a person who said he wanted the war and wanted to kill Russian soldiers. I listened and then asked why. He said because they came to our land, they killed our people. They want to steal our freedom; we can't just give them everything. I told him it's wrong for them to come and kill; it's equally wrong for you to wish to kill them. If you go into Russia and kill Russians, or if you do anything that distresses the Russian people, remember, wrong will always remain wrong, no matter how many people start doing it. The history of war, its past, present, and future, only offers loss. This loss could be due to people, vast social resources, relationships, and the bloodstains on the social consciousness. This will expand society's cruelty and create a victim mentality, which is like a long-lasting fear for any society."

Excited, Natasha asked, "Did he understand then?"

"After that, he began to listen to me, and even his anger subsided a bit."

"Anger is natural, but it should be against war."

"It's the media that creates anger, keeps showing us the truths dictated by the capitalists."

"If you don't mind, explain all this to me in more detail," Natasha requested.

"Imagine, one person says it has rained outside, and everything is wet. Another says it hasn't rained, and everything is dry. How many perspectives do we have to view the outside? Tell me?"

"Two perspectives," Natasha replied.

Sandhi continued, "That's where the magic of the media starts. Some media will go with the first perspective and some with the second. Both will influence you and your decisions. You stop thinking because what is shown to you includes your interpretation, but that interpretation also belongs to a particular group. In the end, without opening the windows of our minds, we accept one of these perspectives as truth and form our opinion. Opening the window and checking the weather outside is such a simple task. Similarly, thinking is simple, but the various perspectives spread by the media in society are meant to stop us from thinking. The robbery here isn't just about money; it's about you dropping your weapons of discernment and accepting whatever the media tells you."

Natasha exclaimed in surprise, "That's very dangerous!"

Sandhi responded, "Yes, it's hazardous, but combating this requires proper education, which isn't impartial anymore."

"There are so many ways to manipulate society."

Laughing, Sandhi said, "Yes, because there are many influential people within society, and a constant battle for resources continues among them. Those who live without being distracted or fighting will live in peace and love."

"But we are fighting this war."

"We must oppose every wrong act happening, but our method of fighting should be nonviolent," Sandhi said, standing up and laughing more vigorously. "Otherwise, think about why such a simple, meaningful, and attractive idea as love is missing from society."

Here's the translated version of the dialogue, preserving the original emotions and tone:

"Yes, it's gone, and day by day, a selfish commercial war is taking its place, and you are driven by the passion to change this equation."

"Maybe the war that takes away my sleep will give us peace."

"What did you do all night?"

"I was still thinking about that war doctor who was smoking a cigarette. I remember him saying that we need to explain to the people here and the people of Russia that the war should stop, as there is no benefit to it. I spent all last night thinking about how to explain this to the people there and what we can do so that the people understand. I thought that the people of Russia wouldn't want war either; it might just be a handful of people who want it in the name of nationalism. I felt we should talk to the person who can stop the war, so I've written a letter, and I will send it to them and share it via social media."

Natasha happily says, "This is a very good way; at least it will start a thought process. But who have you written this letter to? Who is the person who can stop this war?"

"I have written this letter to the honorable Vladimir Putin."

Natasha says in surprise, "A letter directly to President Putin!"

"Yes, we need to awaken consciousness, and for that, we need to directly say something so that people understand our idea of peace and its social necessity."

"We can also make this letter public after sending it to President Putin. We can make many copies and distribute them among the people so they know that we are not just talking to him but to every person related to the war."

"Yes, that would strengthen our approach. I am ready," says Sandhi as she stands up.

"Wow, we have planned so much, but you haven't read me the letter yet. Please read it to me first; I'm also eager to hear it."

Sandhi returns to her desk and starts reading the letter, and Natasha sits up straight to listen.

Kharkiv,

March 9, 2022,

Honorable Vladimir Vladimirovich Putin,

4, Staraya Square,

Moscow, 103132

Russia

Greetings, President Putin. I am writing this letter to you as a citizen of the global village and as the President of the great nation of Russia. In this respect, our relationship can be likened to that of a father and daughter. Beyond the father-daughter relationship, I want to express something very important to you: I consider myself a friend to all religions, customs, regions, colors, and genders equally.

I do not believe that anyone should be enemies with another. This letter is written out of a concern for humanity. The most compelling reason for me to write to you is the violation of human dignity, particularly in the context of the war between Ukraine and Russia.

I trust that you also believe in the principles of humanity. The entire world adheres to these principles and critically assesses your actions. You are well known as the one person who can stop this war at any moment and prevent any further degradation of human dignity.

I am not aligned with the opposition factions that have formed against you; I still respect you. Stopping the war can prevent human values from being reduced to mere tales of cruelty, and civilization will continue to regard you as a guardian of human values.

My analysis of your actions suggests that this war may seem necessary to Russia, but Russian soldiers are also losing their lives. Deciding whether this operation is more important than your people is up to you. I cannot wish you victory because your experiment has already caused great distress to the ordinary people on both sides.

Every nation is unwittingly caught in the throes of this war. If you suspend it, you will be the first on the global stage to prioritize humanity over conflict in this era of power. You might take land and bodies through war but cannot capture souls.

Would you want to continue a futile war where power transfer is merely physical, not psychological? Even if you win, will the people regard you as their president after they have forgotten the deaths of their children, spouses, parents, and grandparents? I apologize, Mr. President, but your war is based on weaponry. If you fire a shot, so can anyone else. If you win this war, tomorrow, another might begin to separate Ukraine from you.

I am familiar with your wisdom, and I know you would not want this war to turn Russia and Ukraine into a permanent furnace of inhumanity, scorching people long after you are gone.

If there are unresolved issues, why not use nonviolence and non-cooperation, methods my country used to overcome an empire where the sun never set? My plea for peace may seem too much if you have interests that are only fulfilled after war and death, but it means everything to the millions who are in war, have loved ones in war, or are affected by it.

Finally, I am reminded of some words by W, responsible for making Russia a great power, about war. He said we should understand the class character of war. If I look at the class character of the Russia-Ukraine war, I see a clash of capitalism on both sides, where workers are armed and directed by capitalists. This war will further divide human society into classes and perpetuate all kinds of exploitation by man against man and nation against nation, which is entirely contrary to the socialist ideals of Russia. The likelihood of more brutal wars in the future remains.

Once again, as your daughter, I implore you to stop the war and triumph for humanity.

Your civic daughter,

Sandhi (Global Citizen)

After reading the letter, Sandhi becomes silent, but Natasha keeps watching her. Sandhi asks, "What's wrong? Won't you say something?" Natasha responds, "What can I say? Now, the whole world will speak, Sandhi."

"What will the whole world say?"

"The world will say that we want peace, which is our right."

"How was the letter, Natasha?"

"I don't know how you wrote such a profound letter. More than the writing, it's how simply you've stated such extraordinary things. This letter will be historic, Sandhi. It will sprout new seeds of love and peace on the hard soil of war, and its tree will provide shade to a united consciousness for peace. Reading this letter has given me even more energy for our cause."

Natasha quickly starts getting ready, and seeing her, Sandhi, despite feeling tired, begins to feel rejuvenated and starts preparing, too. Natasha asks Sandhi, "Where are we going today? We've already covered all the nearby places, holding meetings where people have started talking against the war. The discourse is being prepared for prioritizing peace."

Sandhi thinks momentarily and says, "Remember we spoke to Alex at the 'Hope Refugee Camp'? He said he would talk to the people. Let's go there today and see if we can hold a meeting."

"Alright, let's go to 'Hope' today."

Both get ready and head to the refugee camp. On the way, Sandhi says, "Did you see the debris in front of the house?"

"Yes, I see it every day. What about it?"

"The debris is diminishing day by day."

"Yes, you are right."

After a pause, Sandhi says, "It seems people are taking away things they can use, or maybe the flocks of eagles have eaten up everything human."

Natasha says nothing. She looks back at the debris again and then starts walking ahead, lost in thought. Not far from the refugee camp, Natasha tells Sandhi, "Our previous meetings went well. We must conduct this meeting very carefully, too, especially since many separatists in this camp also support the Russian army. They might oppose the war, so we must respond to them carefully."

"No matter what anyone says, the idea we stand for is a broad humanistic idea built on the truth, and such ideas never fail. Ideas might be obscured temporarily, but they will shine through someday."

They reach the camp. People recognize them as soon as they arrive and start talking to them. Alex waves at Sandhi from a distance, and she waves back to greet him. Alex comes over to Sandhi.

"How are you, Alex?"

"What could be wrong with me? I'm fine... just spreading your ideas."

"These aren't my ideas; they are perennial ideas that have always existed in society. We choose war when we're led astray."

"Yes, that's what I believe too."

"So, can we hold the meeting today?"

"People want to hear you. They want to talk to you more about your ideas."

"Does everyone agree with what I say?"

"Not everyone, but yes, many do."

Gohen arrives and shakes hands with Sandhi. Sandhi says, "Gohen, we've come to hold a meeting today. Will you help me gather people?"

Alex tells Gohen, "Tell everyone to come out for 15 minutes."

Alex instructs Sandhi, "You stand on this slightly elevated concrete platform, and the rest will stand before you."

"Alright."

Natasha also arrives after meeting with Alex and Gohen. She had been talking to the women in the camp earlier.

Sandhi asks, "Alex, approximately how many people will be at the meeting?"

"About 400."

Natasha and Sandhi look at each other. Gohen asks, "What happened?"

Natasha says, "Nothing, we just haven't held such a large meeting before. At most, we've had 200-300 people."

Alex laughs and says, "You can do it. What you'd say to 200 people, you'd say to 400, right?"

"Absolutely."

"Gohen and I will gather the people while you talk to these folks."

Amber and Sherin come outside; Sandhi goes to meet Sherin and bends down to talk to her. Sherin says, "Today, I'll get to hear your speech. I'm curious about what you will say."

Amber adds, "She explains things well; I've heard her informally one day."

Sherin responds, "If you can understand her, then she can make anyone understand."

Amber laughs and says, "What are you saying, Grandma? Don't you ever joke?"

Alex and Gohen gather everyone, and then Alex tells Sandhi, "You can start now."

Sandhi looks at............?

Natasha is standing right below the concrete platform. In the front row of listeners is Sherin in her wheelchair, and behind her, the entire refugee camp is standing, looking at Sandhi. Some are talking to each other, while others are staring at Sandhi. After standing on the platform and observing the crowd, which is mostly still talking among themselves, she takes a few seconds and then begins speaking.

"My dear Ukrainian brothers and sisters, none of you here have a home anymore, and our homes have been taken by war, taken by the violence it has bred. Peace will not be found at Kharkiv's Svobody Square; war is created by humans who look just like you and me, so we must also foster peace. You might think that those who started this war are powerful, but let me tell you, if they were mighty, they would have resolved their issues through dialogue. War is the easiest solution for the powerful to resolve their problems; the hardest is to talk and settle matters. Dialogue is the solution to everything, but those who were assertive and impatient chose not to opt for dialogue and instead chose war!

We all have grown up in different environments, received different educations, had different hopes, and felt different about various ideas. How can I assume there won't be ideological clashes? Clashes are widespread, but it's not common for clashes to result in thousands or millions dying, forcing people to live in refugee camps. That's not merely a clash. Whether the war is thoughtful or thoughtless, it's seriously impacting the populace. Couldn't these conflicts have been resolved without war? They could have, but some lacked the resolve, which is why we face this war.

There was a time when defeating your opponent meant victory, but now, even after defeating your opponent, you lose in many ways. This is what we see in this war... both Ukrainian and Russian soldiers are dying, and no one is genuinely benefiting, only losing time and power. The right place for anger and hatred is in the trash. Throw them away because we will fall far behind if we spend too much time on these emotions. The most significant division at this time is not between nations; it is between two ideologies, which is a more extensive division than between countries. If they have war, we also have peace and love.

In today's world, no wall can separate a human rights crisis in one part of the world from a national security crisis in another. So, if people in Ukraine don't have their homes, if people in Ukraine are dying, it will affect people living in Russia as well; they, too, will be affected by this tragedy.

The 21st century will be the most dangerous in humanity's history because some ideas will try to undermine society. Many nations will inflict excessive violence on other countries, spreading illogical and uncivilized hatred and suspicion motivated by an insatiable personal thirst for power and resources. In response to all these apocalyptic moments, only one idea will stand tall: the concept of love.

We can only defeat war with love and quiet war with peace. War is not a choice; it is an imposed act of violence that historically marks you as inhumane. The start of any massacre begins with the killing of one person, and they have killed so many of our people, but we must not expand this massacre; we must shrink it and end it. When they started this war and began causing problems in maintaining the dignity of life, they caused a disaster for their entire nation. What I say today in terms of peace will one day be heard by the entire world, and perhaps the whole world will agree that peace will provide solid and probable security for your future. War will destabilize, disorganize, and invalidate it.

Our soldiers are fighting for the families they left behind, and we stand before an excellent task remains. Let us dedicate ourselves to that task, to peace, to love, and from the honored dead, to draw more vital inspiration for the objectives of peace and the safety of human society for which they sacrificed their lives. They fought because they wanted our safety; we will fight because we want peace, which will provide protection. We firmly resolve that we will not let the sacrifice of thousands of souls go in vain. After them, we will never let anyone die in war; we will strive to the best of our ability. God, with this nation, will give us another independent thought that will bind us with love. Ukraine will be reborn, and all our people, myself, you, and every Ukrainian, will end the war with love. Peace will be established, change will occur, and there will be faith in love and peace."

After Sandhi's speech, there was no murmur; people just stared at her. Suddenly, a clap sounded, and the entire field erupted with applause and joy. Everyone started saying, 'My faith is with love and peace... My faith is with love and peace.' The clapping continued for a long time; people kept talking about the speech. They continued discussing and clapping. Some people began to stop the clapping, and after a while, the clapping finally ceased.

A person told Sandhi, "I just found out that the Russians have bombed a maternity hospital in Mariupol. These people are killing women and children.. How will you teach them peace?"

Hearing the question, Sandhi paused, then said, "I'm just finding out from you that Russian planes have dropped bombs on children. This proves that they lack humanity and have crossed all bounds of inhumanity, but if we stoop to their level, we will also become inhumane. If we don't forgive them, we will keep attacking each other like this. We don't want revenge from anyone; we want a change in their thinking."

With Sandhi's answer, everyone gathered around the concrete platform. People lifted Sandhi and started chanting, 'Ukraine will remain with love... Ukraine will remain with love.' When Sandhi was in the air on people's shoulders, she felt as if she could see her father and mother's faces in the sky, as if they were smiling at her.

"Will anything be alright when everything is dying? People are dying, the joys connected to them are dying, the memories associated with them are dying, and the conversations about them are dying. Only war is alive."

Kharkiv

March 9, 2022

Time: 4:00 PM

People at the refugee camp had lifted Sandhi onto their shoulders, and soon after, Natasha was lifted, too. Natasha and Sandhi looked at each other. The sun had emerged from the clouds, illuminating their faces even more. The voices around them spoke only of peace and love. It was a lively atmosphere that the camp hadn't seen for a long time, perhaps for the first time.

For the first time, the refugees were able to experience peace and love within themselves beyond their immediate troubles. As Sandhi swung in the air, she wondered whether her letter to President Putin would have any impact. She didn't know whether her meetings would influence anything, but she knew one thing: for a moment, she had made the refugees feel that if the Russians had guns, they had love. To think that love is an emotion that can act as a remedy for war, which could empower these weakened and broken people, giving them hope, was a significant achievement for Sandhi. Because all the refugees felt weak and helpless, at least she had handed them a torch of ideology that held the central theme of a future world, which could lead them to enduring peace and love over time.

Sherin told everyone, "Put them down… I want to speak with them."

Alex also appealed to the crowd to lower them down. After a while, the people took them down from their shoulders. After getting down, Sandhi kissed Sherin first, who said happily, "I told you that you are courageous, and today, you have raised the banner of love even higher with that bravery."

"It wouldn't have been possible without you. Alex, Gohen, Amber, and Natasha have helped me a lot. I am just a product of your efforts, nothing more."

While everyone was talking to Sandhi, Amber was intently listening to her. Amber interjected, "What you said today is utterly pure and true, but these things will move forward very slowly; we need something to speed up this caravan."

Sandhi laughed initially and then said, "When I was little, I, too, wanted rapid changes in everything, but that's impossible. I understand that when suffering is great, we want change more quickly. But in reality, it's not possible. Yet, there's still that little girl inside me, and I have her solution in my pocket."

Natasha looked at Sandhi, gesturing to ask what she had. Sandhi took the letter she had written to President Putin from her pocket. Everyone was surprised to see just a piece of paper and wondered how it could accelerate change. Looking at Alex and Gohen, Amber said, "How can this accelerate change?"

Sandhi assertively said, "This is your voice. If you all repeat this together, it will have an impact. Perhaps this is the voice of all Ukrainians, whom a handful of people have tried to silence."

Sherin asked, "What are you saying? Speak clearly... What is on this page? What is on this page?"

"This is a letter I have written to President Putin, pleading with him to stop the war."

Alex asked, "But why would he listen to your plea?"

"I don't know if he will listen, but I want to make sure I try. Maybe he won't agree, but this letter will be very loud to him."

Alex questioned, "It will be loud... what do you mean by that, Sandhi?"

"I will send it to him and take this letter to the public."

Alex's eyes sparkled. He said, "You mean to say you will take this letter among Ukrainians?"

"Yes... not just to the Ukrainian public but the whole world will read this letter, and afterward, at least people will talk about how the Ukrainian people have the weapon of love to establish peace."

"That makes sense," (although there was a hint of doubt on his face, showing he wasn't fully convinced about the impact of the letter). "Can I see the letter?"

Sandhi handed him the letter, and Alex read it aloud, perhaps wanting everyone nearby to know that this letter was not just a way to bring peace. Contrarily, as the letter progressed, confidence began to appear on people's faces. Sandhi was watching everyone's faces. Natasha and Sandhi looked at each other. Alex read the letter and hugged Sandhi, saying, "Nobody thinks about us; when will we get our home? Nobody thinks about that; our children are sitting outside, under the sky where planes are flying to kill them, and now you, from another country, are here among us trying to bring justice for people like me."

"It's not about the country; I admit I was born in India, but as a human, I see that you are suffering, so how can I use my citizenship to escape from here? No, that won't happen. My country teaches me to share others' pain and to strive for them. I am a daughter of Gandhi's land. I am not someone who eats her meal and sleeps in her house, but someone who will seek peace, carrying all the covenants together."

Alex asked, "Can I distribute this among the people?"

"Yes."

Alex started running. Sandhi called out, "Listen, Alex."

Alex didn't hear; he just ran off. Sherin said, "He must have asked the camp manager to make more copies."

Sandhi smiled and said, "Good! I wondered where he had gone; this is just a letter... how can he distribute it to everyone?"

Amber grabbed Sandhi's hand and said, "Now I see things picking up speed. Initially, everything seemed slow, but now it feels like Sandhi is fast and precise." Sherin had been watching Sandhi for a long time; Sandhi asked her, "Sherin, do you have something to say to me?"

Sherin, adjusting her glasses, said, "I've heard that no one ignores the words of your Prime Minister. Why don't you also write a letter to him and draw his attention to our problem?"

"That's a good suggestion, Sherin... I will certainly do that."

After thinking for a while, Gohen said, "Can we also write a letter to the American president? They are giving weapons to our president, giving us the courage to fight, so can't they establish peace?"

"It's harder to establish peace than to give weapons for fighting. I'm not saying they shouldn't give weapons or they should; I just want to say they should also talk about establishing peace because, in the end, humanity will lose from war or its occurrence." Sandhi continued, "Gohen, now I think that I should write not only to the American president for peace efforts but also to leaders of the African Union, European Union, and OPEC group, so the importance of peace remains a question on the global stage before all leaders, reminding them of their responsibilities towards humanity."

Sherin said, "If people understand this much, then there will be happiness in Ukraine and Russia."

Sandhi saw that Alex was going around, distributing the letter she had written to President Putin to people who were reading it and feeling hopeful that everything would be alright soon. Sandhi, watching people read her letter, thought that maybe the thing that had always been hidden somewhere in her mind, that very thing she had written, was affecting people's minds, and they were trying to leave behind hatred and violence, trying to follow the path of love.

Alex called out to Gohen, "Gohen, come here; I can't distribute so many copies alone." Gohen also ran over and started distributing some copies. Sandhi watched everyone; people were discussing her letter among themselves.

Sandhi couldn't understand how suddenly everything has changed... the journey from Kyiv to Kharkiv, then from the club to the hotel, then the bomb explosion, then that underground metro station, then the underground room, then Pisochin, then Vladimir's death... Sandhi became silent.

Mentally, no sound came from her mind or her mouth. As soon as she remembered Vladimir, she became utterly disheartened and unhappy with herself, thinking that what she was doing was not enough. As she thought, tears fell from her eyes. As soon as the tears came, people started to appear blurry. Natasha placed her hand on Sandhi's shoulder from behind.

Natasha said, "Don't cry, Sandhi... what you have done will significantly change."

"I don't know what will happen; I just want to try so that I can internally respond to Vladimir. Vladimir asks every day, 'What have you done since my death? How will you end this chain of death? Can you ever end this chain? What was the use of your stay here? Aren't you just giving these people false hope?'"

Natasha said, "Calm down, Sandhi, everything will be alright."

"What will be alright? Everything is dying. People are dying; the joys connected to them are dying, the memories connected to them are dying, and the conversations connected to them are dying. Only war is alive. At every turn, at every intersection, in front of every home stands death, which is bigger than life right now."

"Why are you so distressed?"

"I don't know, but whenever I remember Vladimir, I feel very uneasy," Sandhi says. "Ever since I heard about the Mariupol incident, I've felt very strange. Thinking about their pain makes me feel very weak. They never tire of attacking, and here, only weaknesses are growing. I don't know how long people will hold on to this peace. It will become even more difficult if it takes longer to resolve this issue. Then, even those who are with peace and love today will join the war because they will see no other support than guns to save their lives. Every moment is challenging, and those eager for war are making the war more severe."

Natasha explains to Sandhi, "You shouldn't lose hope. Look at these people and how happy they are because they feel you are the solution to their problems. You shouldn't have shown them that you are the solution if you weren't going to be one. But now that you have, you must become the solution."

"What does it mean to become the solution?"

"It's clear, Sandhi, you are their leader, not the kind of leader who gives speeches and then lives elsewhere. You are the leader of those at war; their emotions and impulses are changing rapidly and will change because the war controls their emotions, not them controlling the war. You are under the influence of war yourself; you have to stay with them, and if they see you like this, it will mean that they will think they are with a weak ideology. They will start to feel that weapons are stronger than the ideology of love."

Sandhi becomes quiet and says, "I've understood the leader's dilemma for the first time; a leader becomes one, and after becoming one, he realizes how difficult it is to keep the promise that I will always lead you. I am fighting because I am human; I don't know when they made me their leader."

"That's what it is, what you have now, you have to fight, Sandhi."

"What's wrong with just being human?"

"Nothing is wrong, but seeing you weak will weaken them."

Sandhi says with despair, "Alright... I will control myself. I will try not to let the war affect my state of mind too much and keep fighting without fear."

"Fighting is our life as common people."

Then they both go to Sherin, who is explaining love to the people, and Sandhi says, "Sherin, we are leaving; there is a lot of work to do."

"Alright, but don't work so hard that you fall ill. Come here." Sandhi and Natasha move closer, and Sherin kisses their foreheads. Sherin says, looking at them, "You both have given us a purpose; we had no purpose. The biggest thing war takes away is hope, which destroys homes, and with homes, it erodes purpose. We do live life; if the family survives, we protect the family from war, but purpose gets lost somewhere. We like to live life straightforwardly. If this straightforwardness breaks for any reason, we get distressed. Tell me, Sandhi, what's bothering us here besides the war?"

"War is the biggest trouble." Natasha says, "Yes, war is."

"Yes, but this war isn't that simple. Every day, it will kill your spirit. You won't feel like getting up in the morning because you know you'll hear some bad news again, but I know all this; I've seen wars, I've seen people renounce war, and then after a few days, I've seen them waging wars again. Humans forget our traumas because life teaches us to forget, and we quickly forget our intellectual vigilance."

Sherin looks up and says, "I don't know when everything will be alright, but you have acted like a bridge. All of us here in this camp know everything you've said today, but even seeing hope, we couldn't grasp it. Hope was visible, but we couldn't reach it. You built a bridge and got us there. Go on, both of you, take care. I am also fighting the war of loneliness, so I was talking to you. Go, work, and become a foundation of global awareness. Keep showing everyone this new ray of hope."

Sandhi and Natasha turn to leave. As they went, Sandhi saw that Alex had distributed all the copies among the people who read them and tucked them into their pockets. Alex was also sticking the pamphlet on the streets. Alex, seeing

Sandhi, leaving, called out from the edge of the road, "Sandhi, wait just 2 minutes for me."

Sandhi steps out of the refugee camp and waits. Alex sticks the pamphlet, and right after sticking it, people come to read it and start discussing it among themselves. After sticking the pamphlet, Alex approaches Sandhi and says, "Sandhi, I heard you're going to write more pamphlets."

"Yes, I'm thinking about it."

Alex, cleaning his sticky hands, says, "Definitely write... I've understood how all this will happen, how peace will come from writing letters, from talking. You write and take my email, send it to me, and I will print many copies here; I've spoken to the camp manager."

Sandhi takes his email ID and says, "Tell me how peace will come!"

"From one person to another, then from somewhere else, and then to another place. The idea of peace will spread, and victory will occur."

"Yes, Alex, victory of peace will happen."

Natasha also smiles, "Yes, victory of peace will happen. It's essential for all of us who desire peace to make others understand that now is not the time to sit quietly; we have to fight against war."

They both leave and reach home, where Hero sits very sadly. They start playing with Hero to cheer him up. After a while, Sandhi sits quietly. Natasha asks her, "What happened, Sandhi?"

"Nothing, just thinking whether I should write a letter to Prime Minister Modi."

"Your country is a powerful nation... if you write a letter, there will be no harm. You are an Indian; when you tell him about the situation here, he will do whatever he can."

"Alright! I'll try to write."

Sandhi goes to the desk, sits down, thinks for a moment, and then something strikes her, and she starts writing.

Kharkiv

March 9, 2022

Honorable Prime Minister Shri Narendra Damodardas Modi Ji,

7 Lok Kalyan Marg,

New Delhi - 110001

Honorable Prime Minister Ji,

I am writing this letter from a place caught between despair and hope in Ukraine. This letter also carries a question that has long lingered in my mind, one that perhaps you can answer. Can we, together as humanity, distance ourselves from the threat of war? Can we stop the war?

These questions arise from the front lines, where Ukraine swings between the despair of ongoing conflict and the hope for an early end. Russia has initiated this war and caused this turmoil. Ukraine stands in defense with its morale and arms, and between these opposing sentiments stand the ordinary people of both nations—fighting leads to death, not fighting leads to death, and even neutrality leads to death. Will the ordinary human ever have the right to live freely with love and peace? Humanity, the ultimate goal of human evolution, literally and ideologically, is now so scarce in the world. Violence is unnatural to the human soul, and peace can only be reached through love. Yet, why is there such a distance between humanity and love? Wars bring inhumane atrocities and foster hate and division, injuring humanity and escalating global unrest. War is the enemy of society; it must be stopped.

Every religion provides guiding principles on how to conduct ourselves, but in Ukraine, I see a lack of these principles. It seems that Ukraine is burning today due to the greed for power and accumulation. Humanity is not just an idea but a way of living where you do not insult the dignity of those around you. This is an unspoken supreme law of humanity, yet it is disregarded here.

I am writing this letter because I am witnessing all this with my eyes. Prime Minister Ji, you initiated 'Operation Ganga,' which allowed thousands of Indian students trapped in the war to escape. I had the opportunity to leave, but I felt it was also my responsibility to fight this war. I have chosen a path of non-violence and have already written to President Putin, urging him to end this war and restore hope to the people of Ukraine rather than despair.

I hope you will also speak with President Putin and contribute to ending this war. Such a contribution will be forever remembered by humanity. Remind President Putin that every individual possesses a spiritual essence, which inspires us to nurture life around us, not extinguish it. It's essential to remind him that our goal of uniting with nature and thriving can only be achieved through love. The highest truth is that peace and love are supreme, and if he believes that his victory alone is the truth, he is gravely mistaken. Nature will eventually find peace in its inherent state of tranquility and love. This has happened many times throughout history.

The truth that war is wrong has already spread everywhere. Only those who oppose humanity or aim to remain in power, overriding the people's desire for peace and love, resist this idea. I view this war as a violent action obstructing the free flow of humanity and love, and your support is crucial in stopping it.

Finally, I urge you to tell President Putin that love is the highest morality and to make every possible effort to end the war and restore respect for human dignity and nature so that the rest of the world may learn from this.

Thank you,

Your daughter,

Sandhi

As Sandhi wrote, she fell asleep at the desk. A while later, Natasha noticed that Sandhi had fallen asleep and gently removed the pen and paper, whispering, "Come down and sleep."

Startled, Sandhi woke up and looked at Natasha, who repeated, "Come sleep down here."

"Yes, I'm coming. Read this. I've written a letter to Honorable Modi Ji, uncertain of the future."

"Yes, I will read it," Natasha said as she approached the desk, and Sandhi moved to the bed.

Natasha thought this desk would also be an essential historical artifact safeguarding human values and strengthening the sentiments of world peace and love, perhaps in the annals of world history.

15

"These airplanes, guns, and nuclear bombs are symbols of human sorrow and insensitivity."

Kharkiv

March 10, 2022

Time: 6:00 AM

Sandhi's eyes open. She feels like several airplanes are flying in the sky above. She calls out to Natasha, "Natasha... Natasha!" Natasha responds, "Sandhi, I'm awake; Hero woke me up earlier."

Looking at the ceiling, Sandhi muses, "War is such a strange phenomenon."

"In what context are you saying that?" Natasha asks.

"Can one group achieve collective unity without causing harm to another?"

"That's a very dense perspective. I agree and disagree with you simultaneously," Natasha responds.

"How can you agree and disagree?"

"It's not necessary for a group to exist solely to harm another group."

Sandhi yawns, "It may not be necessary, but in the current global context, every group that exists does so in some way to self-defend its members, whether they are social or political groups. The existence of a group is because it embodies a sense of security. Those in power skillfully manipulate this truth. The biggest truth that gets suppressed is that any task could be easily accomplished if everyone came together. Those in power never want this truth to be revealed because if it were, the impact could also be against the power holders, transforming it into a check on their power. Hence, they resort to things like war to maintain the status quo."

"Then there's no role for ideology in war?"

"I can't say there's no role, but I can say that ideology acts as a shield that prevents us from seeing the machinations of war. I've been traveling and meeting people, listening to ordinary people's pains, and realizing that ordinary people don't have an ideology. They live in their ideal world, believing everything will be alright someday. They don't want to engage in the complexities of the ideology. Their ideal world revolves around the betterment of the situation, not ideology. On the contrary, I've met people from the upper class in India and Ukraine. These people had ideologies. They knew how to profit from and control others. I think ideology is an intellectual weapon used only when one wants to dominate the thoughts of others."

"So, ideology is a slave to power?"

"It appears so. Look at this war. President Putin says he initiated the war because he felt threatened by NATO and that the Ukrainian government was mistreating Russian speakers in Ukraine. On the other hand, President Zelensky says that Putin's attack on Ukraine was wrong and that Russian forces have invaded their land, attacking civilians. The US has its stance of providing arms but not getting directly involved in the war. If you observe these three, their ideologies seem different but believe me; none align with their common people because ordinary people don't want war. If, at the beginning, people in any country wanted war, their media had spread the illusion that the war was already won. The war we are imposing on society everywhere proves that the public is being kept away from the truth because those in power fear that acknowledging this truth would weaken their position. They obscure, distort, and, when necessary, violently oppose this truth to maintain power. War is the ultimate attempt to hide the truth."

Natasha listens and then says, "If ideology can be anything, then what's the problem with having one? Is it harmful?"

"It's not harmful, but its misuse has made it seem dangerous. There was a time when a king's word was indisputable, followed by religion and science in many respects. Any indisputable discussion area should be understood as controlled by a few. Ideology is such an aspect held by a few who implant it into the masses, and the masses live with whatever has been instilled in them. They know nothing about the origins or the outcomes of these ideologies. Ideology is a complex tool because its creation aims to achieve certain outcomes."

After Sandhi finishes, Natasha continues to think. Sandhi looks at her and asks, "What's up? Is there anything you want to say?"

Natasha replies, "There's a lot to say... you shake up my mind. How can we then find a solution to the problems facing humanity? There must be a way to end these issues."

Sandhi, laughing, says, "Only the concepts of love and truth can end all problems. Nothing else will work. Many will oppose, create obstacles, resist, and even want those who are with love to join their path of violence. Like this crucial time for the people of Ukraine, I don't know how long the war will last, but if ordinary people start walking the path of war to stop it, then this war will last a very long time. There is no end to it. Whenever I look at the history of slavery and servitude, it's clear that in those circumstances, humans were not acting according to the laws of love. If they had, they would have inherently loved and not supported any violence. Non-violence involves withdrawing from all participation in violence and only spreading love. Gandhi's ideology of non-violence is nothing but love."

Suddenly, an airplane flies over very low, making a loud noise.

Natasha, startled, says, "Ugh, these airplanes... they're scary; they could drop bombs anytime."

Scared by the noise, Hero barks, and Natasha calms him down.

Sandhi, looking at Hero, says, "These airplanes, guns, and nuclear bombs, etc., are symbols of human suffering and insensitivity. When humanity strayed from love during its development and couldn't find a proper standard to live by, it resorted to crude experiments to console itself for being engaged in something - inventing money and weapons, exploiting nature for profit, and viewing every task with a commercial mindset. Drifting away from nature, these inventions and greed prove that humanity is restless, lost, and anxious. Anxious because even after creating all these, it is still disturbed. It is disturbed because it seeks love, but societal standards have become so materialistic and corrupt, leading humanity into business, wealth accumulation, and competition. Wars show that humanity is unhappy and dissatisfied with this civilization, and its grief is at its peak. War is one of many experiments by humanity that always fails, but each time, it tries harder to succeed, and the result is that eventually, it will likely end humanity unless love saves it."

Taking a deep breath, Sandhi adds, "Despite all these things, it seems that humanity, so dissatisfied, has nothing to comfort or soothe its emotions."

"Humanity has its false pride - accumulated wealth and resources that it flaunts as development. Development merely expresses its defiance, which it imposes on other common humans and nature."

After this conversation, Natasha suddenly says, "I'm thirsty; I need to drink some water."

Sandhi watches Natasha drink water, and Hero rises and sits next to Sandhi. She lovingly strokes him and says, "You show love, it's evident."

"There are many things understood within war that do not seem so clear in times of peace."

"Yes, you may be right."

Sandhi resumes petting Hero. Natasha asks, "Did you write that letter to the American President?"

"Yes, I wrote it, but I need to review and make corrections."

"Alright, make the corrections, and then I'll read it."

Sandhi stands up and sits down at the table.

"I'll make some coffee for you from upstairs."

"Don't go just yet; airplanes flew overhead just a moment ago."

"As soon as the siren sounds, I'll sit under something sturdy. We've gotten used to living like this."

Natasha stands up, and Hero does, too. Then she asks Hero, "Will you come along?"

Hero makes a soft whining sound. Natasha says, "Sandhi, I'll take him along."

"Be careful."

Natasha leaves with Hero, and Sandhi starts revising the letter at the table.

Kharkiv

March 10, 2022

President Joseph Robinette Biden Jr.

The White House

1600 Pennsylvania Avenue, N.W.

Washington D.C. 20500

Dear President Biden,

I am writing this letter concerning the ongoing war between Ukraine and Russia, hoping you are aware of the horrors of this war. Ukraine has no fearlessness; only fear is born from war, and love cannot flourish in fear. This war has plunged millions into a severe refugee crisis, which will likely give rise to numerous other crises in the future.

These crises underscore the degradation of human dignity. While peace is desperately awaited by the war, love is also looking forward to the end of this conflict. The aftermath of this war has made it clear, Mr. President, that while love is essential, it is even more critical to understand whom we are loving.

Russia is showing its love through war and using countless ammunition on the battlefield, but this pressure falls solely on the minor units of society. Millions of families in Ukraine are bearing this burden; some have ended up in refugee camps while enduring it, and others have died as martyrs for their country.

This is a crucial time, an extraordinary period filled with unethical activities that one could never have imagined. It's also a nightmare, but understanding both sides of this scenario is necessary. Under the hot shrapnel and atmosphere of war, there's another layer—of men and women now cold, who once hoped the war would end, a hope unfulfilled even in their dying moments. This cold humanity, lying dead on the battlefield, wished to return to their homes alive.

I am writing this letter to bring humanity back to their homes because their rightful place is not the battlefield but their homes, farms, villages, and cities. Mr. President, your support should not be limited to providing arms to Ukraine; this is my plea. I urge you to strive to end this war as soon as possible. In the paradox of war, we must gain control over the deteriorating condition of humanity; as a man and as a President, your duty should be to soothe the infinite agony of free souls suffering from the torment of war, and millions are looking toward you not just for help, but for the help of peace.

Whatever broken relationships exist between you, Russia, and Ukraine, efforts should also be made to mend them with peace. Establishing justice during these unjust times of war is only possible with peace. It would be best if you strived to give those wounded by bullets a world meaningful with happiness again. Declarations of the end of the world are being made everywhere, and everyone fears the use of nuclear weapons; amidst all these troubles, using a simple and natural emotion is the only way to benefit everyone, and that is the sentiment of love.

Much time has passed since the war began, yet despair, defeatism, skepticism, and those eager for victory are still waging war; we just need to bring those people toward peace with love.

In conclusion, I would say that a significant strike is needed against sorrow and war, but that strike must be strictly non-violent, and your cooperation is expected.

I hope you will give the gift of hope to the Ukrainian people and the world. This gift will also have the power to endure sorrow and commit to providing hope.

Yours sincerely,

Sandhi

After revising the letter, Sandhi waited a bit for Natasha and then showed her the letter upstairs. As she grabbed the stairway railing, Natasha appeared, descending from above. Sandhi stepped aside as Hero jumped down from the stairs. Natasha held two cups of coffee in her hand, and she, too, began to descend. Taking the cups from Natasha's hands, Sandhi said, "I've corrected the letter, Natasha."

"That's great, Sandhi. Maybe now every place and nation will understand the importance of peace."

"I still always wonder if we are having as much impact as needed to establish peace."

"You're starting something, Sandhi... No one has yet begun to work with this truth for this purpose. Any day now, your ideas could ignite a tide of importance for peace and extinguish the flames of war."

Sandhi hugged Natasha and said, "I hope I can do it and end this endless suffering of war. Vladimir would perhaps be happy then. Petrovich might understand love after this. Maybe my father will be proud of my decisions. My mother might recover from the pain of losing her daughter, realizing that her daughter now belongs to many people, a friend to many. This friendship is a bridge to establishing peace in society. I didn't leave everything behind for any hidden personal agenda; I just found myself swept away in the river of pain, seeing no one else addressing the problems with solutions, but Vladimir's death opened my eyes. My heart cried out in pain; I am in this enclosed space because I want to see the common people of Ukraine free."

Natasha replied, trying to shift the topic as she balanced the coffee, "Let me go... My coffee will spill otherwise." Sandhi released her and noticed tears in Natasha's eyes, which she quickly wiped away upon being seen.

"Don't cry, Natasha... Everything will be alright; the war will end."

"And what's in your eyes... Not tears, what is it?"

Sandhi, wiping her eyes while laughing, said, "No, it's just water. Maybe the tears will come the day the war ends."

Changing the subject, Natasha said, "We need to bring this letter to the public."

"I was thinking of giving this letter to Alex. Let's get ready."

"Yes, just a minute."

Natasha started coughing, and the coughing wouldn't stop.

"Are you okay, Natasha?"

"Yes... yes, I'm fine."

Sandhi took Natasha's hand, startled, and said, "You're burning up!"

"It's nothing, I'm fine."

"You're not going anywhere; I'll go alone, understand? Rest properly, and I'll arrange some food on my way back and ask Alex if he can get some medicine."

As Sandhi was about to head upstairs, Hero jumped up and placed his paws on her stomach.

Sandhi told him, "Natasha is not well; stay with her. I'll take you out later."

The hero seemed to understand and stepped down. Sandhi grabbed his face, looked into his eyes, and said, "You are brilliant." She kissed his forehead, then closed the hatch and ascended the stairs.

Sandhi carefully stepped outside and started walking briskly, perhaps more cautiously and faster than usual. She thought about bringing Natasha, but her health was not good. Sandhi suddenly spotted a few Russian soldiers in the distance; she veered off the main path and moved through the buildings on the side. As she walked, she pondered the dangerous thoughts of how she would escape if a Russian soldier saw her, changing every plan of attack into one of survival. So far, many plans have started and ended in her mind because she didn't want to kill any soldier. She thought about how fear is a terrible weapon that compels you to consider whether you could kill someone. "I am fine now, but these thoughts come uninvited like unwanted rain, wanting to wreak havoc."

Sandhi considered how fundamental the emotion of fear is, how it determines what you will do and whose side you will take. Fear dictates the relations of entire states, individuals, and groups, and international relations are formed by fear. As she walked, thinking how statehood itself might be based on a foundation of fear, she realized how many policy mistakes are made in an atmosphere of fear rather than one of love.

Pondering this, Sandhi reached the refugee camp and breathed freedom, knowing the fear was yet to worsen. As she left, Russian soldiers walking past Natasha's apartment heard Hero barking. Drawn by the sound, they approached the apartment, entered, and, after some searching, realized someone was below. Listening to the carpet, one soldier heard a woman's voice below. "Sounds like there are two people down there," he whispered to his comrade. "I'll move the carpet and the hatch; cover me."

The other soldier agreed. As the hatch opened, revealing a dog and a woman below, Hero began to bark fiercely, ready to attack. "Shoot that dog, or it won't let us do our work," one soldier commanded.

Without a moment's hesitation, he fired three shots from his AK-47, each bullet piercing through Hero's fur and flesh. Hero's white coat turned red as he fell to the floor in agony, and the soldiers' boots clattered on the stairs. Natasha stood frozen in shock as the soldiers descended into the room, their wild eyes scanning her body. One moved forward, gun pointed, and commanded, "Let us do what we want, and if you do anything else, you'll have more bullets in you than this dog."

The other soldier grabbed Natasha, tearing at her shirt. Natasha's hands tried to cover herself while the soldier exposed her. The struggle was brief; the soldier hit her shoulder with the butt of his gun, knocking her to the ground. He stomped on her hands as she sat and declared, "Your country and you are both beneath our boots."

The other soldier laughed cruelly and urged, "Make this story interesting."

Hearing this, the soldier said, "You want an interesting story."

The soldier, seizing Natasha's hair, dragged her across the floor and stripped off her remaining clothes. Now, on one side lay Natasha, and on the other, Hero soaked in blood, both sprawled on the floor, while the two soldiers, transformed into monsters of hatred and lust, stood between them. Natasha's eyes, filled with helplessness and despair, were drowning in tears. She kept pleading for them to let her go, citing her illness, but for the soldiers, the battlefield had become Natasha's body. As one of the soldiers was about to lie on top of her, he said, "Whether it's a man, woman, or child, we will spare no one in Ukraine."

The other soldier said, "This war doesn't clarify anything; everything is in doubt here; maybe after we play with her body, our doubts will be resolved."

Hearing this, the first soldier, already engaged in his violent act, began to move faster, fueled by excitement, and Natasha began to mourn her womanhood amidst her struggles. The hatred she felt for the man turned into sobs and tears. She looked into the soldier's eyes and saw him as more unfortunate in his mental state than her own. Consequently, she closed her eyes and ceased all resistance. Once the first soldier had finished, he said to the other, "Now it's your turn to relieve your fatigue." And the eager soldier commenced his assault on Natasha's body, attempting to conquer the woman within her. Moments later, Natasha's body went limp without resistance, her eyes opening to stare at the ceiling. The sound of the Russian soldiers' sexual conquest echoed within her, audible only to her, and the soldiers left her in that state as they walked away, hurling insults. At the same time, Natasha just listened, or perhaps the pain was so intense that she became like a living corpse. The necessity of oppression to transform victory into a reality was the pinnacle of psychological aberration.

As soon as Sandhi entered the camp, everyone began to greet her. Many people approached her, discussing the day's speech and the letter. Sandhi asked Amber, "Where is Alex?"

Amber replied, "I'll go and call him." She left to find Alex and asked Sherin, "Where is Alex?"

"What happened?" Sherin inquired.

"Sandhi is here... she's asking for Alex."

"Let me go outside; I'll meet Sandhi too."

Alex was talking with some people at the other end; as soon as he saw Sandhi, he ran towards her. Sherin also arrived at the scene and saw Alex and Sandhi talking. Sherin said, "Looks like they are discussing something... I'll meet them in a while; it's good to see Alex helping someone."

Amber, watching Sherin, remarked, "Alex is not just helping someone else; he's helping himself and all of us."

Sandhi pulled the letters from her pocket and said, "I'm bothering you again."

Alex responded, "It's no bother... if we want to change the situation, everyone must try together."

Sandhi handed the letters to Alex, saying, "Please type these up and distribute them. These are two letters. During the discussion the other day, many people thought we should seek help from other countries too, so I've written a letter to President Biden of America and another to Prime Minister Modi of India."

"That's very good... now we will try with double the strength to stop the war."

Sandhi smiled and said, "It feels good to see your morale, Alex."

"We can only show courage; the war has taken everything else."

"My effort is to give back to us what you and I have lost in this war."

"Jesus will surely grant us peace."

Without thinking, Sandhi exclaimed, "Long live Baba Vishwanath!"

Then Sandhi asked Alex, "Could you arrange a fever pill?"

"Whose health is not good?"

"Natasha isn't feeling well, so I will head home quickly."

"Okay."

Sherin then called out to Sandhi; Sandhi turned and walked towards Sherin. Alex watched his mother and Sandhi meeting, smiling, and then headed towards the camp office. Sherin and Amber greeted Sandhi warmly. Sherin took Sandhi's hand and began to talk. Sandhi told them that Natasha was ill that day and that she would leave soon.

Alex ran up to Sandhi and gave her a pill, saying, "Give this to her; she will get better."

Sandhi read the pill's name and put it in her pocket. After a conversation, Sandhi said, "Now I must go."

Everyone told her to stay longer, but Sandhi didn't stay and left the camp.

As Sandhi walked rapidly, her mind was consumed by overwhelming worry about Natasha. She couldn't understand why she felt so uneasy. The road to the underground room seemed incredibly long. Her thoughts were filled with dread about Natasha, and despite trying to distract herself, she couldn't shake off the fear. She realized she had been thinking about Natasha, and those thoughts were tinged with fear for her well-being.

Lost in thought, Sandhi reached home. She reflected on how thoughts besieged her daily and considered that thinking was food for the brain—without it, one's capacity to think might atrophy. With this in mind, Sandhi reached the ground floor and saw the hatch open. Peering down, she saw only red—the color of blood—and Natasha lying naked and trapped by it. The sight made her collapse, but the shock did not allow her to stay down for long.

She quickly got up and went down. Hero lay there quietly, with Natasha lying naked beside him. Sandhi placed one hand on Natasha and the other on Hero; both were silent. Silence filled the room, broken only by Sandhi's voice as she softly called out, "Hero... Hero, Natasha... Natasha." Suddenly, Natasha began to sob loudly.

Sandhi cradled her, holding her in her arms. Natasha wept bitterly, and Sandhi gently stroked her back while shaking Hero slightly. Hero remained silent. Natasha screamed, "He probably doesn't care about life anymore; he won't wake up."

Sandhi left Natasha to shake Hero vigorously. Natasha said, "He won't wake up... he was shot with three bullets. That monster shot him three times..."

Natasha's sobs prevented Sandhi from holding back her tears. On the other hand, Hero's unresponsiveness felt like death to them both. Nothing was certain; everything was shrouded in darkness at that moment. Sandhi continued to shake Hero while constantly stroking Natasha's forehead. Suddenly, she stopped shaking and trying to wake him, crying loudly, "Hero... Hero... HERO... HERO!" After staring at him, she, too, began to scream and cry. Sandhi's tears continuously fell on Natasha's face, but Natasha did not wipe them away. They both cried together. Sandhi cried, hand on her forehead, unsure if their tears were mixing. Those tears, mixed with Hero's blood, cursed the downfall of humanity. Sandhi kept stroking Natasha, who, amidst her tears, said, "He didn't let anything happen to me as long as he was alive. He died trying to protect me. Those beasts killed this dog, who harbored human feelings. Look how red his white fur has become, trying to stop the violence."

Saying this, Natasha resumed crying and began to stroke Hero's face.

Sitting down, Sandhi pulled a blanket from the bed and draped it over Natasha, wrapping her up while sitting. Then, crying, she placed Hero's head in her lap along with Natasha's and continued stroking their heads. While stroking, she said, "This war has also shown the atrocities inherent in humanity... alas."

Lying down, Natasha said, "I was sitting here quietly... Suddenly, the hatch opened, and two Russian soldiers came down. Hero lunged at them as soon as he saw them, and one soldier shot him three times. The hero died moaning. They fired bullets at a harmless animal, Sandhi... they fired bullets."

She then narrated how after that, the soldiers raped her at gunpoint. Sitting up, Natasha continued, "Sandhi, it wasn't just rape; they turned rape into a weapon against me. One soldier was repeatedly hitting me with his rapist intent on my body, and I saw despair and doubt in his eyes. One of them was drunk and kept saying he didn't understand this war and what we were doing here on Ukrainian soil. He was hurting me, and I just thought that we both were helpless, but maybe I was more so."

Natasha tearfully said, "He had turned my body into a battlefield; with every strike, he declared, he had come to kill the woman inside me along with your cities, to instill fear in us for thousands of years. I gave up wishing to be a woman, but he also left his humanity here. The way he was using me, twisting my arms, slapping me, kicking my womb, and biting my breasts, I didn't even feel it was a sexual assault but rather him trying to show me that I was weak, that he had more power; it wasn't intercourse, it was a crime of power and domination."

Natasha was narrating everything as she looked ahead. Sandhi was watching her and felt as if Natasha was seeing it all again in front of her. Natasha cries, then falls silent... then cries again and starts to speak, "That other soldier, holding a gun, the one next to him was digging his nails into my bare flesh saying, 'You too must become a man today, I did all this for you, now we are one, the Russians are uniting.'" Natasha, with her hand on her forehead, says, "What kind of unity is this that is fulfilled by tearing apart, ripping, and piercing a woman's body?"

Sandhi, also in tears, says, "I don't know... I know nothing. The more I think about men, and whenever I feel like I've understood them, I turn out to be wrong every time. I've accepted today that all cruelty, violence, chaos, and ruthlessness are purely the contributions of men."

Then, both become quiet for a while... Perhaps they both felt the death of humanity, and this silence was a message of empathy.

Sandhi thinks of the daily decreasing gap between love and violent physical lust wrapped in mentality, a tragic social spectacle of the decline in male-female relationships that can be felt everywhere—in villages, in cities. This guiding perversion extends from corrupt religious leaders to the corridors of political leadership.

To protect the morality of love, whom should the common people follow? To protect women's dignity, whom should they trust? This social fear, taking the form of an institutional crisis, searches for its savior. Where should it establish its trust? This freedom of choice, now challenged by fear, has become the most powerful terror standing in the dark for today's women.

The force done to Natasha had deeply immersed Sandhi in thought. She thinks rape is an enforced acceptance stamped in black ink, where the devaluation of all moral values is smeared from one face to another. It's nothing but a shameful outrage performed by an unfit, defeated mentality against an honest competitor.

After a while, Sandhi says, "It's time to bid farewell to this hero." Natasha starts crying and then, wiping her tears, tries to stand. As she stands, she winces in pain. Sandhi, taking her hand, asks, "What happened?"

Natasha gestures towards her breasts. Sandhi sees teeth marks there. Sandhi closes her eyes and swallows the saliva in her mouth. It takes her time to overcome all this. Then, remembering her God, she comes to Natasha, embraces her tenderly, and holds her close to her heart. After that, she quietly tells Natasha, "Let's get dressed, Natasha."

Natasha wears her clothes over the bloodstains of the hero and moans in pain. She and Sandhi lift the hero. They slowly carried him out of the underground room to where there was debris. Sandhi holds the hero like a child in her lap. Reaching the debris, Sandhi hands the hero to Natasha and starts searching for something, then finds a broken piece of a rocket. She starts digging the ground with this sharp fragment. The intensity with which Sandhi was digging made it clear that her emotion behind the digging was her anger at the war. She soon digs a deep hole, then suddenly collapses from the exertion. She had been gripping the piece so tightly that marks had formed on her hand.

Natasha goes to Sandhi and helps her up. Sandhi gives the hero to her, and now Natasha picks up the fragment and begins to dig vigorously. They soon finish digging the grave.

Sandhi says to Natasha, "Take off the scarf from around my neck." Natasha removes the scarf. Sandhi says, "Spread the scarf." Natasha understood that she wanted to wrap the hero in her scarf and bury him.

As Sandhi wraps the hero, she says, "He always used to stuff it in his mouth. He knew it annoyed me when he did that."

They say nothing more... both hold him and place him in the grave. Natasha opens his mouth, which is covered by the scarf. Then, both start covering him with soil. Suddenly, they stop, look at the hero's face again, and then resume covering him with soil. After completely covering the hero's grave with dirt, both sit there for a while, unafraid, without thinking or understanding. After some time, Sandhi says, "Let's go home." Natasha says, "A part of our home was buried with Hero."

Looking towards the grave, Natasha says, "I can't stay here, Sandhi. I can't stay here."

16

"Consider not the sulfur, coal, and other elements lying in the earth transformed into weapons; they are not to blame. Think about the intentions of the one who crafts these arms, how concerned he was about his own existence, and now, he has placed the existence of everyone at the barrel of a gun."

"Six months later, on October 10, 2022, approximately 15 kilometers from the Russian-Ukrainian border, around 11 PM, in a large underground room, a map of Ukraine lay spread across a large table. The room, equipped with basic amenities, also contained a large bookshelf filled with various books. People stood around the table, deep in discussion. Natasha held a cigarette, Sandhi a pen. Natasha and Sandhi faced each other, with Alex standing next to Sandhi and Ember next to Natasha. Suddenly, Gohen entered the room and asked, 'So, what's the decision? When are we holding the candlelight march at the Russian-Ukrainian border?'

Sandhi responded, 'We are doing it tomorrow at around 9 PM. Have you informed all the refugee camps in Kharkiv that they need to gather?'

'Yes, I've informed them, and many others along the way want to join us too. There should be a large turnout for the candlelight march.'

Alex interjected, 'Sandhi, do you really think this is necessary? It could be very dangerous.'

Looking at Natasha, Sandhi replied, 'Yes, I know it's dangerous, and we might even lose lives, but Alex, we have to take this risk. If we want to secure the future for all humanity, these are the risks we must take. It's been over six months, the war continues, and people have become accustomed to death. Tell me, what should I do? Is there another option? I cherish peace more than my life; if I live, peace for all, and if I perish, peace for me. But we must make an effort. How much longer can we wait for the war to end on its own?'

Exhaling smoke from her cigarette, Natasha said, 'But Sandhi, we are doing something. Even in this war, we have a large group of peace supporters trying their best to make a change. Our people are always upholding the flag of peace.'

'But what have we really achieved for our cause? Still, I must say that we must continue with humanity and non-violence. And yes, those two men standing outside with guns, tell them they either drop their guns or lose me.'

'Sandhi, sometimes you get too stubborn. We are so close to the border, which is why I arranged for this.'

'Weapons remind me of Vladimir and Hero's deaths and how many more Vladimir and Heroes these weapons have consumed.'

Natasha snuffs out her cigarette in an ashtray and heads outside. Sandhi gestures to Ember, who follows Natasha. They stand in a tunnel connected to the room. Natasha, sitting on the ground in the tunnel, lights another cigarette and says, 'I still search for Hero around me; his absence always lingers. But what happened to me? I don't want it to happen to Sandhi, so sometimes I resort to arms.' Ember then walks down the tunnel, opens a massive iron door with a plastic box containing buttons, presses some, and after going out and coming back in, closes the door and rejoins Natasha, saying, 'Let's go back inside... I've told them to leave.'

'Alex's presence has given us a secure location. Otherwise, we would be much more vulnerable,' Natasha remarks as she gets up to head inside. Ember follows, and inside, they see everyone seated. Natasha takes the chair next to Sandhi, who asks, 'Ready for tomorrow?'

'Always,' laughs Natasha, 'except for that one day...'

Changing the topic, Alex asks, 'Sandhi, have you prepared the leaflet we need to distribute tomorrow?'

'Not yet, but I will... I still have time, and I know what I need to write.'

Alex laughs, 'Sherin is really excited about tomorrow. She says that Sandhi will change everything.'

'If it were that easy for me to change everything, I would have done so by now. But I have always learned from my mother to keep smiling.'

Looking at her burning cigarette, Natasha remarks, 'It's this laughter that the war has taken away.'

Banging his hand on the table, Alex says, 'I don't understand why any soldier would fight knowing they could die. Why go to war at all?'

Looking at the map, Sandhi responds, 'The question should be why wars arise at all, why seeds of blood are sown. I think when societal games fail to satisfy a young person or anyone, they become eager to wage war, including issues like unemployment. The problem isn't why they go to war but what they would do without it. A society without purpose breeds purposeless offspring. This is a harsh reality, but it gradually cultivates a mindset of struggle and a desire for victory. What end will such people meet? This is visible upon deep reflection of life.'

Interrupting, Ember says, 'That's not true, people do have purposes.'

Yes, but to sustain life, the purposes imposed on people might help them bring food to the table but not a fulfilling life. With neoliberal globalization, the world's economy is interconnected, and the market has been freed, leaving individuals more isolated and helpless. If we start from 1960, we see that wars have never stopped—from the Congo crisis and the Bajaur Campaign, where Afghanistan and Pakistan clashed, to numerous others... I could go on, but the wars will not stop. We have engaged in nearly 500 wars since 1960, and no substantial action has been taken to stop them. Every country provides reasons before starting a war. Isn't it clear enough to understand why someone would wage war if they see no other option but war? We need to create an alternative as powerful as war, and when I look around, I only see humanity as that alternative. We need to rise above caste, creed, region, gender, and class. Our long-term belief should be in the seeds of educational completion—love, peace, cooperation, and tolerance. Anything less will not secure our future.'

Alex, looking up at the ceiling, says, 'It seems only time will teach humanity how to abandon war and resolve its issues.'

Extinguishing her cigarette, Natasha says, 'Not just time, but patience too... Wars often result from a lack of patience, though I, too, lose patience when I can't find solutions to my problems. But we must have patience, or everything will be destroyed.'

Sandhi, looking at Natasha, adds, 'If everyone fought only for their beliefs, there would be no wars. We often fight for others' beliefs. My view might be personal, but it's correct that we should struggle for our beliefs ourselves, not others. Look at this war... many are fighting for one man's belief, and many of them must be doubting by now, on both sides.'

Ember awkwardly says, 'If we only stand for our own issues, then what's the point of society?'

Just then, a man enters and shows a poster that reads, 'War is a social crime; stop the war.' Everyone looks intently at the poster. After a moment, Sandhi says, 'The world is divided into two—those who are with love and those who are not. Society was not formed to plunge itself into war but to tell you when you're being partial. Society's concept is like that of grandparents—it will always guide you with love. I know society isn't functioning on this concept because the market has trapped it in various temptations. But there will always be voices from society that will tell you if you're wrong.'

Natasha, with renewed hope and a loud voice, says, 'We must not be discouraged... there are always possibilities for joy in society; we just need to find them and try to bring laughter to everyone.'

Laughing as he leans back in his chair, Alex says, 'There will be a lot of noise in that effort.'

Standing up, Sandhi says, 'Society has failed to teach us some things, like how to identify who is a foe and who isn't. Because of this mindset, we love our closest friends, parents, and family with eternal human love but fail to love our enemies because loving an enemy depends on intellect and mental capacity, and society and your family teach you to use your intellect to decide the mental capacity of others and how they will behave. This isn't a divine quality... you just need to understand that hating them won't achieve anything other than leading to a fight. Loving them is essential so you can try to understand them instead of spending time focusing on their flaws. Understand why they are the way they are; society doesn't teach us to spend time on understanding our enemies, on what waters have nourished their roots, which paths they have walked, and what environments they have come from. This should be the scientific basis for forming a perception of any personality and where the process of development can be corrected.'

Ember says in astonishment, 'Are you saying we should understand what President Putin is doing... what is there to understand when thousands are dying, rapes are occurring, and you say we should understand them, not fight them? What kind of reasoning is that?'

Sandhi laughs, then turns serious and says, 'If you think you can reestablish human civilization with reason, forget it—it won't happen. Only love will bring peace, and don't apply logic to it. We've seen where logic has gotten us. Just understand that without love, we are living in a benumbed civilization. If civilization is to retain its human dignity, love is absolutely necessary.'

Standing up, Alex laughs, 'Benumbed civilization! You and your words, Sandhi.'

'If you look into the womb of happiness, Alex, you'll find love. "One who reads love is learned," that's the most beloved child of civilization we've pushed away because materialism has taken its place.

Love's earnings were meager, but love will take care of its aging grandmotherly civilization until the end.'

Gohen says, 'Sandhi, your words are just theoretical, nothing more.'

Sandhi, standing by the table and placing her hand on it, says, 'Just theoretical, Gohen? This isn't just a battle between theory and practice; it's a battle between love and war. All religions say everything in the universe is created by God, so tell me, whose expression is your enemy, if not God's too? Every expression must be understood with love and patience; that's how humanity will come through. I said before that war is easy, but humanity is difficult because it has completely fled, and now we have to coax it back. The last time I saw Petrovich and walked away, I was very upset because my mind was telling me I still couldn't hate him, and I started to hate myself because I still loved him. It took me a long time to realize that human love often turns into hate due to a single action, but the universality of love is the true purpose and form of love.'

'That may be, but war has its place, and love has its own. The situation in Ukraine is improving because of the war, Sandhi.'

'Gohen! Just answer one question.'

'Yes, ask.'

"You are afraid of war; you are afraid of the consequences of war; what if you lose? I mean, if Ukraine loses."

"I don't even want to think about what will happen."

"So, it means you are afraid. As long as fear exists, you can't hold anything else inside. You will just live in fear but with love. When you assimilate love, you will live only in love, without fear, and then you can truly embrace any emotion. Otherwise, you will feel everything subconsciously. War is a contagious disease; in war, we are morally afflicted, and because of this moral degradation, we unwittingly start to desire war. Gohen, call it theoretical or practical, but this is the simple reality."

Natasha first looks at Gohen, then at Sandhi, and says, "But how will all this happen, Sandhi... How is it possible? I can't see it happening, it's been 6 months of war. How will all this be?"

As she walks around the room, Sandhi starts to speak, "Whenever we stray from our daily path, we feel that we are doing something wrong, that perhaps we won't reach the right place, but believe me, life itself is happiness, not death. As long as we are alive, there is a chance for happiness. Our civilization has been going on for 6000 years; it wakes up every morning, moves, searches for something, and then sleeps at night. Sometimes, it stays up all night and stays awake all day; perhaps walking so much has become important. It has lost its fundamental purpose. Whenever we ask it questions, it starts listing its actions, like development, human understanding, human intelligence, human inventions, etc. It doesn't tell how many people it has killed; it doesn't share how much sorrow it has distributed. It needs to pause and think about where it is going; otherwise, we all will fall into a massive pit, and then only those with power will emerge, meaning you and I are done for. This civilization has divided everything, and subjects like science, economics, sociology, marketing, history, and political science have overly dissected things to understand them, and by dividing, everything has died. When everything was united, everything was powerful; now everything is separate and fragmented; the whole is the truth."

As soon as Sandhi finishes speaking, two people enter and hand Alex a small piece of paper and a poster. Reading the paper, Alex informs Sandhi, "A thousand candles, six dozen packs of matches, and eight gas lighters have also been ordered." Then, he and Gohen examine the poster closely before laying it out for everyone to see. Reading the poster, Sandhi says, "The entire structure of war and its components are enslaved. If not, why isn't their opposition vocal? Why isn't history rewritten to state that fools have waged all wars? After all, for whose benefit were all these wars started or waged? The true beneficiaries of war are always finding reasons to mislead the common people. Those involved in violent conflicts are fools and have waged wars for their interests. Initially, wars were needed for change; now, wars are needed to maintain that change, and then wars to keep the change fresh."

After finishing her talk and taking a sip of water, Sandhi continues, "And many wars would have been waged simply because many could not fight and would fall behind, but whenever they regain strength, they will wage war to claim their share, and this process will continue, wars will keep happening, and history will keep recording them according to the whims of kings or high positions. Unnecessary desires are a major cause of human dissatisfaction. Science will continue to frustrate, economics will keep inventing new methods of looting, political science will market fear, and sociology will remain entangled in caste, civilization, culture, species, and gender. We will never be unified until these fragmented subjects incorporate love into their disciplines. Life will go on, but we will not learn to live."

As more people enter the room, Sandhi pauses to hear someone whisper something in her ear, then resumes speaking as they leave. "Our parents send us to school with the expectation that we will achieve something great. We go to school burdened with the weight of our bags and the desire to score high marks, and there we take on the goals of our teachers to become someone important; that's all we learn. We spend our lives chasing after that 'important person,' and one day, that person stands in front of a war with the same backpack he carried in his childhood but still filled with fear, helplessness, and resentment towards society because by then he will have realized that everything he did was meaningless. Now, his life depends on someone else pulling the trigger. Only love can save him, but that's not what the entire subject and school teach. The false reassurances of a report card are constructing a false society, incapable of telling you that you are on the wrong path."

Natasha, standing up, says, "This civilization and its people don't want to understand anything fully, and their confidence is based on falsehoods, such as their nation being mighty, the whole world bowing down before their nation, their culture being very refined, one nation having the highest GDP, another having the best technology, one's parliament being very organized, another's army being powerful, etc. This kind of confidence creates infallibility, and every country's media is spreading this confidence, further creating an irrefutable mindset that disrupts your independent thinking, focusing your attention on all these trivial matters. The real utility is in love; after loving, one's confidence will be without pretension. It will not be arrogant; it will have nothing to prove and does not need proof of being good. Human problems and sorrows are not due to a lack of human needs but because of this dream in which we exaggerate human needs. Pain, freedom, happiness, and sorrow have their limits."

Sandhi, nodding, adds to Natasha's point, "I'll add one more thing to what Natasha said: in this postmodern era, being clever means a mixture of cunning and wickedness. So whenever someone tells you to be smart, they say be cunning and wicked."

Amber, with more confidence this time, says, "According to what you all have said, it seems we don't know anything; the whole civilization just stands there; this is our and this civilization's conscience."

Sandhi, walking towards Amber, says, "Call it whatever you will, but this is the supremacy of our ignorance or knowledge."

Alex, placing the posters down, says, "Why were we given so much freedom that we can pick up a weapon and kill someone?"

Natasha, laughing, replies, "Don't blame freedom, Alex. It's not about freedom; it's a mistake in understanding freedom."

Sandhi says, "Alex, picking up a weapon and killing someone isn't just an irrational act; it's not freedom. But with the same freedom we can kill, we can also give flowers."

Sitting back down, Alex says, "So the problem is in the choice, not in freedom."

Natasha adds, "The problem is in consciousness; when our consciousness starts seeing someone with hatred, we think of killing them, proving them wrong, or harming them. What's happening in this war? Some people's consciousness is of war, but it's presented as everyone's consciousness, and we start waging war without listening to our consciousness. Still, when the pain intensifies and the danger to our lives begins, then we realize our consciousness is saying we don't want this war. The state starts listing the benefits of war, telling us why war is necessary. The state writes laws about non-violence but engages in violent activities. It's easy for the state to write laws because it has to look after its interests. Still, it can only truly implement them when it shapes the educational system to enable people to make decisions through thinking and discussion. The state watches over the people, and the people should watch over the state, so blind devotion to any state is like moles digging at its roots. Only by critically observing a state's actions can a truly beneficial state be formed, which is lacking almost everywhere in the world today."

Sandhi says, "If looked at extensively, nothing is truly free; my initial statement that nearly 500 wars have been fought is evidence that no one's freedom is completely unimpeded. If we look at it historically, there are reasons behind wars, and behind those reasons, there are other reasons, and the immediate reasons for wars are a combination of all these reasons. When Archimedes understood why a bucket rises in water, his thought was not entirely independent historically, and it was the result of his prior thinking and reasoning. The revelation of war is never immediate; the seeds are always hidden in history, so why don't we plant only love so that the coming generations see a lasting love, not a transient one."

Gohen says, "It's easy to blame humanity and civilization when wars are waged, and lives are lost, but we say nothing; we don't praise it when the same civilization spreads love."

To address Gohen's skepticism, Sandhi explains that the complexities increased by society day by day continuously create worry, discontent, and the pressure to live life effortlessly among people, and that's why it spends the least time on something as natural as love because all these conditions collectively extinguish their physical and mental health along with their innate creative energy. Civilization has adapted just for love; love is a natural product of society, so we don't praise it because doing so is natural. Ancient cave paintings spread worldwide and are fundamental signs of civilization's love and creativity. This natural desire has been sacrificed to social complexities."

Natasha, slightly agitated, says, "Before we die and fail to find answers to our questions before we can understand why we are here, what our purpose should be, why we should love, why peace is necessary, why love is necessary, what fears we have, what will end with fear—among all these questions, only one thing is certain: death. And before our mortal bodies burn and our ashes become useless to future generations except to cloud their eyes and create another mirage of life, giving birth to skeletons like us to be struck by the same questions again."

Sandhi starts walking again and says, "Our destiny to know the truth is filled with obstacles, with numerous doubts around the world that will acquaint you with various truths. Truth has now taken merely a factual form, and we can mold this form in any way. People sitting in high positions construct the truth for us and you, which makes us happy or sad as we think and see."

Amber shakes her head and says, "I don't understand; I'm confused."

Alex says, "I'm becoming aware listening to all this, and you're getting confused; perhaps what we already have in our minds also depends on how we'll handle knowledge and truth, in what form we will take it, whether we'll use it for the good of people or to destroy them, or just carry out our actions in confusion."

Amber, in despair, asks, "With all these discussions, can we forget the deaths of our husbands and sons? Can we stop being hurt, Sandhi?"

Sandhi replies, "The wounds on your soul will heal by giving joy to someone else because, in the end, the sorrow of the soul heals only by including love in life. Just as a physical injury heals by the life existing in the body, that same life will heal the soul's wounds; trust this... give something of your life to another, and the healing will begin. We can't apply ointment to our backs; someone else will do it. We all make up society by joining backs; you apply ointment to my back, and I'll apply it to yours. Until we meet each other's spiritual edges, soaked in love, the flow of humanity won't commence."

Suddenly, the tunnel shakes, following an explosion. Alex stands up and says, "They will never understand this love; they only understand weapons."

Taking a deep breath, Sandhi says, "Think about how weapons were made, the transformation of elements like sulfur and coal in the earth... It's not their fault. Think about the intent of those who make weapons, how consumed they were with selfish fear for their existence, and now they've put everyone's existence at gunpoint. Weapons can do nothing if you're committed to winning; they are just weapons. We, too, are committed to war, but our weapon of war is nonviolent. We must conquer ourselves before defeating them."

Putting her arm around Sandhi's shoulder, Natasha says, "Yes, we must first conquer ourselves, but even after conquering ourselves, we must think about what we want to win, why we are acting, and for what purpose we are acting."

Looking first at Natasha and then at everyone else, Sandhi says, "I said at the beginning that the lack of employment forces many to enlist in the army, and some enlist just because they love their country. Employment is such a condition that you're considered a very irresponsible citizen if you don't have it. I also said that all events are interconnected and historically linked. As written in the Gita, actions should be performed without desire for the fruits of action. However, employment is the opposite, dependent only on attachment; how much salary one receives is a much more important question than what you do and think. Acting and working have become a compulsion in our society. This compulsion keeps us active and visible; civilization could decline, and our social standing could fall if we're not active. But I think if a person could find that blank page that lies between activity, work, and employment but is vacant, where one can celebrate inactivity, think a little about the rush to act, like everyone else, I too must act, whether my compulsion is making me do something wrong. By being inactive, could he be useful to society because no one has spread love? Everyone is busy but not spreading love, so should their unloving activity also be considered active, or should they be considered inactive and thus useless to society, present yet absent."

Natasha, laughing again, says, "War is merely a hobby for some people, and some just spend their lives in bunkers, where avoiding shells and bombs is their only activity. What entertainment it is for people; why have we invented different ways to kill humans."

Sandhi says, "As long as we think about change through violence, the permanence of change will only occur through non-violence, through love."

Amber curiously asks, "So will there be no change, or will everything remain the same even after the change?"

Natasha looks at Sandhi and says, "No one will remember the change of this time, the patriotism of this time, the sacrifices and so-called bravery of this time. Many people's lives will have been lost in this war. You and we will also stay away from all these matters. We will only be affected by those reasons that threaten our lives; the rest is for journalism and people in high positions on both sides."

Sandhi looks at her watch and says, "We should sleep now; I must write something for tomorrow. Anyway, it's 2 AM." Alex, neatly arranging all the posters, says, "It felt good to have these discussions; many confusions in my mind were resolved."

"It was necessary to have these discussions for tomorrow and to tell people many solutions."

Amber cheerfully says, "Now I'm not confused; things are quite clear."

Sandhi gets up from her chair and goes to her bed, saying, "That's very good." Sandhi stands and goes to her bed while everyone else slowly heads to their rooms through the tunnel.

Sandhi begins writing on a piece of paper beside her bed; Natasha, smoking a cigarette, says goodnight to Sandhi, who replies and adds, "Tomorrow is a big day for us."

"Yes, Sandhi, it's big. Tomorrow, we will be where we need to be."

Sandhi continues writing, engrossed with her pen and paper.

"Grasping the roots of the banyan tree, I have leaped over and measured the definitions of progress, and now I am at peace within myself, for I live for others."

October 11

About 15 kilometers from the Russian-Ukrainian border

Time: around 8 PM

Everyone gathers in Sandhi's room, where she sits with her eyes closed. As everyone settles into chairs, she remains with her eyes closed, all eyes on her, dressed in a white shirt and a white jacket. The room is littered with posters advocating peace and opposing war, with phrases like "You want war, we want peace" and "You crave blood, we desire laughter." Gohen made and neatly organized these posters, holding one that read "Peace is power."

Sandhi finally opens her eyes, looking around as if seeing everyone for the first time. Alex asks, "What were you doing with your eyes closed?"

"I remember and thank Kashi Vishwanath for showing me this day and helping me get here."

"Do you fully trust in God?"

"I trust every source from which love emanates."

Natasha, placing her hand on Sandhi, says, "That's why she trusts me." Gohen adds, "That's why she trusts me too." Amber says, "That's why she trusts me as well." Alex concludes, "That's why she trusts me, and we all trust you, Sandhi."

Sandhi smiles and says, "Thank you all for trusting me and acknowledging that love flows through me."

Everyone smiles. Natasha asks, "So what do we do now?"

"What have you thought, Alex?"

"We'll leave from here and meet the rest of the group a short distance away. There, we'll light our candles and then proceed to the border. Some will hold posters, others candles. Some of us will chant the slogans written on the posters. Sandhi, you'll lead, Natasha and I will be at the back. Amber will be with you, and Sherin will join us from the front. Gohen and I have posted everywhere about today's candle march. I expect a large turnout, from doctors to soldiers. I've clearly stated in the posters: no weapons allowed. I'll personally ensure no one brings any."

"Great, Alex... everything's ready then."

"Yes."

Sandhi asks Gohen, "Are the posters ready?"

Gohen loudly replies, "The posters are ready to spread peace, Sandhi."

"Everyone, join hands." They form a circle, and Sandhi says, holding hands, "Let's start with a prayer to God."

"Should I start the prayer?" Natasha asks.

"Yes, you start," everyone agrees.

Natasha begins, "O Lord, you have distributed the fortunes of life to us all in different ways, but we ask for no more. We only wish to see children playing with their toys in open fields, women carrying their laughter on their faces, recognized for more than their bodies, recognized by their families, and men feeling love for their wives and children as they go to work. O

Lord! We want farmers to touch their soil again, their sweat to moisten the earth rather than soldiers' blood. We desire victory for the will to live, not death from the causes of war. People should not visit hospitals because a soldier from another nation shot them at someone else's command. O Lord! We all want to sing songs of peace, not of victory."

Everyone says, "Amen." Sandhi concludes with, "Om Shanti."

They open their eyes and embrace each other. Sandhi announces, "Everything is ready."

"All set," everyone responds in unison.

"Let's march to establish peace," Gohen declares.

Alex excitedly adds, "Let's show the Russians at the border what they think is not the future; only peace is."

They all exit the tunnel, stepping outside. Sandhi takes a deep breath and says, "It seems even the moon will make our candles whiter tonight and spread peace."

"It's a full moon tonight... everything is as white as snow," Natasha remarks.

Alex joyfully says, "Along with us, the moon will march and shower the nectar of peace."

They stroll. Ukrainian soldiers they met on the way, the snow on either side and the full moon above casting moonlight made it seem as if they were all walking on a path of peace, everything draped in a white sheet. In her white attire, Sandhi seemed almost to blend into nature—the moonlight, the snow, and her outfit created a strange harmony.

Ukrainian soldiers gradually joined their group, some without weapons and some with guns, and they also greeted Sandhi. Their circumstances compelled them not to abandon their arms but to momentarily participate in Sandhi's peaceful method. It was perhaps a victory, a semblance of one, or a testament to how mentally fragile a human can be, dropping one weapon to pick up another, not to defeat an external enemy but to confront the foes within their mind, stirring doubts about their lives and futures.

Alex tells Sandhi, "Seeing all this, it's easy to govern without war, like horses returning to their stable. There is no need for worry... the people manage everything, and the ruler takes all the credit for good governance. But when the horses don't return, the ruler's troubles begin, for he must explain what happened. Why didn't the horses come back? Did they not know the way, did they lose their path, or, tired of his rule, did they go elsewhere? How will his chariot run without horses?"

"It won't... it absolutely won't. Governing in war isn't easy, but we should also consider who made it so hard. Everyone was moving and happy because they had a purpose, for themselves and society."

Gohen had distributed the posters; everyone held them, though they were not unfurled.

"Many soldiers can be seen on the road with weapons," Alex notes as they walk.

Amber proudly says, "I have a weapon in my hand, too, this poster."

Hearing this, everyone laughs. Sandhi talks to herself, reflecting on the significance of this day. "Today is significant for me; the trust I've instilled in people for peace must not break. I was probably alive just for this day—to speak for the people, bring them to them, and secure peace for them. I've left my love, my elders, all for peace and love, for the people I don't even know, whom I've never seen. These people around me, whom I know and have seen, are the faces of peace for me. Beyond them, I have nothing in this world, and who knows how those I've left view me, whether they understand what I'm doing or see me as a selfish person who abandoned her family and loves to change everything.

I've changed completely. Sandhi, who once drove through the lanes of Banaras, is now leading a candle march in Ukraine. I'm not the same, but my soul is still the same. I seek justice; I want smiles on people's faces. Can those I left behind grasp this plain truth? My everything is here now—some truths, some people, and a struggle I'm fighting for everyone or perhaps just for myself. I couldn't bear losing Vladimir, couldn't stand my mother toiling all day in the kitchen, couldn't bear my father talking about Gandhi but not following his teachings, couldn't tolerate my uncle and aunt chasing money, couldn't bear my friend staying subdued at home, couldn't bear leaving Manikarnika Ghat... My inability to accept these things has brought me here. I'm walking through this cold for a change. If I had tolerated it, I'd be warm in bed but helpless, powerless, not thinking of change but of war because those who can't change always have a battle raging inside them, and those caught in that war are incapable of change."

Their war might be more challenging than a war of weapons, but it is still a war; everyone must fight their own battle, and if the soul isn't strong, you may blend into the dust. Otherwise, even in dust, you can resonate with the steps of others. Whatever I have done is mine: my mistakes, thoughts, and all of mine. I am proud of losing everything and gaining nothing because I still fight for truth while the world struggles with selfishness. I don't understand why they want to fight such battles. How can one live without fighting for the truth? Whether human or animal, struggle is your destiny as long as there is falsehood. There is a big difference between violent and nonviolent struggles. It is this struggle that will make you human. Perhaps it has already made me human, or am I still that old woman who is afraid, or the woman who pays attention to clothes, or the woman who can leave everything for her own sake, or the woman of the tribe who is more adept in the jungle of problems than men, holding onto the banyan roots and leaping across the definitions of development? I have measured them. Now, I am at peace within because I live for others.

Alex tells Sandhi, "We must wait a bit; people will arrive soon."

"Yes, we will wait; how many are coming?"

"I can't give an exact number, but there should be quite a few."

"Why do you say 'maybe,' Alex?"

"With the war atmosphere and the harsh cold, I'm unsure if people will gather the strength to come here. I can't say for certain."

"I don't know how many will come, but however many there are, it will be enough, and they will believe in our ideology."

Soon, there is the sound of scraping, and a wheelchair appears, Sherin coming alone. Seeing Sherin, Sandhi, and others are happy, but Sandhi feels a bit sad that after all this effort, only an old woman in a wheelchair is coming. Sandhi bows her head in disappointment and tries to muster courage within herself.

She closes her eyes and remembers her family. Just then, Natasha grabs her hand, and before Natasha can speak, Sandhi, with her eyes still closed, says, "Natasha, I'm fine, but I don't understand what we lacked, whether we failed to convey the importance of peace, perhaps our efforts were weak."

"Open your eyes, Sandhi; you might not see what I'm seeing."

Sandhi opens her eyes and is stunned to see a sea of people swaying before her. "Gohen, how many posters do you have?" "Not enough to make so many," he replies.

Alex runs to Sherin, Sandhi runs too, and the others rush towards the crowd. Sherin stops her wheelchair, Sandhi touches her feet, and Sherin asks, "What is this, Sandhi?"

"In our culture, when someone is about to do something good, the younger person touches the feet of the elders, and the elder blesses them."

"Then let me think what blessing I can give you." Sherin decides, "Touch again," and Sandhi touches her feet again. Sherin says, "Go, Sandhi, make a treaty of humanity and peace."

Sandhi rises from touching her feet, tears in her eyes. Sherin says, "Don't cry, Sandhi... now it's the turn of those who fight to cry."

"Yes, Sherin... let's go."

Sandhi, Sherin, and Amber led the procession. Gohen was in the middle, distributing posters as they walked, and Natasha and Alex tied up the entire procession at the back. Sherin raised the first slogan, which was not on any poster. She said loudly with her nearly toothless mouth, "Give me death or give me peace," and almost everyone echoed it. Alex started shouting different slogans written by Gohen.

The crowd's steps were filled with determination and desire, each step pushing them towards an unprecedented event. The event made it clear that ordinary people together could do something extraordinary. Everyone's steps matched effortlessly. They were all in different clothes and unarmed, but their march signaled they had formed an army of peace.

Sandhi was leading the entire procession, and Natasha, at the end, was proving that even the last soldier was not weak. As they chanted, they battled internally with fear, loss, gain, war, and peace, struggling with the mentality that prevented them from believing they could find peace. Living daily through rockets, missiles, bombs, and tanks, fighting the sounds of those weapons, battling the siren that tells you you're weak, survive or die. They were together to overcome this emotional terror, and a siren would sound somewhere today, but they had resolved to write their destiny, standing before guns with a poster of change in their open hands.

Natasha tells Alex, "We should light the candle now; there isn't much distance left."

Alex moves from the back to the front of the procession and asks Sandhi to stop. Everyone stops. Gohen pulls out several bundles of candles from a bag and distributes them. He lights Sandhi's candle first, and Sandhi lights Sherin's candle from hers; Sherin lights Amber's, and soon everyone's candles are lit.

The consciousness that Sandhi had awakened had now become light, and everyone's faces were glowing. The lighting of these candles was not ordinary; it was a flame born out of courage and many deaths. There was no wind in the air, and their steps were plodding, the fire of the candles flickering with their brisk movements.

Peace also comes in this way, slowly but with persistent effort, holding tightly to the nonviolent ideology in hand, not letting go so that your mind is illuminated only by this light. Sandhi had no poster in her hand, but slogans were continuously on her lips; this procession was against the war, and no one there was hired; all came at the call of their consciousness. The slogans were now bullets, and soldiers also chanted with the ordinary people. Gradually, they arrived very close to the Russian border; Russian soldiers were watching them, and so were the Ukrainian soldiers.

The media was there, too, in their giant vehicles with canopies coming along. Suddenly, Petrovich emerges from the media vehicle and talks on the phone. Petrovich's gaze falls on Sandhi, and he keeps walking in front of her repeatedly so that Sandhi can also see him. He was waving at Sandhi, but before Sandhi could reach the border, a large crowd was already there. As soon as the crowd saw Sandhi, they started chanting her name. On his microphone, Petrovich says, "So many people, and they're all shouting the name of one girl... Sandhi... Sandhi... Sandhi." Petrovich adds, "It seems like 'Sandhi' has become synonymous with peace."

Petrovich was also thinking that the girl who had cried seeing a murder was sobbing; that same girl was so fearless today that she was with hundreds of people at the Russian border, trying to convince the Russians to choose peace over war. The peace sentences written on the posters were also running in the media. The media was talking to Russian soldiers, too; many Russian soldiers were not speaking openly, but many were covering their faces, saying they, too, did not want war; they wanted peace, and they were being pushed into war. This news ran on TV channels in Ukraine and worldwide; Petrovich was not alone. There were many other media vehicles there. The people in the procession were not stopping; they were still shouting, 'Sandhi, Sandhi.'

The media now used large cameras and countless microphones, branding familiar people as peace messengers and injecting them with sensational news.

In war or peace, countless people cannot live without this injection, who have so much war within them that they want to hear talks where there is the most shouting. Helga was also in the crowd gathered before Sandhi arrived, shouting Sandhi's name. Still, Sandhi was only surrounded by ordinary people, by those Ukrainian women who now wanted their daughters to be like Sandhi.

Society has lost such common standards that they can genuinely call their leader, which were once very common but are now unique. If they exist, these standards are either corrupt or supporters of a specific ideology, but because they have status and power, parents have to make their children unique. This madness for the special is strange worldwide. Without thinking, be like this one, be like that one. No one says to be human first, then love.

Helga's voice wasn't reaching Sandhi. Russian soldiers were watching the people and their fearless demeanor with their guns raised. Many Russian soldiers were jumping to see if they could see the person everyone was following, and that too unarmed. Many who saw Sandhi couldn't understand if she was that girl or someone else because the special couldn't be so ordinary. They don't meet the public that closely, so why is she special? What threat do those exceptional ones have from the public? The leaders of the people don't go near them; they need cars and security and use elections as a chance to meet them.

But here, Sandhi is fighting for peace, sitting in the car of hopes, within the security of ordinary people. Around her are guns, soldiers, another nation's border, and a crowd of people who have understood that everything is easy; just being a human is necessary, most necessary to relate to the problems—being one in difficulties, purposes, intentions, and defeats. No one in that crowd had won, and all were defeated... yet they harbored a desire for peace because all their desires together had become a continent of hope where all were equally defeated.

Amid resounding slogans, Sandhi signals for silence. Seeing Sandhi's gesture, Gohen and Alex tell everyone to be quiet. The procession becomes completely silent, as if everyone wanted to listen to Sandhi. Petrovich's camera closely shows Sandhi's face, which has become quite thin and frail. Before Sandhi walked the path of peace, her body had been subjected to emotional strain, thoughts, and fear, and then she became Sandhi, who was now running in Petrovich's camera.

Various TV camerapersons stood, asking the crowd to give them a little space, and the crowd reluctantly gave them some room. Sandhi starts to speak, holding a paper that Gohen and the others were about to distribute. After her introduction, Sandhi joined her hands in praying for Kashi Vishwanath. It begins her statement, "Today, on the soil of Ukraine for peace."... Suddenly, a drone appears in the sky, a slate-colored drone moving at a rapid pace, and the next moment, it crashes to the ground where Sandhi was standing.

A terrible explosion occurs. Wrapped in a cloud of smoke, the explosion devastates all of Sandhi's efforts for peace. Along with Sandhi, shreds of several other people fly into the air and fall back to the ground, shrouded in smoke. Nothing was organized; there was chaos, blood, burned flesh, despair, a stampede, and unrest was again stretching itself. Pieces of the drone that hit the ground had flown and stabbed people, showing how weapons are enemies and what science is creating. A weapon killed a woman who wanted to spread peace; there was no face there responsible for breaking the peace dreams of so many people. A suicidal machine took everything: all hopes, all trusts, the flood of peace; everything ended in the blink of an eye, except for the papers Sandhi had written, which were flying in that cloud of smoke after the drone attack, and there was Sandhi's last word, 'peace' silently begging for forgiveness from the attack noise and Sandhi's flesh shreds.

A stampede began as soon as the drone fell, and Sandhi's consciousness was quieted. Those for whom peace was unique were now gripping each other in fear. Amber and Gohen were rushing towards Sandhi, and Natasha, too, was coming towards Sandhi, but by then, Sandhi had been shattered into many small pieces. After the attack, the blood of ordinary people was very clearly marked on the white snow like red ink on a white page, just ink... making no sense. Helga ran towards Sandhi, but where Sandhi had been, there were now pink papers written by Sandhi. Helga, crying, picks up a pink paper and bursts into sobs. A tear from Helga falls on the paper, with Ukraine written there, and the paper says –

"To all the citizens of the world! Countless times, your elected leaders have dragged you into wars under the guise of nationalism. In today's world, amidst all the chaos and disorder, it is easy to become agitated and distressed. Countless wars have occurred because of those who impose wars on the common people to cover up their failures in governance. The war between Ukraine and Russia is not just any war. You have seen this countless times as soldiers, as fathers, as mothers, and as families who have died for the sake of war. Governments have always justified war, placing guns in your hands, hunger in your stoves, and your bodies in the crematoriums. Your existence has been thrown into the pit of death many times, and your entire being has been limited to war alone. Historically, you have never benefited from wars; wars were never meant for you; wars have always been the result of the selfish and irresponsible intentions of two irresponsible people. You have always been kept far from peace and kept fighting, being told that war is necessary. No matter how necessary war may seem, it can never be justified because it is fought over the existence of humanity, mothers' lullabies, wives' kisses, children's toys, and farmers' fields. Who needs such a war? Only those select few who are frightened by the independent existence of ordinary people or who want to destroy them and share their resources with their capitalist friends. The stains of war on human dignity can now only be cleaned by peace. I call for the end of all wars through a final peace war, which will be waged on the strength of nonviolent efforts, in which the collective vow of all humanity will be the sacrifice, and from that sacrifice, peace will flow unceasingly."

Om Shanti,

Sandhi (Peace Messenger)

www.ingramcontent.com/pod-product-compliance
Lightning Source LLC
LaVergne TN
LVHW091622070526
838199LV00044B/897